ROUTLEDGE LIBRARY EDITIONS:
WELFARE AND THE STATE

I0131234

Volume 12

PRIVATISATION AND THE WELFARE STATE

PRIVATISATION AND THE WELFARE STATE

Edited by
JULIAN LE GRAND AND
RAY ROBINSON

Routledge
Taylor & Francis Group

LONDON AND NEW YORK

First published in 1984 by George Allen and Unwin (Publishers) Ltd

This edition first published in 2019
by Routledge
2 Park Square, Milton Park, Abingdon, Oxon OX14 4RN

and by Routledge
711 Third Avenue, New York, NY 10017

Routledge is an imprint of the Taylor & Francis Group, an informa business

British Library Cataloguing in Publication Data
A catalogue record for this book is available from the British Library

ISBN: 978-1-138-61373-7 (Set)
ISBN: 978-0-429-45813-2 (Set) (ebk)
ISBN: 978-1-138-60356-1 (Volume 12) (hbk)
ISBN: 978-1-138-60362-2 (Volume 12) (pbk)
ISBN: 978-0-429-46896-4 (Volume 12) (ebk)

Publisher's Note
The publisher has gone to great lengths to ensure the quality of this reprint but points out that some imperfections in the original copies may be apparent.

Disclaimer
The publisher has made every effort to trace copyright holders and would welcome correspondence from those they have been unable to trace.

Privatisation and the Welfare State

Julian Le Grand and Ray Robinson
(editors)

London
GEORGE ALLEN & UNWIN
Boston   Sydney

George Allen & Unwin (Publishers) Ltd,
40 Museum Street, London WC1A 1LU, UK

George Allen & Unwin (Publishers) Ltd,
Park Lane, Hemel Hempstead, Herts HP2 4TE, UK

Allen & Unwin, Inc.,
Fifty Cross Street, Winchester, Mass. 01890, USA

George Allen & Unwin Australia Pty Ltd,
8 Napier Street, North Sydney, NSW 2060, Australia

First published in 1984

© Introduction and Editorial selection Julian Le Grand and Ray Robinson, 1984; © individual chapters Alan Walker, David Donnison, Nick Bosanquet, Robert Sugden, Alan Maynard and Alan Williams, Peter A. West, Christine Whitehead, R. M. Kirwan, Maurice Peston, Mark Blaug, Stephen Glaister, Graham Crampton

British Library Cataloguing in Publication Data

Privatisation and the welfare state.
1. Public welfare—Great Britain
I. Le Grand, Julian II. Robinson, Ray, 1944–
361.6'0941   HV245
ISBN 0-04-336079-3
ISBN 0-04-336080-7

Library of Congress Cataloging in Publication Data

Main entry under title:
Privatisation and the welfare state.
Bibliography: p.
Includes index.
1. Great Britain—Social-policy—Addresses, essays, lectures. 2. Welfare state—Addresses, essays, lectures.
I. Le Grand, Julian. II. Robinson, Ray V.F.
HN390.P74   1984   361.6'1'0941   84-12492
ISBN 0-04-336079-3
ISBN 0-04-336080-7 (pbk.)

Set in 10 on 11 point Times by Preface Ltd, Salisbury, Wilts
and printed in Great Britain by Billing and Sons Ltd, London and Worcester

Contents

About the Contributors

MARK BLAUG is Professor of the Economics of Education at the University of London Institute of Education. He has also taught at the Universities of Yale, Manchester and Chicago and acted as a consultant to UNESCO, OECD and the World Bank. His published works include *Economic Theory in Retrospect* (1968), *An Introduction to the Economics of Education* (1970), *Education and the Employment Problem in Developing Countries* (1973) and *The Methodology of Economics* (1980).

NICK BOSANQUET is Lecturer in Economics at the City University. He is the author of *After the New Right* (1983). His recent research has been into the costs of special needs housing and the recruitment and training of young workers in the NHS. From 1974 to 1982 he served as a councillor in the London Borough of Camden, including a spell as chairman of its Social Services Committee.

GRAHAM CRAMPTON is Lecturer in Economics in the Faculty of Urban and Regional Studies at Reading University. After studying Mathematics and Economics at Cambridge, he spent a year at Harvard, and worked at Brown University, Rhode Island, for two years on models of US urban areas. His research interests include the economic analysis of urban spatial structure in general, as well as the policy issues of public passenger transport and local government finance.

DAVID DONNISON is Professor of Town and Regional Planning at the University of Glasgow. He was Professor of Social Administration at the London School of Economics from 1961 to 1969, Director of the Centre for Environmental Studies from 1969 to 1975, and Chairman of the Supplementary Benefits Commission from 1975 to 1980. His most recent books are *The Good City* (1980), written with Paul Soto, *The Politics of Poverty* (1982) and *Housing Policy* (1982) with Clare Ungerson.

STEPHEN GLAISTER is Cassel Reader in Economics at the London School of Economics. He has published books and papers in applied microeconomics with a specialism in transport economics. He has been an editor of *Economica* and has acted as advisor to the Department of Transport, London Transport, the British Railways Board and the Parliamentary Select Committee on Transport.

R. M. KIRWAN is a member of the Department of Land Economy in Cambridge University. From 1974 to 1976 he was a member of the Policy Unit at 10 Downing Street and subsequently Senior Economic Adviser in the Department of the Environment, working on the reform of housing policy and finance. Between 1976 and 1980, he taught at various universities in the United States.

JULIAN LE GRAND is Lecturer in Economics at the London School of Economics, having previously taught at the universities of Sussex and California. He is the author of *The Strategy of Equality* (1982) and, with Ray Robinson, of *The Economics of Social Problems* (2nd edition, 1984), as well as of many articles in academic journals. He is currently in receipt of a Nuffield Fellowship to write a book on the policy implications of theories of social justice.

ALAN MAYNARD is Professor of Economics and Director of the ESRC–DHSS Centre for Health Economics at the University of York. He has written numerous articles on the economics of social policy and is the author of *Health Care in the European Community* (1975) and co-editor of *The Public–Private Mix for Health* (1982).

MAURICE PESTON is Professor of Economics at Queen Mary College, University of London. He has been a member of the Council for National Academic Awards and of the Social Science Research Council. He has also been special adviser to the Secretary of State for Education and Science and the Secretary of State for Prices and Consumer Protection. He is editor of *Applied Economics*.

RAY ROBINSON is Lecturer in Economics at the University of Sussex. He has also taught at the Universities of Leeds, Massachusetts and California, and been a visiting Research Fellow at the Australian National University. He is co-author, with Julian Le Grand, of *The Economics of Social Problems* (2nd edition, 1984) and author of *Housing Economics and Public Policy* (1979).

ROBERT SUGDEN is Reader in Economics at the University of Newcastle upon Tyne. He was previously Lecturer in Economics at the University of York. He has written numerous articles on the economics of social policy and philanthropy, cost–benefit analysis and welfare economics. He is currently writing a book on the ways in which social co-operation might evolve in a community without government.

ALAN WALKER is Lecturer in Social Policy at the University of Sheffield. He is currently conducting research on the family care of elderly people and redundancy in the steel industry, and is about to embark on a study of a new departure in the formal care of the elderly in Sheffield. His publications include: *Unqualified and Underemployed* (1981), *Disability in Britain* (1981), edited with Peter Townsend, *Public Expenditure and Social Policy* (1982, editor), *Community Care* (1982, editor) and *Social Planning* (1984).

PETER WEST is an economist with the Bloomsbury Health Authority. He was previously at the University of Sussex and St Thomas's Hospital Medical

School, and has also taught at the University of Bath and the London School of Economics. He has written numerous articles on the economics of health and is co-author, with J. Cullis, of *The Economics of Health* (1979).

CHRISTINE WHITEHEAD is Senior Lecturer in Economics at the London School of Economics. She worked on the Housing Policy Review between 1974 and 1976 and was adviser to the House of Commons Environment Committee from 1979 to 1983. Her research is mainly in the field of housing economics, on which she has published *The UK Housing Market* (1974) and a number of papers in academic and policy journals. She is currently working on a research project at the Department of Land Economy, Cambridge, examining changes in the structure of the housing market in the 1980s.

ALAN WILLIAMS is Professor of Economics at the University of York. He has written many books and articles on the economics of the public sector generally, but with a particular interest in health and personal social services. He was at one time Director of Economic Studies at HM Treasury Centre for Administrative Studies (the forerunner of the Civil Service College), and was also a member of the Royal Commission on the National Health Service.

Preface

Since the election of the Conservative government in 1979, privatisation of the welfare state has become a major issue. Yet, when we discussed the issue in the summer of 1982, it seemed to us that there had been no systematic contribution to the debate over privatisation from those economists who specialise in the area. Accordingly, we decided to organise a seminar series at which economists and others interested in the welfare state could subject some of the claims being made for privatisation to critical scrutiny and reassess some of the basic arguments in support of the welfare state. Three half-day seminars were subsequently held in May 1983 at the International Centre for Economics and Related Disciplines, London School of Economics and Political Science.

In the event, the form of the seminars differed from our original idea in two ways. First, although the majority of the participants could be described as sympathetic to the ideals of the welfare state, they none the less represented a far broader range of opinions than we had anticipated. (Indeed, one very clear consequence of the seminar series was to show that privatisation is too complex an issue to be dealt with adequately in terms of the simple for/against, public/private dichotomies in which it is often discussed.) Second, the seminar was not confined to economists but included participants from political science, social administration, philosophy and other disciplines with an interest in social policy. Moreover, participants were drawn from both academic institutions and the civil service.

This book has grown out of the seminar series. It is not, however, simply the published version of a set of seminar papers. Although each of the six papers presented at the series has been included, they have been revised in the light of points made during discussion and of the needs of a wider readership. Moreover, seminar participants who identified areas in which the debate could be extended have also been invited to contribute chapters to the book. Finally, we have provided an introduction that is intended to indicate the scope of the debate on privatisation – as it affects the welfare state – which the subsequent chapters develop at more length and depth.

We are most grateful to A. B. Atkinson, Director of the International Centre for Economics and Related Discipline, for encouragement and financial support for the seminar series. Also our sincere thanks to Angela Swain who organised the series with superb efficiency; to Prue Hutton, the Administrative Secretary of the Centre; and to Pauline Hinton of the University of Sussex who coped with the trying task of typing edited material in her usual faultless manner. Finally, our thanks to the 30–50 participants who attended the various seminars; although, regrettably, too numerous to mention individually, their ideas have contributed markedly to the form of this book.

JULIAN LE GRAND
RAY ROBINSON

Privatisation and the
Welfare State

1 Privatisation and the Welfare State: An Introduction

JULIAN LE GRAND and RAY ROBINSON

In recent years the 'welfare state' has been the object of a sustained intellectual attack. A substantial body of economists has for some time been uneasy about the public provision and tax financing in the United Kingdom of certain commodities that are provided through the private market system in some other countries. Throughout the 1960s and 1970s their views were promoted through a series of publications from the Institute of Economic Affairs, but they remained – as far as mainstream policy decisions were concerned – an academic curiosity. The election of the Thatcher government changed all this. Since 1979, the government's commitment to a private market philosophy has led to a series of proposals or decisions designed to replace the 'welfare state' systems of collective provision and finance with more privatised systems. Examples include proposals to introduce private insurance funding to the National Health Service, contracting out hospital cleaning and catering, education vouchers, replacing student grants by loans, running public transport on a break-even basis, the sale of council houses and, as part of the return to Victorian values, the replacement of state redistribution by private charity. As this process gathers momentum, there is an urgent need to subject the claims made for privatisation to serious scrutiny, to establish the allocative and distributive consequences, and to reassess some of the fundamental economic aims of welfare state provision. This is the aim of this book.

In this introductory chapter we set the scene for the individual contributions that follow. We begin with some facts and figures concerning the rise – and recent fall – of the welfare state. This is followed by a discussion of the meaning of the term 'privatisation', and then, to open the debate, we present a review of the principal arguments, both for and against. The review is not designed to offer a conclusion; rather, it is more a taxonomy, designed to place the following chapters in context.

THE RISE AND FALL OF THE WELFARE STATE

Although there is no precise definition of the bounds of the welfare state, it is possible to specify the main programmes that are normally identified as parts of it. First, there is the social security system, which makes income transfers from taxpayers to benefit recipients in the form of cash payments. These include the social insurance based programmes emphasised in the Beveridge Report (1942), through which individuals' contributions provide entitlement to benefits (i.e. sickness benefits, short-term unemployment benefits and retirement pensions), and also increasingly – in the face of continuing high levels of long-term unemployment – non-contributory payments such as supplementary benefits. Second, there are benefits in kind, which are provided via free health care, education and various personal social services (e.g. the services of social workers, home-helps, meals-on-wheels, etc.) Third, there is a range of price subsidies designed to reduce the cost to consumers of certain commodities deemed socially desirable. These include rent subsidies, housing improvement grants and public transport subsidies.

The long-term growth of public expenditure upon these programmes has been well documented (Sleeman, 1979; Gordon, 1982; Judge, 1982a). Judge (1982a, p. 31) estimates that social expenditure rose by almost 250 per cent in real terms between 1951 and 1979; this represents an increase in its share of GNP from 16.1 per cent to 28.3 per cent. Recent figures contained in *The Government's Expenditure Plans 1983/84–1985/86* (HMSO, 1983a) show that expenditure on the welfare state – defined in terms of the categories shown in Table 1.1 (which are slightly different from those used by Judge) – accounted for about 25 per cent of GNP by 1981/2. As the table shows, nearly one-half of the total budget was accounted for by the social security system: of this, approximately 43 per cent was spent on retirement pensions, 17 per cent on supplementary benefit payments, 12 per cent on child benefits and 6 per cent on unemployment benefits. Spending on health and personal social services, and on education and science, accounted for about one-fifth of total expenditure each, while transport and housing represented about 5 per cent each.

Since the mid 1970s, the rate of growth of welfare state expenditure has been severely checked and in some sectors expenditure in real terms has actually fallen. This process, which arose initially because of the perceived need to limit public expenditure in the interests of macroeconomic policy, has been accentuated by recent policies on privatisation. Table 1.2 presents indices of the levels of real expenditure for the main welfare state

Table 1.1   *Welfare state expenditure, 1981/2 (current prices)*

	£ million	% of total
Education and science	11,828	19.7
Health and personal social services	12,751	21.2
Housing	3,137	5.2
Social security	28,510	47.4
Transport	3,898	6.5
Total	60,124	100.0

Source: *The Government's Expenditure Plans, 1983/84–1985/86*, Cmnd 8789-1, HMSO, February 1983, Table 1.7, p. 11.

programmes 1977/8–1982/3 and planned expenditure for 1983/4. The most striking feature of the table is the scale of reductions in housing expenditure: planned expenditure in 1983/4 is only a little over 40 per cent of the 1977/8 level. Education has also suffered reductions in real expenditure in recent years with a 5 per cent cut planned for 1983/4. Only in the social security sector has there been an increase in expenditure, particularly since 1980/1. Expenditure plans for the government's current planning period (i.e. up to 1985/6) are now only published in cash terms. However, with no programme planned to increase its cash budget by more than 12 per cent over the two-year period 1983/4–1985/6, it is clear that government plans include little scope for any expansion of real resources devoted to the welfare state. Privatisation is clearly designed to cater for an increasing proportion of welfare needs.

THE MEANING OF PRIVATISATION

In the most general sense, any privatisation proposal involves the rolling back of the activities of the state. The latter vary widely from welfare area to welfare area; and so, therefore, do the former. Hence, in order properly to understand the various meanings that the term privatisation can take on, it is necessary to have some method of classifying the different activities of the state.

The state can involve itself in an area of social and economic activity in any of three ways: provision, subsidy or regulation. That is, it can provide a particular commodity itself through owning and operating the relevant institutions and employing the relevant personnel. It can subsidise the commodity by using public funds to

Table 1.2 *Welfare state expenditure, 1977/8–1983/4 (1977/8 = 100)*

| | Outturns | | | | | | Estimated outturns 1982/3 | Planned 1983/4 |
	1977/8	1978/9	1979/80	1980/1	1981/2			
Education and science	100	99.7	98.2	101.2	99.2		98.5	93.3
Health and personal social services	100	102.7	105.1	113.5	115.1		116.5	116.8
Housing	100	94.5	102.1	85.2	54.2		41.4	42.7
Social security	100	106.9	107.8	110.1	120.9		128.1	129.3
Transport	100	97.5	101.0	99.5	101.4		105.0	99.1
Total	100	93.8	104.2	105.6	101.6		109.1	108.2

Source: The Government's Expenditure Plans 1983/84–1985/86, Cmnd 8789-1, HMSO, February 1983, Table 1.14, p. 17.

lower the commodity's price below the one that would otherwise obtain; sometimes, the price is lowered to zero, the commodity being provided free. Or the state can regulate the provision of the commodity, regulating its quality, its quantity or its price.

In most of the activities encompassed by the welfare state in Britain, it uses all three. For instance, under the National Health Service, the state provides health care through the public provision of hospitals and the employment of general practitioners; it subsidises health care by providing it free, or largely free, at the point of use; and it regulates the quality of the providers of health care through qualification requirements. In education, the state regulates the quality of schools through an inspectorate; it also regulates the quantity of education provided by, *inter alia*, compelling children to attend school between the ages of 5 and 16. It owns and operates most educational institutions, from primary schools to universities. And it provides most education free, or largely so; in some cases (such as most students in higher education), it even pays people to attend.

The quality of all types of housing is regulated through a variety of statutory requirements, concerning layout, appearance, structural soundness, sanitation, etc. Otherwise the form of state intervention varies between tenures. Council housing is, of course, state provided; council tenants have also traditionally been subsidised, through general subsidies and rent rebates. In the private sector, rents are regulated, while poor tenants have been subsidised through the rent allowance scheme. (Assistance to tenants, both public and private, has recently been combined in one scheme – a unified housing benefit.) The owner-occupied sector is subsidised through direct grants, such as those for house repairs and improvements; it is also heavily subsidised through various 'tax expenditures', such as the exemption of owner-occupied houses from capital gains tax, and the non-taxation of imputed income.

In the personal social services, social workers and residential homes for children, for the mentally handicapped and for the elderly are provided and subsidised by the state. The quality of the service is regulated, through qualification requirements and inspections.

Most public transport undertakings are owned and operated by the state; they are also heavily subsidised. Private undertakings, such as private coach operators, are regulated.

This categorisation of state activities can even be carried through to its activities in the social security field. State social security serves two functions: the provision of insurance against loss of income due to sickness, unemployment and old age, and the redistribution of private income. The state can thus be viewed as 'providing' two commodities:

insurance and redistribution. In each case, it regulates the quantity provided, through its use of eligibility requirements; and, of course, it subsidises them through its use of public funds to pay the relevant benefits.

Having described the various ways in which the state can intervene, we are now in a position to classify the various kinds of privatisation. Not surprisingly, they parallel the three types of intervention. First, there are forms of privatisation that involve a reduction in state provision. Examples include the sale of council houses, the closing of local authority residential homes, the expansion of privately provided medical care, the contracting out of hospital cleaning and catering, and most education voucher schemes. Into this category also fall proposals for privatising the social security system, such as relying more heavily on private insurance companies to provide sickness and other 'insurable' benefits or on private charities for redistribution. Second, privatisation can involve a reduction in state subsidy. Examples here include the reduction in subsidies to remaining council tenants, the introduction of charges (or an increase in existing ones) for services received under the National Health Service, the replacement of student grants by student loans, and reductions in subsidy to public transport. Third, privatisation can imply a reduction in state regulation. Examples are the lifting of restrictions on competition between private and public bus companies, and the easing of rent controls.

However, privatisation schemes differ not only in the type of state intervention whose reduction or elimination they require. They also differ in what is proposed in its stead. Some propose simply the replacement of the state by the market; the relevant service should be undertaken by profit-maximising entrepreneurs operating in a competitive unregulated environment. Other schemes involve the replacement of one form of state activity by another: a reduction in state provision, for example, coupled with an increase in regulation of private providers. And yet others want to encourage the activities of organisations that are neither the conventional profit-maximising firm nor the state enterprise: charities and other non-profit-making voluntary organisations, workers' co-operatives, consumer co-operatives, community associations.

Thus, privatisation can take many forms. A simple interpretation, such as the replacement of the state by the market, will not suffice. The kind of state intervention to be replaced must be specified; so too must be the type of non-state institution that will replace it. For this reason, it is not easy to argue about the merits and de-merits of privatisation in the abstract; the arguments will vary according to the types of state and private activities involved.

PRIVATISATION: FOR AND AGAINST

The case for privatisation rests upon the supposed deficiencies of the various forms of state intervention and on the ability of some form of privatised system to remedy them. In particular, the welfare state is said to have failed to achieve some of its aims, such as the promotion of economic efficiency and of social justice (usually interpreted in terms of greater equality of one kind or another), while at the same time it has adversely affected other ideals that society might have, such as the preservation of individual liberty. Privatised systems, in contrast, are said to be both efficient and conducive to the exercise of liberty; it has also been argued that they are on occasion more equal. Views such as these come from a large number of sources. Among the principal critics of the welfare state are Friedrich von Hayek, Milton Friedman, the 'Public Choice' School developed from the work of James Buchanan, Anthony Downs and Gordon Tullock, and the writers associated with the Institute of Economic Affairs. A detailed description (and ascription) of their arguments can be found in Part I of Bosanquet (1983). In what follows we elaborate these views and put forward some of the counter-arguments. (Many of the issues are discussed in more detail in Le Grand and Robinson, 1984.)

Efficiency

The welfare state is said to create inefficiency in two rather different ways. First, it is argued that state social services encourage a wasteful use of resources by both their suppliers and their consumers. Second, the welfare state is supposed to damage the productive power of the economy through its effects on the incentives to work and to save. Although the second charge could be also levelled at state subsidised social services, it is usually confined to the social security system.

The inefficiency of state social services varies with the type of state intervention considered. State *provision* is supposedly inefficient because services are not supplied at minimum cost. Individuals in state organisations pursue their own interests in the same way as individuals in private ones do; they all want jobs that are rewarding (in terms of money, status and power), satisfying and as secure as possible. However, in their pursuit of those ends, public employees are not faced with the same constraints as private ones; in particular, their 'firms' cannot be driven out of business or be taken over, even if they provide an inefficient service. Hence they will engage in practices that serve their own ends at the expense of their clients. Hours of work will be reduced, work practices will be inefficient, wages will be too high, other elements of remuneration such as pension schemes wil be too generous, and so on. Generally, resources will be wasted because the public sector lacks accountability.

This argument has been criticised as taking simultaneously too pessimistic a view of public employees' activities and too optimistic a view of those of private employees. To assume that public employees *never* consider their clients' interests is as naive as assuming that they never consider their own. And private employees, particularly of large corporate firms, often seen their own interests as quite different from making profits for the shareholders.

In addition, there are many specific areas within the welfare state where *a priori* reasoning would suggest that private provision would be inefficient. If users of a service lack relevant technical or other information (as, for instance, in the case of medical care), then this will permit monopoly exploitation by private providers (Le Grand, 1983, pp. 67–70). If there are economies of scale in production (as, for instance, in public transport), then a competitive market will degenerate into a monopoly. If people's desire to give to charity rests only on their concern for the recipient's welfare, then they will be tempted to 'free ride' on others' contributions and hence not enough will be given. And there are various technical problems associated with private insurance markets that make it likely that they will fail adequately to provide for sickness, old age and unemployment insurance (Layard and Walters, 1978, pp. 382–7).

Not surprisingly given the difficulty of measuring 'output' (and therefore the cost per unit output) in the social services, there have been very few empirical studies of the relative efficiency of public and private provision in the areas concerned. One exception is Spann (1977), who examined the relative efficiency of public, voluntary and profit-making hospitals in the United States. He found that different kinds of provision seemed to make little difference to quality, but that private provision 'might lower health care costs slightly' (p. 88); however, he emphasised the tentative nature of his conclusions. A study that was just in the area of the welfare state was that of public and private Canadian railroads (Caves and Christensen, 1980; discussed in Millward, 1982); this found no significant difference in efficiency between the two.

Other comparisons of public and private enterprise have concentrated upon areas outside the direct concerns of the welfare state, such as electricity and water supply, and refuse collection. Millward's careful review of this evidence (1982) shows that private enterprise superiority could be established only in the case of refuse collection; indeed, many of the other studies found clear evidence that costs were lower in the public enterprises. Millward suggested that what appeared to be crucial was not so much the form of ownership, private or public, but the degree of competition to which the enterprise was subject; and this is perhaps the most significant lesson to be learned from this literature. (Symptomatic of the difficulty of making definite statements on the issue even outside the welfare state is that Millward concluded from this review that the studies as a whole did not provide significant evidence of private superiority, while another recent review of the same evidence – Borcherding *et al.*, 1982 – came to the opposite conclusion.)

The inefficiency associated with state *subsidies* arises because their existence encourages users to demand more of the services concerned than they would if they were charged the true cost. The value of the extra services demanded (as measured by the amount that people are willing to pay for them) must be less than their social cost. Hence, if the extra services are actually provided, there will be inefficiency, with services being provided that cost more than they benefit. If the extra services are not provided, then some arbitrary rationing method must be used to cope with excess demand (such as queues or waiting lists). This will inevitably result in some people with high valuations of the service not receiving it, while others with much lower valuations do; hence again there will be inefficiency.

The principal defence of welfare state subsidies on efficiency grounds is that the services concerned confer external benefits. An external benefit arises when the use of a service by an individual confers benefits not just on that individual, but on others as well. Examples are immunisation from, and treatment for, infectious diseases; house improvements (raising the value of neighbouring houses); the political and cultural benefits from education; and reductions in traffic congestion associated with public transport. There is also a wider class of external benefit, known as 'altruistic' or 'caring' externalities, where people derive satisfaction simply from knowing that others are receiving the medical care they need, an appropriate education, proper housing, and so on.

If such external benefits exist, then a private market will under-supply the service concerned (relative to the efficient level). If people are forced to pay the full cost, then they will be tempted not to use the service themselves but to 'free ride' on others' use of it. So instead of paying to get immunised (or treated) people will rely on others getting immunised (and treated); house-owners will wait for their neighbours to improve their houses before improving their own; people will use cars instead of public transport; and so on.

One difficulty with this argument is that in some cases the magnitude of the relevant external benefits does not seem to be very great. For instance, infectious diseases take up less than 5 per cent of the National Health Service budget. In other cases, sizeable external benefits could exist, but might be better served by alternative means of state intervention (such as, in the case of education, enforcing common curricula in schools or, in the case of transport, introducing a system of road pricing). Ultimately, the importance of external benefits and the best way of dealing with them are again empirical questions; however, little of the relevant work has as yet been done.

Inefficiencies associated with state *regulation* vary according to the type of regulation. There are three principal kinds: that designed to promote quality, such as qualification requirements for practising medicine; that designed to affect quantity, such as compulsory schooling; and that designed to affect price, such as rent control. The first, it can be argued, is used as often to protect individuals and firms from competition as it is used to preserve quality; and, in so far as this occurs, it creates inefficiency by raising the costs of production. The second compels people to consume either more or less than they want to and hence creates inefficiency through frustrating consumer desires. The third lowers (or raises) the price that would have obtained in the market, and thereby creates excess demand (or excess supply). If it creates excess demand, then there is the problem of arbitrary rationing; if excess supply, the problem of unused or unemployed resources.

There is an enormous literature on the economics of regulation (for a review, see Joskow and Noll, 1981), very little of which has to do with the welfare state. The major form of regulation within a welfare area whose effects have been studied extensively is rent control. The results suggest that it has led to excess demand at the controlled rent level and contributed towards the long-run decline in the supply of private, rented accommodation (Robinson, 1979, Ch. 6).

The final area of alleged welfare state inefficiency is the effect of the social security system on the incentives to work and to save. Cash transfers are supposed to prevent people from taking up jobs, or from working as hard as they might when in employment. The provision of benefits in times of unemployment, sickness and old age makes it unnecessary for people to save against these eventualities. As a result, both work effort and savings fall, leading to lower levels of economic production than would otherwise occur. An extreme example of these disincentive effects in action is the so-called 'poverty trap'. The existence of both means-tested social security benefits and means-tested social services can lead to an individual who starts work losing benefits equal to or greater in value than his or her gain in earnings. Such people are facing a marginal tax rate of 100 per cent or more, and therefore are said to be 'trapped' in their situation (see Deacon and Bradshaw, 1983, Ch. 8).

Again, the impact of the welfare state on incentives is an empirical question that cannot be resolved *a priori*. The available evidence (mostly American) has been extensively surveyed by Danziger *et al.* (1981). By amalgamating the results of a large number of studies, they produced 'guesstimates' of the overall effect of the US social security system on the supply of labour and savings. They estimated the reduction in work effort, compared with that which would have pertained in the absence of the social security system, as 3.3 per cent; the equivalent figure for annual private savings was towards the lower end of the range 0–20 per cent. Although neither of these numbers seems large, the US system is significantly less generous than the British; it is possible that equivalent calculations for Britain might show up some greater effects.

Equality

Most people, on both sides of the debate, would agree that the cash transfers component of the welfare state is broadly equalising (Danziger *et al.*, 1981; Central Statistical Office, 1982). The criticism that the welfare state is *inegalitarian*, therefore, is generally confined to the social services and, within them, to the 'universal' services. These are services or subsidies available to everyone who wishes to use them without a means-test; they include most medical care under the National Health Service, most of the education system, tax relief to owner-occupiers, and public transport. An extensive recent review of the evidence (Le Grand, 1982) showed that the better-off almost invariably used such services to a greater extent than the poor, and concluded that such services had failed to achieve equality – however defined.

To acknowledge that the welfare state has failed to achieve equality is not, however, to imply that a privatised system, of whatever kind, would necessarily do better. In fact, the presumption has to be that it would do worse. Most privatised systems are likely to create distributions of the relevant service that more closely reflect the market distribution of private income and wealth. Of course, if the savings from reducing subsidies to the universal services were used to bolster the incomes of the poor, then the eventual outcome might well be more equal than under the present system; but that is a big 'if'.

There are none the less certain subsidies whose withdrawal would almost certainly create greater equality. Subsidies to university education, owner-occupation and public transport (particularly railways) are among the most inegalitarian uses of public funds; if they were withdrawn and the savings used to increase everyone's incomes equally, the poor would be better off and the rich worse off.

Even if the savings were used to increase the income of the rich by *more* than the poor then, so long as the absolute increase for the rich was not more than five times the increase for the poor (universities), six times (owner-occupation) and ten times (railways), the poor would still be better off as a result (Le Grand, 1982, pp. 131–2). Subsidised social services are at best an imperfect instrument for promoting equality.

Liberty

There is a variety of ways in which the welfare state is said to be illiberal or coercive. Individual preferences for diverse services are overruled; the taxation necessary to fund the welfare state's activities is coercive; recipients of welfare benefits have to conform to specific regulations and conditions; the welfare state creates a psychological condition of 'dependence', thus reducing people's ability to make their own choices; producers' interests predominate at the expense of consumers' liberties. More generally, there is a broad libertarian case against state power of whatever kind; any accretion of power to the state must imply a corresponding reduction in individual liberty, and therefore is to be deplored.

Whether liberty is affected adversely by the welfare state will depend in part on the definition of liberty chosen. If it is defined negatively, as the absence of coercion, then there is generally a presumption that various state activities will reduce liberty. If it is defined positively, however, as the freedom to do what one wants and accomplish one's goals, then the welfare state may be regarded as increasing liberty – particularly those parts of the welfare state that help the poor. (The distinction between positive and negative liberty is due to Berlin, 1969).

There are major philosophical questions here that we do not have the space adequately to consider. (For recent discussions of these issues see the special issue of the *Journal of Social Policy*, II (2), April 1982, particularly the contribution by Goodin; and Heald, 1983, Ch. 4.) However, there is one point that is worth emphasising. The state is not alone in taking decisions on behalf of private individuals; other private individuals do so as well. In particular, parents take decisions on behalf of their children; later, those children may have to make decisions on behalf of their elderly, confused parents. In both cases, individuals are deprived of the right to make their own choices: liberty, in the negative sense, is infringed. Now, many libertarians would like a lot of the decisions currently made by the state to be returned to the family. Yet the powers of the family do not seem intrinsically less coercive than the powers of the state. Indeed, many of the welfare state's activities can be viewed as protecting individuals against the tyranny of their families. This is perhaps clearest in the case of social workers, much of whose time involves protecting children and old people from decisions made, or actions taken, by their families. There are many other examples of the state intervening wholly or partly on behalf of those vulnerable to their families: compulsory education, regulation of old people's homes, allocation of council housing according to numbers of children, to name but a few. In short, many of the welfare state's infringements of liberty are simply replacing one agent of coercion (the family) by another (the state); and, in the abstract at least, there is no reason – on libertarian grounds – necessarily to prefer one over the other.

Community

We conclude with a positive defence of the welfare state that involves an objective that has not been raised in the discussion so far: that of community. For many people, the concept of the welfare state embodies a principle of collective provision and finance that they find preferable to the individualistic forms of behaviour encouraged through private market systems. Thus the welfare state serves to develop a sense of communal interest rather than self-interest. Such an objective is difficult to deal with within the conventional Paretian system because it implies that a 'community', and its level of social welfare, is in some sense more than a function of individual utility levels. (The concept of a 'caring' externality – Culyer, 1980, Ch. 3 – is an attempt to capture an element of this concept within the Paretian framework, but it fails to deal with it adequately.) Moreover, the objective also implies that the method of resource allocation is a source of social welfare *per se* independently of its output. But these difficulties only reveal the limitations of the Paretian system: that many people do feel a sense of community in their preference for, say, the National Health Service over private medicine is a matter of empirical fact. As such, the privatisation of certain health care services will tend to jeopardise the realisation of this objective.

A particular aspect of this view was expressed most persuasively by the late Richard Titmuss in his book *The Gift Relationship: From Human Blood to Social Policy* (1970). Titmuss viewed non-market, welfare state institutions as providing opportunities for altruistic behaviour; that is, they provide individuals with the opportunity to engage in acts for the 'common good' without any motive for personal gain. (He developed this argument in the context of voluntary blood donation, but it has general application to a whole range of social policy areas.) For Titmuss, privatisation proposals would restrict individuals' rights to act altruistically, actions that he regarded as ethically superior to the market pursuit of self-interest.

CONCLUSION

This introductory chapter has endeavoured to set the scene for subsequent discussion. No attempt has been made to reach an agreed position. Rather, we have sought simply to identify the main areas of debate. The chapters that follow will take up particular issues in more detail. Even here no simple consensus will emerge. The individual authors often differ in their judgements about the probable outcomes of various privatisation proposals. More importantly, their preferences regarding the relative importance of the objectives of efficiency, equity, liberty and community also differ. What they have in common is a shared commitment to the highest standards of academic debate. The reader of this book can thus expect to gain a far deeper understanding of the issues involved in privatisation as it affects the welfare state than is offered by much of the current political debate.

PART I General Principles and Strategies

Despite much simplistic political rhetoric that suggests otherwise, Chapter 1 has shown that the subject of privatisation is an extremely complex one. In one sense it represents a partial re-emergence of the longstanding general debate about the respective merits of market and non-market systems of resource allocation. As such there might be thought to be a large body of theoretical and empirical evidence on which conflicting claims may be assessed. This is not the case, however. Much of the theoretical literature deals in terms of polar extreme 'ideal' types: perfectly competitive market systems versus pure state provision and/or finance. If it has done nothing else, the contemporary debate surrounding privatisation has awakened people to the realisation that there is an enormous range of public/private organisational structures that require specific analysis in terms of their operation and performance. To date, the theoretical literature has not been able to deal adequately with this diversity. Similarly, as Chapter 1 has shown, the already sparse empirical evidence on the relative performance of public versus private organisations is not suitable for assessing this heterogeneous set of welfare state organisations. Thus, although the established debate between 'Marketeers' and 'non-marketeers' – and its particular form in relation to the welfare state – provides a useful context within which privatisation may be examined, it needs to be extended and modified to cope with many of the specifically contemporary concerns.

Part I of this book endeavours to contribute towards this process. Its four chapters indicate in terms of general principles and/or strategy some of the important issues that need to be confronted in the current privatisation debate.

In Chapter 2, Alan Walker sets the scene by providing an overview of the political economy of privatisation. He shows that there has long been a mixed economy of welfare that does not correspond to the simple public/private dichotomy upon which much of the current debate is based. Privatisation is thus seen as an extension of the existing limits. Walker is in no doubt that this is undesirable. He argues that the case for privatisation rests upon the subordination of 'social' concerns to narrow economic objectives, and that its social costs – in terms of efficiency, inequity and social segregation – are unacceptable. He concludes by outlining an alternative strategy for the socialisation of social services based upon universal, de-professionalised and locally accountable services.

The preference for locally based institutions is shared by David Donnison. In Chapter 3 he argues that, in the light of the failings of many old-style state services, the questions posed by the privatisation debate needed to be asked – even though the Thatcher government's response to these questions has been 'barbaric'. As an alternative, he points to progressive responses to the same questions. These include the decentralisation of public services; the development of economic opportunities through local enterprise boards and similar locally based organisations; the growth of locally based enterprises in which public service replaces private profit as the primary objective; and the development of community-based projects relying upon local involvement. Donnison leaves no doubt that such an agenda poses a number of yet unresolved problems of its own. For example, the appropriate constitutional structures, the degree of local autonomy and the cost-effectiveness of such schemes all require investigation. But, most important of all, he calls for the reassertion of a more compassionate ideology around which a consensus may be built; an ideology that will bind these projects together and form the basis for a more civilised society in the future.

Nick Bosanquet is also concerned to use the privatisation debate positively in order to propose new 'mixed' forms of service provision. Thus in Chapter 4 he starts by discussing reasons why the old style of tax-financed, state-owned, centralised bureaucracy is unlikely to be suited to the needs of the future. These reasons include increased difficulties in raising tax finance; the stifling of managerial initiative; inflexibility in employment conditions; diseconomies of scale; and the failure of large-scale, selective assistance schemes. These features are contrasted with new 'mixed' enterprises – represented at present by, for example, housing associations and voluntary hostels for the mentally handicapped – which are typically small and owned and managed independently of the public sector, although dependent on public as well as private and voluntary funds. Their greater flexibility in terms of managerial autonomy and employment conditions enables them to cater for changing user needs more efficiently. Bosanquet argues that in the future the public sector will, in many social welfare areas, need to adopt a rather different role: one of an entrepreneur promoting the growth of mixed enterprises through advice and the allocation of development funds.

These arguments suggest that the private non-profit and voluntary sector is destined to assume a greater role in the provision of welfare services in the future. If this is the case, a better understanding of the operation of this sector is clearly desirable. This is the concern of Robert Sugden in Chapter 5, who examines the contribution that economic theory can make to understanding voluntary activity. He starts by arguing that voluntary organisations are suppliers of what economists term 'public goods'. He then proceeds to show how the existing theory of public goods yields absurd predictions about voluntary behaviour. To illustrate, the theory predicts that a person currently donating, say, £10 per year to Cancer Research will, if faced by an increase in income of £100 and knowledge of the fact that Cancer Research has suffered a drop in income of £100 from its total income of several million pounds, devote the entire increase in his personal income to the charity! In the face of such implausible predictions, Sugden sets out to develop a more convincing theory of voluntary activity. Although this is only at an early stage at the moment, he is able to identify a series of economic and social motivations for charitable and voluntary behaviour. In the final part of the chapter, Sugden discusses the advantages of the voluntary sector in comparison with other forms of economic organisation. His conclusion is that the voluntary sector is ideally suited to the provision of a diverse range of public goods in the same way that the private market economy is designed to cater for heterogeneous tastes in the case of private goods.

2 The Political Economy of Privatisation

ALAN WALKER

INTRODUCTION

Why is it that after more than thirty years of steady growth in collectively provided social services the government has advocated and, in some instances, set about reducing the role of the state? What is privatisation intended to achieve? What are the implications of the development of this embryonic policy, particularly for those whose living standards are composed entirely of, or buttressed by, the social wage? This chapter is intended primarily to provide answers to these questions. In the process I shall discuss some of the general issues in the privatisation debate that are dealt with in more detail in relation to specific welfare state services in the second part of the book.

Of course the case against the privatisation of social services starts from the assumption that collective provision is potentially more egalitarian, socially responsible and democratic than similar services provided by the private market. Whereas a moral assertion along these lines might have sufficed thirty, or even ten, years ago, it will no longer. This is *not* simply because public policy-making is gripped by a 'cost-effective imperative' (Davies, 1980). In fact, the argument that privately provided services are more cost-effective than similar public ones is a matter of ideological belief that is, at best, unproven (Millward, 1982). It is also a recognition of the important critique that has developed in recent years around the restricting, unjust, undemocratic and contradictory features of the *experience* of public welfare provision (Wilson, 1977; Gough, 1979; LEWRG, 1980). It is not sufficient to support collective provision unquestioningly, as one would a football team. There are important deficiencies in the welfare state, which have been exploited by the right-wing proponents of privatisation. I am concerned, therefore, not with a straightforward defence of collective social services but, rather, with the further question: what alternative policies are there to counteract the deficiencies of the welfare state that the privatisation debate has exposed but that privatisation does not attempt to tackle and, in fact, may exacerbate?

In this chapter, then, I consider the strategy of privatisation in the context of the mixed economy of welfare. This indicates that it is not the radical departure that some of the more alarmist reactions have suggested. The idea of a continuum of public and private services is employed to underline the interconnection and interdependence of the two forms of service. This is followed by a discussion of the rationale underlying privatisation and its distributional implications. I go on to examine the divergence between economic efficiency and social equity that underlies privatisation. The chapter then turns to the potential impact of privatisation and particularly its social costs. Finally I outline an alternative strategy intended to increase the effectiveness and the efficiency of the social services, which unlike privatisation gives priority to the former. As a starting point it is worth reminding ourselves of the collectivists' case for the social services.

THE CASE FOR COLLECTIVE PROVISION

The full-blown collectivists' case for public social services is based in large measure on a critique of the free market as individualistic, undemocratic, unfair, inefficient and the source of social divisions and inequalities (Tawney, 1964; Townsend, 1967; Titmuss, 1968, pp. 138–52).

The advantages of public social services, by contrast, are, first, that they promote social purpose rather than individual self-interest, social integration rather than individualistic differentiation. According to Titmuss (1970, p. 255),

The ways in which society organises and structures its social institutions – and particularly its health and welfare systems – can encourage or discourage the altruistic in man; such systems can foster integration or alienation.

Secondly, collective control of social services, through a democratically elected government, militates against the exploitation of those in need of services by suppliers seeking to maximise their profit rather than the social good. Since some social service provision is often concerned with life or death situations, the clients of these services may be in a particularly weak position to resist the exercise of monopoly power. The provision of health care is the most obvious example of the dangers of any criterion other than that of need intervening between the demand for and delivery of social services (Titmuss, 1970; Abel-Smith, 1976). Because the state operates to some extent to protect citizens from such exploitation, collectively provided services also entail a partial redistribution of power; a point I shall return to in the latter part of this chapter.

Thirdly, collective services can distribute resources according to need, that is, according to 'social' as opposed to narrow 'economic' priorities (Walker, 1982a, p. 20). Social justice is more likely to be promoted by such services because it is only through collective provision that social costs or 'dis-welfares' can be spread throughout the system. Under a private market system of risk spreading, vulnerable high-risk groups would be excluded (Titmuss, 1970; Walker, 1979).

Fourthly, public control is needed to provide regulated, standardised and efficient services. Because of the inherent contradiction between the profit motive and meeting need, public regulation of private services is not sufficient to ensure that services operate in the interests of those they are supposed to serve (Le Grand, 1983, p. 69). Under the aegis of the state, economies of scale are possible (see, for example, Knapp and Missiakoulis, 1982) though in practice often difficult to achieve, as is demonstrated by the protracted negotiations between the Department of Health and Social Security and pharmaceutical companies to reduce the price of the drugs supplied to the National Health Service.

Finally, public social services can counteract the natural tendency of capitalist enterprise to increase inequalities in the distribution of resources, status and power. The state can guarantee minimum incomes and standards of provision, and it is the only institution that can ensure the application of distributional justice throughout society. Both left and right of the political spectrum agree that equality (however that is defined) is impossible without public intervention in the form of 'social services' (Le Grand, 1982, p. 10).

The fact that the welfare state, as institutionalised in Britain and other western capitalist societies in the immediate post-war period, has not achieved this goal, or fully realised any of the others outlined above, does not negate the case for collective provision or undermine its potential as a vehicle for distributional justice. Instead it suggests that these aims have not been pursued wholeheartedly; this is evident in both the coverage and organisation of the welfare state.

Apart from major deficiencies in the structure and operation of benefits and services – such as their bureaucratic inflexibility and lack of responsiveness to the needs of claimants and clients (see, for example, Lister, 1977; Piachaud, 1979; Burghes, 1980; Walker and Townsend, 1981) – it should be noted that the purpose of the welfare state is not solely to promote welfare. Despite the close association between the Labour Party and the Beveridge welfare state (Abel-Smith, 1983, p. 11; Walker, 1983), it was developed not on the basis of socialist principles, but more as an extension of democratic citizenship rights (Marshall, 1963, p. 302). It is certainly not intended, in its present form, to create social equality, as any claimant of supplementary benefit would readily testify; rather it is intended to guarantee certain minimum rights. Titmuss (1968, p. 191), for example, disassociated himself from those who believed that the welfare state was created for 'deliberately redistributive' reasons or that its effects would be 'significantly egalitarian'.

Although the dominant social construction of the welfare state in capitalist societies is a limited, liberal one, it does not represent the only possible form that collective provision might take – This is one of the main assumptions underlying this chapter.

THE MIXED ECONOMY OF WELFARE

Discussion of privatisation usually starts from the assumption that it marks the end of an era of (Butskellite) consensus on the role of the state in the provision of social services (see for example, Hastings and Levie, 1983). While there are important elements of truth in this (namely, that privatisation is one part of a radical social strategy and that it is pursued more single-mindedly than at any other time in Britain's post-war history), three important factors are often overlooked.

In the first place, ever since the creation of the infrastructure of services known collectively as the welfare state, social services have been provided by a range of *both* public and private institutions. In addition to these 'formal' services, there are also a large number of 'quasi-formal' or voluntary services such as the WRVS meals-on-wheels, as well as the 'informal' sector of family, neighbourhood and friendship networks. This complex reality remained obscured for so long largely because of the restricted construction of social services as public services, which dominated social administration until very recently (Donnison, 1975; Walker, 1981a). If, instead, one defines social services functionally, in terms of their aims or intentions rather than their administrative boundaries, then all attempts to attain similar social ends would be encompassed and not just those of the state. Thus,

social services are those means developed and institutionalised by society to promote ends which are wholly or primarily social. The ends include social justice; freedom from oppression; prevention of disease; abolition of poverty and squalor; integration in the community; harmony between races; equality of educational opportunity; full employment and especially social equality. (Townsend, 1975, p. 28)

Secondly, the two systems of public and private welfare do not exist in isolation but are interrelated (Heidenheimer *et al.*, 1976, p. 276). Decisions taken in one sector can have important implications for the other. The reliance of the private sector of health care on the public sector for trained personnel is one example of this interrelationship (see Chapters 6 and 7 below). Other examples are the coexistence of compensation for industrial injury through the tort law and social security systems (Walker and Townsend, 1979); public and private pensions (Reddin, 1983); the allowance paid by social services departments to private nursing homes for the accommodation of elderly people; the payment of foster parents in the informal sector by social services departments in the formal sector.

Thirdly, the distinction between the two sectors of formal services is rarely a simple one of private versus public, market versus non-market principles. Market mechanisms and assumptions are a common feature of public services. There are, for example, charges for home-helps and school meals, and rents for council houses (Judge and Matthews, 1980). Just as common is state regulation of private services – the provision of residential accommodation for elderly people, for instance.

Rather than a simple dichotomous framework of public and private institutions, social services consist of a wide range of sometimes overlapping provisions. This 'mixed economy of welfare' (Webb *et al.*, 1976, p. 5) is typified by housing, with a dominant private sector, large public sector and significant charitable sector. Not only does the state directly provide housing, in return for the payment of rent, but it also subsidises the private sector through tax relief on mortgages, improvement grants and the sale of council houses. In the personal social services, the vast bulk of caring tasks are provided, informally, by kin, neighbours, friends and volunteers. For example, more than twice as many bedfast and severely disabled elderly people live in their own or relative's homes as in all institutions put together (Townsend, 1981, p. 96).

This plurality of social service provision might be represented diagrammatically on a continuum stretching from the public sector, through private and voluntary provision to the informal sector. It is more helpful for our purposes here to imagine a continuum of *formal* services with two polar extremes: wholly public services, collectively organised and financed, on the one hand, and wholly privately run and funded on the other. Although the debate about public and private welfare is often based on these two ideal types they are, in practice, relatively rare. Ranged between them are the more common forms of service provision. There are predominantly public social services with residual private provision and/or market principles playing some role in the distribution of public welfare. Examples are education, social security, personal social services and health. In contrast, there are predominantly private services alongside smaller public sector provision in the same sector, and/or public subsidies underlying the finance of private welfare. Examples are housing and employment services. Looking at this continuum from the perspective of the organisation of state intervention it can be seen that there are three principal forms of activity: direct provision, subsidy and regulation. Discussions about privatisation tend to be concentrated on the former.

Drawing the line between public and private services

These various systems coexist and are to some extent interdependent, but the observation of a mixed economy of welfare should not obscure the fact that these forms of welfare provision are different in important respects. In the public sector, benefits and services are funded wholly or predominantly on the basis of general taxation and administered partly on the basis of non-market criteria such as need. In the private sector, benefits and services depend on individual contribution and are administered according to market principles, primarily the profit motive. The different forms of provision are not entirely substitutable for each other – between either the public and private sectors or the formal and informal sectors. To attempt substitution, therefore, means providing a different form of service, which may entail costs or benefits for the clients of that service, a crucial point that is overlooked entirely in official pronouncements and one to which I shall return later.

Much of the debate in social policy about different types of services revolves around the borderline between them, although it is sometimes difficult to discern precisely (Higgins, 1981, p. 156). The position of the borderline between public and private provision has an important bearing on the supply, nature and social perception of social services. Privatisation represents an attempt not only to shift the demarcation line between public and private services and establish a 'new balance' between them (Judge, 1982a, p. 15), but also, thereby, to change the character of those services, particularly those in the public sector. Moreover, while it may well entail the dismantling of certain aspects of public welfare services, in a broader context it is concerned with the restructuring of social services, especially the balance between the public and private finance.

The conception of a continuum of publicly and privately organised and funded social services contrasts with the simple model of either purely public or purely private welfare that tends to dominate much of the discussion in this field (Seldon, 1980; Labour Research Department, 1982). Thus privatisation is not simply a matter of the full transfer of ownership from the state to private enterprise (Levie, 1983, p. 28) – although this model is appropriate in the field of nationalised industries and panders to the needs of political rhetoric (Treasury, 1982, p. 1). In the social services, privatisation (or privatism) more often takes the form of a partial inroad into the public sector. This may consist of the takeover by private enterprise of specific ancillary services, such as school meals or laundry services; more common is the introduction of charges or a self-financing criterion. In this context then, privatisation represents the introduction or further extension of market principles in the public social services. Because of the difficulty of drawing a precise dividing line between public and private provision, the term privatisation is defined here in a much broader sense than is often the case. It is intended to underline the point that a service does not have to be totally controlled and administered by the private sector for (partial) privatisation to be carried out.

So, privatisation is not delineated simply by the particular ownership or management of services; there are elements of it in predominantly public services. Nor is it the introduction of cash payments that marks the essence of privatisation; nurses, social workers, home-helps and so on are paid for their labour and it is not unreasonable to expect that informal carers, such as 'housewives', should also receive financial rewards for their services. This is a matter of shifting the nature of the boundary between formal and informal care. Privatisation may be said to take place when responsibility for a service or a particular aspect of service delivery passes, wholly or in part, to the private sector and when market criteria, such as profit or ability to pay, are used to ration or distribute benefits and services.

The idea of a mixed economy of welfare is an elaboration of the 'social division of welfare', through which Titmuss (1963, pp. 35–55) identified functionally similar social services in three separate sectors of welfare. Within the social division of welfare, the cost of providing benefits and services falls, directly or indirectly, on the whole population (Titmuss, 1968, p. 192). In the informal sector, the cost is borne more directly by individuals and families (Walker, 1982b, pp.

32–4). The social division of welfare thesis is important for an understanding of why privatisation of social services is likely to widen social inequalities, and it is considered at greater length later in this chapter.

A comparative perspective

A comparison of similar social services in different countries on the formal sector organisation and finance continuum emphasises the range of possible mixtures of public and private provision. A study of health care expenditure in 1975 in ten western developed countries with similar population sizes revealed that the USA stood alone at one extreme in having less than half of its total health care bill paid from public funds. At the other end of the continuum, the UK, Sweden and Italy were overwhelmingly publicly financed. Between these extremes, West Germany, France and Canada were three-quarters reliant on public finance, and Switzerland, the Netherlands and Australia were two-thirds publicly financed (Maxwell, 1981, p. 59). The most famous study of differences in the operation and effects of publicly and privately financed social services is Titmuss's (1970) account of blood donation in Britain, the United States, Russia, South Africa and Japan. On the basis of estimates for the twenty-seven countries for which information was available in the early 1960s, he concluded that only in Britain and Eire and 'two or three other countries in the world' was the system almost entirely voluntary with no payment of any kind to donors. At the other extreme were Japan, Sweden and the United Arab Republic, where all or nearly all donors were paid. Most countries had a mixture of paid and unpaid donors, including the USA and USSR, both with 50 per cent paid donors (Titmuss, 1970, pp. 174–6).

This comparative perspective puts the discussion of privatisation in a broader context. As Higgins (1981, p. 139) points out, what is considered to be a normal organisational approach to meeting need in Britain is often abnormal elsewhere, and vice versa. So, for example, an important debate in the field of health care in the UK concerns whether public services should be transferred to the private sector; in the USA, the parallel debate surrounds the opposite question: should private responsibility be transferred to the public sector? Countries might also be compared on the basis of their different forms of fiscal and occupational welfare (Kaim-Caudle, 1973; Higgins, 1981, pp. 136–44), and also the different balance between them in terms of public welfare. This approach would overcome the obvious difficulty of assessing the role and function of social services solely on the basis of officially recognised public expenditure (see, for example, Wilensky, 1975).

The position that any nation occupies on the continuum between public and private welfare (in so far as it is possible to aggregate welfare provision) rests primarily on dominant values and ideologies, including attitudes towards the role of the state, individual freedom, private enterprise and paid employment (George and Wilding, 1976; Mishra, 1981). These depend, to a considerable extent, on the particular balance of the conflict between the dominant and subordinate classes in that society. Since this balance may change over time, the importance attached to different values underlying public policy also changes and so, in turn, does the mix of public and private services (Tawney, 1964, p. 124). Privatisation is one manifestation of these social changes and of the increased prominence given to individualistic values – just as the institutionalisation of the welfare state in the immediate post-war period reflected a different balance of class relations and the collectivist values it promoted.

This sort of dynamic (as opposed to static) analysis suggests that, rather than being an inevitable response to changed circumstances, the end product of a progressive road of reform or the result of ideological consensus about the mixed economy of welfare (Klein, 1980, p. 33; Gladstone, 1979, p. 3), privatisation is based on the ascendancy of a particular set of values and beliefs in the long-term structural conflict between social classes in Britain. This development, therefore, is certainly not immutable and may be mitigated by a change in the balance of power between different classes as a result of a general election or trade union pressure, or by interest groups campaigning in relation to particular services. Less convincing, as I shall go on to argue, is the suggestion that the strategy of privatisation itself could backfire and turn out to be a very short-lived phenomenon (Heidenheimer et al., 1976, p. 276; but see the second edition 1983, p. 331).

THE RATIONALE FOR PRIVATISATION

The strategy of privatisation is one manifestation of recent changes in the balance between different political ideologies (policies aimed at the domestication of women are another). But what are the values and assumptions underlying the strategy and what is the explicit rationale used to promote it?

I have already referred to the fact that privatisation is not a new phenomenon. The importation of market principles into the public

social services – privatism – has a long history and some elements of a
free market of welfare were built into the original framework of
services, for example in the provision for voluntary insurance in the
social security system (Beveridge, 1942, p. 143). The post-war period
of often uneasy Butskellite corporatist consensus witnessed a
fluctuating dividing line between public and private forms of
provision and a great deal of often heated discussion about the role of
public and private welfare (Lees, 1961; Friedman, 1962; Powell,
1966; Titmuss, 1968; Seldon, 1980). What is relatively new is the
social and economic strategy, currently being pursued, that is
designed radically to shift the fluctuating balance between public and
private welfare much further in favour of the latter than at any
previous period in the history of the welfare state.

There is not room here to trace the development of the current
Conservative ideology (see, for example, Gamble, 1979; Golding,
1983) or to explore the factors that contributed to the change in
economic and social policies in the mid 1970s (see O'Connor, 1973;
Walker, 1982a, pp. 7–11). Suffice it to say that the doctrine of
monetarism, or 'new classical macroeconomics' (Cross, 1982, p. 2),
lays blame for the inflation of the mid and late 1970s mainly on the
size of the public sector. Thus, the first sentence of the 1979–83
Conservative government's first White Paper on public expenditure
asserted that 'Public expenditure is at the heart of Britain's present
economic difficulties' (Treasury, 1979, p. 1). The key element of
economic policy, therefore, is the reduction in the size of the public
sector in order to make room for private sector investment to expand
– what Miller (1978) has referred to as the 'recapitalisation of
capitalism'.

Privatisation of the social services has an important part to play in
the recapitalisation of capitalism both in reducing the size of the
public sector and in providing ready-made markets for the private
sector. Privatisation of the social services, or the potentially
profitable parts of them, represents a direct gain to the private sector,
which may secure long-term contracts for cleaning, and so on, and
may undercut union-negotiated rates of pay. In some cases,
privatisation has been carried through, even though it was more
expensive, beause of the government's commitment to reduce the
size of the civil service (Labour Research Department, 1982).

The profit-making potential of privatisation depends to a
considerable extent on public sector support. Among the
shareholders of the two leading cleaning services are the Post Office
pension fund, the West Midlands County Council, British Airways
and London Transport pension funds. The public sector also provides
direct subsidies to the private sector. For example, nursing agencies

may increase their profits by relying on the public sector to bear some of their administrative and other costs. Private hospitals draw on publicly trained medical personnel. These hospitals are no longer the sole province of non-profit-making charities in this country. For example, in the five years to January 1981 American Medical International and Humana received an average yearly return on equity of 16 per cent and 24 per cent (Politics of Health Group, 1982, p. 19). The Pritchard Services Group – the largest supplier of hospital services in Britain (and the second largest in the USA) – increased its pre-tax profits by 73 per cent between 1980 and 1981. It is clear, therefore, that the privatisation strategy is of considerable benefit to private capital. By contrast, the workers employed by private contractors are often part-time and low paid. For example, the 14,444 UK employees of Pritchards earn an average of £30 per week (NALGO, 1983a).

Of course, the Conservative strategy is not based simply on the interests of private capital and the prescriptions of economic theories; there is also the characteristic *laissez-faire* aversion to the public sector. So cuts in public expenditure and privatisation are intended to strengthen individual incentives and enlarge 'freedom of choice'.

There are, then, two main strands to the policy of privatising social services.

On the one hand there is a reduction in the welfare activity of the state. Three main assumptions underpin this aspect of privatisation. In the first place there is the belief that public services stifle individual initiative and responsibility. In the words of the former Secretary of State for Social Services, Patrick Jenkin, 'our statutory services should be a safety-net, not a blanket that smothers initiative and self help' (House of Commons, 1981). Secondly, with the significant exceptions of defence and law and order, the assumption is that the private sector is necessarily more efficient than the public sector: 'what the state can do the private sector can do better' (Golding, 1983, p. 9). Thirdly, the non-productive public sector is held to be a costly burden on the 'productive' private sector. The main argument here is that increases in public expenditure, and more especially the taxation needed to finance them, 'crowd out' an equal amount of private spending. In the words of the last Conservative government: 'Higher public expenditure cannot any longer be allowed to precede, and thus prevent growth in the private sector' (Treasury, 1979, p. 2). For these reasons it is argued that the frontiers of the public sector should be rolled back. In other words, less government means more capitalist enterprise and individual self-help.

On the other hand, there is a drive to increase the efficiency of the public sector. This does not mean necessarily improving the *effectiveness* of public services in meeting need; indeed, in official statements on privatisation the needs and interests of the claimants and clients of the welfare state are given scant attention. The main aim is to reduce the size of the 'bureaucracy' in the social services. Yet, in the NHS at least, increased expenditure on administration is required in order to achieve a more efficient use of resources (Maynard, 1983, p. 36; DHSS, 1983). Of course, there is a link between efficiency and effectiveness. Indeed, the cost-effectiveness imperative might provide a much-needed challenge to the complacency that grips some sections of the welfare bureaucracy; but it is not the most important criterion of effectiveness in the delivery of social services. The current efficiency drive is not concerned with the central issue of how to determine priorities based on need in the social services, from which are derived both efficiency and effectiveness. Instead, the standards of commercial efficiency are applied to the social services on the assumption that the same criteria of efficiency should be used in assessing the effectiveness of both sectors. For example, Lord Rayner has been imported from Marks and Spencer to judge the 'efficiency' of different Whitehall departments. Commercial consultants, such as Price Waterhouse, have been used by some local authorities to assess their social services departments (see, for example, Price Waterhouse, 1982). Another aspect of this efficiency drive is the use of selectivity and the price mechanism to ration resources and target them on cases of 'genuine need'.

Both of these complementary aspects of privatisation entail the wider assertion of market forces in the public social services, in the belief that the private market is a superior mechanism of allocation. Both reflect and extend the re-legitimation of 'economic' or least-cost efficiency that is an integral part of the recapitalisation strategy of the Conservative government. In the realm of social policy this means, in Titmuss's (1970, p. 14) stark terms, 'the philistine resurrection of economic man'.

Privatising the public burden

At the heart of the privatisation strategy is the assumption that the public sector is wasteful, inefficient and unproductive. This model of welfare characterises expenditure on public social services, especially those with redistributive intent, as a burden on the economy (Titmuss, 1968, pp. 124–5). It has exerted a significant influence on both official and public attitudes to expenditure on state social services over the whole of the post-war period, and is one of the main reasons why elements of privatism were built into different parts of the welfare state from the outset.

The 'public burden' thesis underscores both of the strands of privatisation outlined above and is, therefore, crucial to an understanding of the rationale implicit in this policy. This is clear in the desire to 'roll back the frontiers' of the welfare state. Less obvious, perhaps, is that behind the drive for greater efficiency is the same belief that the public services are both unproductive and wasteful of resources by providing benefits to those who, it is argued, are not in genuine need. Thus the 'deceptively simple and romantically appealing' (Titmuss, 1968, p. 132) argument for selectivity in the distribution of benefits and services is a diluted version of the *laissez-faire* case for the full privatisation of the *finance* and organisation of services.

The 'public burden' model of welfare is supported by the crude division between productive economic relations and unproductive social relations (and, therefore, between economic policy and social policy) and the presumption of supremacy of the former over the latter (Walker, 1982a, pp. 12–14). Narrowly defined 'economic' objectives such as profit maximisation and economic growth are considered automatically to be legitimate, while 'social' objectives such as health and community care must secure legitimacy in the policy system, and are believed to rest ultimately on economic policy for their achievement (Pinker, 1974, p. 9). This view of social policy as the 'poor man's economic policy' (Miller and Rein, 1975) restricts severely the scope of social policy's contribution to social development. Equally it sustains the over-simplified division between the public and private sectors – even when the 'private' sector receives subsidies and the 'public' sector charges for its services.

These divisions are reflected in the statistics of economic accounting. Non-marketed goods, including public social services, are represented in the national income statistics in terms of expenditure not output. Statistically, therefore, there can be no productivity gain from the activities of these services. So, by convention, the more a society spends on public services, such as education and health care, the *lower* is its rate of economic growth (Glennerster, 1983, p. 11). Ironically, as Miller (1978, p. 6) points out, this represents a reversion to Marx, in that only some forms of economic activity are said to produce value; in this case, the public sector is by definition unproductive.

Although the public burden thesis may be criticised on a number of grounds (see Sleeman, 1979, pp. 87–93), it has exerted a strong influence on attitudes to public expenditure and taxation. It is, therefore, an important factor in the legitimation of privatisation and its apparent widespread acceptance by the public. In a recent small-scale study of attitudes to public services in Chester, Sheffield and London, it was found that some forms of privatisation were welcomed because they implied increased efficiency and effectiveness' (NALGO, 1983a, p. 9). The overall impression of ambivalence to public social services was mirrored in a survey of 240 adults in Kent in 1981. Of those aware of private schemes, 70 per cent thought that there should be freedom of choice and 60 per cent said they would use a private health service or send their children to private schools (Taylor-Gooby, 1983, p. 52).

ECONOMIC EFFICIENCY AND SOCIAL EQUITY

A major factor in the belief that private social services are, or would be, more efficient than public ones (and therefore in the case for privatisation) is the subordination of what might be termed social equity to economic efficiency. (To avoid confusing readers trained in economics I have substituted the term 'social equity' for my earlier usage 'social efficiency' – Walker, 1984.) The prefixes 'economic' and 'social' are intended to denote the primary focus of each of the concepts. They are in fact two very different concepts. This does *not* mean that they cannot be used in conjuction with the assessment of different policies, that they cannot be equated to some extent or that they are the only factors underlying policy. It is important, however, to highlight the dominant concerns of different policy prescriptions. Privatisation is concerned wholly with a narrow form of economic efficiency and its pursuit may have serious consequences for social equity (a point I return to later).

Economic efficiency is the 'least-cost' notion of efficiency (Culyer, 1980, p. 22). It is achieved 'when the value of what is produced by any set of resources exceeds as much as possible the value of resources' (Haveman and Margolis, 1977, p. 10). Clearly, social services would not be efficient if market value were the main criterion. For example, the economic product derived from the provision of home-help support to the elderly is, to say the least, difficult to measure in these terms and to relate to national production. However, regardless of whether or not such gains exist, they are assumed not to by the conventions of economic accounting. The related concept of *Pareto-efficiency* assumes, similarly, that the market is politically neutral and that the distribution of original income is fair (Mishan, 1967). Both concepts automatically undervalue the contribution of social services to development and growth.

'Social equity', in contrast, is concerned with the impact of policy changes on the distribution of resources, status and power between different groups in society. A socially equitable policy is one that maximises equality within this framework. It is not simply a matter of distributional justice in the spread of incomes and wealth; the distribution of status and power too should be subject to the same criterion. Thus social institutions such as those of the welfare state would, ideally, reflect this aim and set out to minimise any stigma and humiliation associated with the receipt of benefits and services.

There may be a conflict between the goals of economic efficiency and social equity. A project that meets a cost–benefit criterion may also make the poor worse off (Mishan, 1977, p. 101). A government may pursue economic efficiency as a priority, for example in the privatisation of the social services, but the outcome of this policy will not necessarily be a fair or just distribution of resources. At best, those in a relatively weak position (because of low skill, poor education, physical or mental disability) are likely to be further disadvantaged by the operation of the market, however 'efficient' it may be. If the criterion automatically overrides social priorities, then inequalities in the distribution of resources, status and power are likely to grow wider.

The assumption that the market mechanism is superior to non-market systems of allocation follows from the subordination of the equity concerns of social policy to the efficiency concerns that dominate economics and economic policy. Social policy has been assigned, by Keynesians and monetarists alike, to the role of intervening in a natural order of economic relationships to modify their outcome in the interests of 'social' goals. In both capitalist and state socialist societies, social policy has operated primarily as a 'handmaiden' (Titmuss, 1974, p. 31) to the economy (Ferge, 1979, p. 50). In Britain, the post-war settlement and the development of the welfare state took place within the framework of this sort of economic hegemony. Thus, many of the assumptions that Beveridge brought to his study of social insurance were based not purely on social welfare considerations 'but on the prejudices of official economic opinion' (Kincaid, 1973, p. 43). In particular, the necessity to limit the Treasury contribution was crucial in the decision to set benefits at a very low level (Beveridge, 1942, p. 177). Similar examples could be adduced from other sectors of the public services.

Proposals by the current government to privatise some parts of the social services are to some extent legitimated and encouraged by this legacy and by the failure of successive Labour governments to establish alternative principles of distribution as a basis for social development. The proposals are in large part, after all, an extension of some longstanding trends in the management of the social services, rather than a complete break with the past. The fact that the simple division between economic and social policy is false and misleading has been exposed elsewhere (see, for example, Walker *et al.*, 1983). The distinction between economic and social objectives is equally misleading (Abel-Smith, 1967). However, as long as this distinction is maintained, and with it the subordination of social to economic policy, the case for some form of privatisation of the social services will recur constantly, on the grounds that the economic efficiency assumptions underlying privatisation are more important than the social equity assumptions underlying collective provision. The large measure of ambivalence towards public services revealed by surveys and opinion polls is not at all surprising in view of the relative weight given, in public policy and the media, to the goal of economic efficiency as opposed to social equity.

THE SOCIAL COSTS OF PRIVATISATION

I now turn to the consequences of privatisation. Other contributors will discuss specific services in detail; this chapter is concerned with general questions and principles. Privatisation of the social services is likely to enlarge inequalities in the distribution of resources, reduce the efficiency of public services and widen social divisions.

Before discussing these consequences, it is necessary to point out that this analysis is based on a comparison between the two extremes of the formal social services continuum outlined earlier. Public social services already contain important elements of privatism that militate against the distribution of collectively financed benefits and services according to need. In other words, they are not directed primarily at social equity. My argument therefore is not only that privatisation would damage public services and, more importantly, their clients, but also that the public services are already defective in important respects. The question whether or not privatisation addresses these deficiencies is reserved for the concluding section of this chapter.

Privatisation and inequality in the distribution of resources

The contention that privatisation is likely to widen inequalities in the distribution of resources and life chances rests on an analysis of the distribution of social costs and the operation of the social division of welfare.

The term 'social costs' usually refers 'to all those harmful consequences and damages which other persons or the community sustain as a result of productive processes, and for which private entrepreneurs are not held accountable' (Kapp, 1978, pp. 13–14).

These include the social consequences of rapid technological change and the effects of production on employment, health and pollution. They are, in the main, the unconsidered side-effects of production. In a private market, producers charge and consumers pay for only the direct costs involved, whereas indirect costs or 'externalities' are passed on to the public at large. It was, of course, the recognition of this problem that prompted the earliest state intervention to regulate industry and protect public health. Social costs do not fall evenly on the public, but are differentially distributed, being borne disproportionately by the working class (see Townsend and Davidson, 1982).

The concept of social costs might be extended to encompass social insecurities and dis-welfares that arise outside of, and not as a direct result of, the process of production (Titmuss, 1968, p. 133). These include the social consequences of the government's economic policies (Walker et al., 1983), the ownership and management of pension funds (Minns, 1980) and even the class structure (Sennett and Cobb, 1974). They are the intended, as well as unintended, consequences of the particular forms of social and economic policies adopted by different societies. For example, since the mid-1970s in Britain, governments of both the main political parties have consciously chosen economic priorities and policies that have created widespread economic insecurity amongst workers and their families and large-scale unemployment and underemployment (Sinfield, 1979; Burghes and Lister, 1981). These social costs have been borne disproportionately by already disadvantaged groups such as people with disabilities, the low paid and so on (Walker et al., 1983).

The question for society, as Titmuss (1968, p. 133) argued so forcefully some fifteen years ago, is whether these social costs should be met by collective social services or whether they should be allowed to 'lie where they fall'? Equally, should the risks attendant on the class structure, economic system, process of production or government policy, which fall most heavily on the weakest groups in society, be underwritten collectively or individually?

Under the *laissez-faire* system of the nineteenth century, social costs were a matter primarily of individual responsibility. Privatisation reflects the same individualism. Underlying this strategy, then, is an individualistic explanation of need and deprivation – one that contradicts the known facts about the causes of social deprivation. Social problems such as unemployment, ill-health, disability, low pay and poverty are not primarily a matter of individual fault but of social creation (see, for example, Walker, 1980, 1981b). Moreover, even if there is an element of individual fault, the conditions in which it occurs are usually socially constructed, and it is often impossible therefore to draw a strict dividing line between the two contributory elements. This suggests that the case for privatisation resolves into an argument for forcing individuals to bear the cost of socially created problems and deprivations. Thus, according to Titmuss (1968, p. 134), 'universalist services are in part the consequence of unidentifiable causality'; they are partial recognition that many of the vicissitudes of life are beyond the control of the individual.

The socialisation of the financial cost of social problems means that the living standards of those affected are buttressed by a social wage. As I have indicated already, this is not to say that public expenditure on the social services creates greater equality; indeed, the evidence shows that some of it does exactly the opposite and supports inequalities (Townsend, 1979, p. 222; Le Grand, 1982, p. 128). The abolition of public social services in favour of private ones would, however, undoubtedly worsen this position.

The social division of welfare thesis is central to an understanding of why privatisation would widen inequalities. If the public social services are privatised, those who can afford to do so will purchase welfare services in the private market, while those who cannot will have to rely on a residual public sector. At the same time, the better-off will still be able to secure a disproportionate share of other forms of benefits and services (primarily in the form of tax concessions) through the fiscal and occupational sectors of welfare (Sinfield, 1978; Field, 1981). While the share of public expenditure on the social services might shift in favour of lower-income groups, privatisation nevertheless means that public expenditure on meeting social need will be switched from the one sector of the social division of welfare that attempts, in part at least, to distribute resources according to need. What is intended is a partial redistribution of resources from the public social services to the hidden fiscal and occupational sectors, in which higher-income groups automatically gain a greater subsidy than lower-income groups. Of course, the 'privatisation' of certain state subsidies, such as tax exemptions received by owner-occupiers for mortgage interest and capital gains, and subsidies for rail transport, would *reduce* inequalities in the distribution of resources between different sectors in the social division of welfare (Le Grand, 1983, pp. 72–7). This is not, however, the intention of current privatisation proposals.

There is another important respect in which privatisation would increase inequalities. Privatisation is a euphemism for cuts in the total amount of public expenditure devoted to the social services. It is by no means certain, however, that the private sector will provide the same level, quality and coverage of services as the public sector.

Moreover, because of the introduction of market criteria, distribution will be based, in part at least, on ability to pay. After privatisation, therefore, the distribution of resources on social services is not likely to reflect the same order of social priorities as under a predominantly public system.

An indication of the implications of privatisation for social justice can be gauged from what happens currently as a result of cuts in public services, in either gross or real terms. In this case, social costs and disadvantages do not simply disappear, they must be borne by the individuals and families concerned. For example, cuts in personal social services resources for the care of the elderly mean that the cost of providing this care falls not on the private sector but on the informal sector, and in particular on female kin. Indeed, the existence of the informal sector was used as a justification for cuts in the personal social services by the last Secretary of State for Social Services (Social Services Committee, 1980, pp. 99–100). Privatisation is likely to exploit the informal sector of care further by assuming that care will be provided in the absence of payment. Thus, like cuts in some public services, it will be more 'economic' simply because it is inadequate (Opit, 1977, p. 33).

Another consequence of recent reductions in public expenditure is the reinforcement of local variations in the provision of health, housing and personal social services. In the provision of home-helps, for example, some authorities have introduced flat-rate charges, some continue to provide an unlimited service free of charge and some provide a limited service free to each client. At the same time, the national shortfall of home-helps in relation to the official target is nearly 50 per cent. So, privatism does not necessarily imply an improvement in either the quality or quantity of the service received by social service clients.

Privatisation and efficiency

One of the main arguments in favour of privatisation is that it would increase the efficiency of the social services. I have already indicated that an economically efficient policy outcome is not necessarily socially equitable. Even on its own terms, privatisation would not automatically result in a more efficient or effective use of resources.

In the first place, privatisation and the growth of private insurance companies would result in enormous replication of provision and administration. In comparison with public monopoly, imperfect competition might give more choice but this would entail unnecessary duplication and, therefore, the waste of resources. Moreover, the extension of choice may itself be illusory, because private markets tend to provide choice between similar goods. This is especially likely to be the case in the social services because there are severe limitations on the extent to which they can be treated as market commodities (see, for example, Abel-Smith, 1976, pp. 45–57). In his classic study of blood donation, Titmuss (1970, p. 205) applied four basic criteria – economic efficiency, administrative efficiency, cost per unit to the patient and quality per unit – 'which economists would themselves apply' in order to assess the relative advantages and disadvantages of public and private provision. He found that on all four criteria in the USA 'the commercialised blood market fails': it was highly wasteful of blood; it was administratively costly and inefficient, and more bureaucratic; the cost per unit of blood was much higher than in the UK; and the quality of blood was much lower.

Secondly, privatisation of the social services would entail a strong incentive for those who hold considerable power to exploit the clients of those services. The consumers of services such as health care, education and personal social services are usually characterised by uncertainty and lack of specialised knowledge. This puts the professional groups working in those private services in a powerful position to recommend unnecessary treatment or services and thereby exploit the clients' ignorance. Where a private entrepreneur holds a monopoly over some form of provision in a particular area, for example a school or nursing home, or controls an emergency service, there is a dangerous opportunity for exploitation (Le Grand, 1983, p. 69). It is not that there is a natural inclination on the part of social service professionals to exploit their clients, but that in a private market they would be positively encouraged to do so in order to maximise their profit. Thus, contrary to the myth of consumer sovereignty:

> In commercial blood markets the consumer is not king. He has less freedom to live unharmed; little choice in determining price; is more subject to shortages in supply; is less free from bureaucratisation; has few opportunities to express altruism; and exercises few checks and controls in relation to consumption, quality and external costs. Far from being sovereign, he is often exploited (Titmuss, 1970, p. 206).

It is, at best, questionable whether a privatised service is actually more economically efficient or cost effective than a similar one provided publicly. So the recent assessment of Birmingham's social services department by the consultants Price Waterhouse (1982, p. 14) argued against the privatisation of the department's laundry service. There is no evidence that private hospitals are more efficient than NHS ones (Maynard, 1983). Research that indicates that private or voluntary services are cheaper than statutory ones have usually not compared similar services (see Knapp and Missiakoulis, 1982).

Privatisation is certainly not economically efficient when viewed from the perspective of the overall use of scarce resources. For example, if efficiency was the main aim in the NHS, then management, evaluation and information resources would be increased rather than cut: 'greater efficiency can only be bought at the cost of some greater administrative costs' (Maynard, 1983, p. 36). Paradoxically, however, the privatisation of the social services would be more 'efficient' by adding to national production. As I indicated earlier, this would be the automatic result of the purely statistical transfer of 'unproductive' social services, including some unpaid volunteers, to the 'productive' sector (Titmuss, 1970, pp. 205–6).

Judged in terms of social equity, there is no doubt that privatisation would increase inequity. There are serious difficulties associated with the assumption that collective welfare will be maximised by the pursuit of individual welfare. In particular, there is the presumption 'that self-interested actions have socially benign results' (Hirsch, 1977, p. 119). One example is the role of prevention. The state has a vested interest (tempered in practice by other interests) in preventing socially generated problems such as disability and ill-health. The private social service system has no such interest and little chance of operating on a common front to promote it. Its economic interest lies in reducing preventive action and increasing dependency. If the state were left with the task in a predominantly private system we might expect private social services to occupy a similar role to the tobacco companies on the issue of the prevention of smoking. This provides further indication of the potential waste of resources (particularly human resources) under private, individualistic market welfare.

Doubts about the criteria for the allocation of resources to individual clients can be extrapolated to the societal level. In comparison with public social services, resources would not be distributed equitably according to social priorities, particularly need. In an imperfectly competitive system of market welfare, the distribution of services would be based, in part, on a 'tyranny of small decisions' (Hirsch, 1977, p. 106). Overall then, privatisation would be likely to reduce the effectiveness of the use of total national resources spent on the social services.

Privatisation and social integration

Privatisation of the social services would increase social divisions and reduce social integration. There are three factors to be considered here.

First, it would add considerably to the power of corporations such as insurance companies (Titmuss, 1963, p. 238). At the same time, it would remove the potential for an effective challenge to be mounted against the monopoly power of welfare bureaucrats and professionals. As a result, unless strict regulation was enforced, the power of consumers would be reduced even further than at present. Privatisation, therefore, would remove an important element of social accountability. Although this has been inconsistently and inadequately established throughout the public sector, the potential for effective accountability and redress remains. Under a private market it is usually only those who can afford it, or who have the protection of a trade union or other body that can, who are able to secure accountability retrospectively through the courts.

Secondly, privatisation would increase the division between those with sufficient resources to buy services in the private market and those forced to rely on the residual public sector. Residual, selective systems of welfare make the poor stand out more conspicuously than universal ones (Higgins, 1981, p. 153). This entails a 'humiliating loss of status, dignity [and] and self-respect' (Titmuss, 1968, p. 129). Such services also encourage the view that the recipients are a public burden. Thus clients are likely to be stigmatised and increases in expenditure on their services hotly contested. (Privatisation is not concerned with freeing resources for the public sector because there is little doubt that, as soon as the private sector is established, public services would be cut back.)

Another aspect of the division between public and private systems is the impact on the staff of public services. The change from a predominantly public to a predominantly private system is likely to have a severe impact on the morale of the staff left in the public sector as they see resources diminishing and services worsening.

Thirdly, elements of social integration in common social services would disappear. Self-interest diminishes altruism and privatised social services might be expected to affect adversely voluntary effort and the availability of informal care by emphasising individualistic values. This highlights the fundamental fallacy underlying much of the case for privatising the social services and also for a more pluralistic mixed economy of welfare. It is falsely assumed that one form of service can fully substitute for another – in this case private for public. As Hirsch (1977, p. 93) points out, however, this 'does not allow for a change in the nature of the product according to the method of provision'. Once one set of services based on values such as social integration and community is replaced by another reflecting different values, such as self-interest, the nature of the service and its social consequences will have been transformed (Titmuss, 1970, p. 199). Of course, this would be considered to be a positive advantage in a right-wing social strategy aimed at reasserting market principles of distribution in the social services (Taylor-Gooby and Dale, 1982, p. 259). Thus, as Titmuss (1970, p. 225) has argued, social services may be used to foster self-interest or altruism.

TOWARDS THE SOCIALISATION OF SOCIAL SERVICES

In large measure, privatisation might be seen as an ideological response to a perceived damaging tendency in universal public services – the introduction of mechanisms of allocation and distribution that challenge market principles and militate against self-interest and consumerism. It is claimed, falsely, that privatisation would increase efficiency and consumer choice; the wide, tacit, public acceptance of at least some measure of privatisation is based in part on the belief that private provision actually is more efficient. Equally it reflects important deficiencies in public social services, deficiencies that social service clients and others may be tempted to believe that privatisation might overcome.

All public social services are not universal. Most of them contain elements of privatism in the form of charges, or selectivity in the form of means-tests. In recent years these elements have increased as a result of government cuts in the social services. For example, charges in the personal social services have been extended in many authorities and greater use has been made of private residential care. In education, school meals charges have been increased or parents have been expected to provide mid-day meals. It is likely that these changes, along with the general rundown of public services, have contributed to a reduced public commitment to the welfare state.

Public social services are not geared solely to meeting need. They also function as social control agencies, for example in the regulation of housing conditions, in sustaining the work ethic and in promoting certain family relationships. As such, they often stigmatise and further marginalise claimants and clients. They encourage dependence rather than independence. In the care of the elderly for example, there are powerful vested interests in the perpetuation of forms of residential care that manufacture dependency (Walker, 1980). The public social services are also characterised by the unequal relationship between bureau-professionals and clients, relations that may be patronising and authoritarian. As a result, the services are often unresponsive to client need (see, for example, Goldberg and Connelly, 1982). Equally, those working in the social services, such as social workers, are often put in impossible positions by being expected to tackle structural problems with meagre resources. It is not surprising, therefore, that many clients hold a confused view of the welfare state:

> The ways in which we interact with the state are contradictory – they leave many people confused. We seem to need things from the state, such as child care, houses, medical treatment. But what we are given is often shoddy, or penny-pinching, and besides, it comes to us in a way that seems to limit our freedom, reduce the control we have over our lives. (LEWRG, 1980, p. 8).

There are, then, major deficiencies in the public social services – such as their potential for promoting social equity and social justice. The privatisation strategy, however, is addressed not to any of these deficiencies, but rather to a domestic desire to reduce the size of the public sector. It has thus worsened the position for the clients of public services. If pursued still further it is likely to increase the stigma associated with public welfare, reduce the quality of the social services and prevent the planned distribution of public expenditure according to need.

What is to be done? It is tempting to conclude that the privatisation strategy itself might backfire when the economic and social costs of that action become apparent (Heidenheimer *et al.*, 1976, p. 276); but that position overlooks the strong ideological motive behind privatisation and the fact that the social costs of the strategy are themselves privatised and atomised. It may well be that the extension of market principles throughout the public social services would introduce an element of consumer power. If the evidence of health care in the USA is anything to go by, however, that is unlikely. More likely is that privatisation would add to the power of bureau-professionals and the tyranny of insurance executives. The result would be 'a socially irresponsible collection of corporate welfare states for some citizens, but by no means all' (Heclo, 1977, p. 24). Any element of consumer power for the better-off would be bought at the expense of the increased powerlessness of those forced to rely on the residual welfare state. Furthermore, contrary to expectation, the introduction of direct payments may actually make consumers *less* critical of services (Hirschman, 1982, p. 44).

In order to overcome the fundamental problems in the public social services sketched above, an alternative strategy to privatisation is required. The outlines of such a strategy may be traced here (for a detailed account see Walker, 1983). The 'socialisation' of social services would be aimed at extending universal principles at the expense of privatised welfare. Examples would be in health care and pensions. The goal would be truly universal services; that is, for the community and not separate client groups, distributed according to need rather than ability to pay. They would be based on small local areas, as far as possible, to enable democratic involvement and control. This would help to counteract paternalism and dependence. For example, community-based units for the whole range of personal social services clients, including short-stay residential provision and outreach services, might be combined with other community facilities. Clients would be involved in the management of services. Services such as health care and social work would be de-professionalised to enable clients to become less the passive recipients of welfare and more the active participants in social services. Power would be decentralised, and the rigid hierarchical division of labour in the social services would be reconstructed.

Clearly this is a radical strategy that is quite incompatible with the assumptions underlying privatisation. It is intended to illustrate the direction that is necessary in order to create social services that are effectively social in operation as well as in finance. It would undoubtedly reduce the freedom of choice of those who are able to purchase welfare; but it would enlarge the freedom of others and provide the basis for a socially equitable distribution of national resources.

The question remains, however, what is to be done about efficiency in the socialisation of social services strategy? The key issue for the future of the social services is how to maximise the effectiveness of the social services in meeting need and, in doing so, to secure the most efficient use of resources. So far, the proponents of privatisation have failed entirely to address this issue. It has been assumed that more privatisation automatically means greater efficiency and, at best, efficiency and effectiveness have been equated. I have already noted the fact that privatisation is aimed not at improving the effectiveness of services in meeting need, or indeed at increasing efficiency in the use of resources, but rather at a very spurious form of cost-effectiveness that assumes that the less spent on the public sector the better. To dismiss privatisation is thus not to dismiss the importance of efficiency. The socialisation policy proposed here places greater weight on the effectiveness of services in meeting need than on narrow economic efficiency. The efficient use of resources is nevertheless essential if priorities are to be met effectively. Services must be planned, managed, audited and evaluated more effectively, which will probably require more rather than less expenditure on administration. This pill is likely to be too bitter for the right-wing supporters of privatisation to swallow.

CONCLUSION

A key question now confronting social policy and society is whether the social costs of economic policies and socially created disadvantages are to be socialised or privatised. The case for privatisation rests in part on an individualistic explanation of social problems, and therefore allows that social costs should lie where they fall. This also reflects a narrow economic theory of efficiency that puts market relations above distribution on the basis of need. The case for universal public social services stems from observation of the construction of deprivation and dependency and, in turn, from the desire to promote social integration and the allocation of resources according to principles of distributional justice.

In conclusion, it is worth remembering that public social services were provided on a universal basis precisely because the private market was unable or unwilling to do so:

> If these services were not provided for everybody by everybody they would either not be available at all, or only for those who could afford them, and for others on such terms as would involve the infliction of a sense of inferiority and stigma. (Titmuss, 1968, p. 129).

Supporters of privatisation have overlooked or ignored this fundamental fact. Moreover, the privatisation strategy is not aimed at overcoming any of the main deficiencies in the scope and delivery of services. It is, therefore, at best a diversion from the long overdue task of rethinking the welfare state and, at worst, one that increases the inadequacies of the public social services.

ACKNOWLEDGEMENTS

I am extremely grateful to Ray Robinson, Eric Sainsbury, Adrian Sinfield and John Westergaard for their helpful comments on an earlier draft of this chapter.

3 The Progressive Potential of Privatisation

DAVID DONNISON

INTRODUCTION

The questions posed by the present government's attempts to 'privatise' public services needed to be asked, even if some of the answers given by this regime have been barbaric. This chapter briefly outlines the main aims and forms of Conservative 'privatisation' recently initiated, and the initial response of their critics, and concludes that these responses are often even more conservative – with a small 'c'. It then outlines four developments now taking shape in the local administration of public services. These are beginning to modify a functional or service-oriented style of government by giving it a stronger economic orientation, area focus, and community base. They may offer more constructive responses to some of the defects to which 'privatisation' was addressed, but many problems will have to be resolved before they can take root effectively. Six of those problems are briefly discussed in the next section of the chapter. By practical experiment and careful thought a richer array of alternatives to Conservative initiatives can be generated. Some speculative suggestions illustrating the forms these alternatives might take are offered in conclusion.

CONSERVATIVE 'PRIVATISATION'

'Privatisation' is a word invented by politicians and disseminated by political journalists. It is designed not to clarify analysis but as a symbol, intended by advocates and opponents of the processes it describes to dramatise a conflict and mobilise support for their own side. Thus it is a word which should be heavily escorted by inverted commas as a reminder that its meaning is at best uncertain and often tendentious.

'Privatisation' of the social services initiated by regimes of the right takes many different forms. They include the shedding of work from public services to private contractors (the Home Office's Police College at Bramshill is now guarded by security men employed by a subsidiary of an American multinational); the encouragement of private sector competition with public services (the big commercial hospital – also American – now being set up in Southampton opposite the medical school and its NHS hospital is an example); the sale of public assets to private owners at artificially low prices (the disposal of the City of London's flats in the Barbican to their generally rather well-to-do tenants is a striking instance); policies for securing a larger share of the costs of public services from their users (by imposing or increasing charges for admission to art galleries and swimming baths for example); and the abolition or reduction of public services, carried out with the assumption that private provision of some sort will fill the gap (the drastic cut-back in provision of school meals for example). All these forms of 'privatisation' upset rather long-established equilibria and are therefore likely to have further economic and social repercussions. Where the normal school meals service has been abolished altogether, the sandwiches that the authority is still compelled by law to provide for children living on supplementary benefit must become a grotesque social stigma of the latter-day poor laws. Commercial hospitals will not prosper unless private medical insurance prospers: since very few people can afford to meet the costs of hospital treatment from their own pockets, some collective provision for the sharing of risks has to be made. But some of the main insurers suffered losses in 1981. Thus the government will be pressed, and may agree, to provide financial support of some kind for the industry in order to keep it and the private hospitals in business.

The examples of 'privatisation' I have picked are conservative, not in the sense that they prevent change – on the contrary, they are bringing about a lot of changes – but in the sense that they express the aspirations and operate within the assumptions of a long-established view of the world. Central to that view is the conviction that the price mechanism and market relationships usually provide the most efficient ways of allocating resources and managing affairs. Many conservatives go further and say these relationships are morally superior – healthier for society.

Academics – who have played their over-simplifying parts, along with the politicians – often assume that choices will normally have to be made in this debate between equity and efficiency, and that these choices range public enterprise and the soft-hearted left on one side against private enterprise and the hard-nosed right on the other. Reality is more complex, however. The arguments advanced by

William Beveridge and others of his generation for national insurance
and a national health service were as much concerned with the
inefficiency of friendly societies, private insurance, the private and
voluntary hospitals, as with their inequity. They were expensive ways
of providing an inadequate service. Meanwhile, the belief that the
state will operate more equitably than the market is convincing only if
it can be based on the assumption that government will be
accountable to a central, fair-minded, popular consensus. In many
parts of Northern Ireland, for example, local administrators can be
fair or democratically accountable but not both. Higher levels of
government present problems too: it is noticeable that the Roman
Catholic minority provides approximately its proportionate shares of
solicitors and medical general practitioners (professions supplying
services in a kind of market – even if it is largely a publicly funded
one), but it provides far less than its proportionate shares of judges,
barristers, hospital consultants and senior public administrators
(professions more heavily dependent upon the state for their work
and their appointments). Uncertainty about the fairmindedness of
governments, present and future, may explain why tenants of the
Northern Ireland Housing Executive have been more anxious than
public sector tenants in Britain have been to buy the houses they live
in.

THE CRITICS' RESPONSE

It is time we turned to the left and the opponents of 'privatisation'.
They argue that public enterprise can be more efficient than the
private sector and solve problems of distribution which the private
sector can do very little about, thus creating a fairer, a more equal
and a more efficient society (see Chapter 2). Here, too, strong moral
principles are involved: the profit motive, many people feel, has no
place in the management of services concerned with things like
health, education and public order.

However, the people who turn out to demonstrate against
Conservative proposals for privatisation have mixed motives. Some
are consumers of public services. But people find it much easier to
organise collective action as producers than as consumers. Thus many
of the demonstrators are defending personal interests: they work in
the public services and their jobs may be threatened, along with
familiar working routines. That may explain why the political
response to what is called the 'attack upon the welfare state' has thus
far focused mainly on restoring the previous regime – with knobs on,
as it were. Proposals to outlaw private education, private practice

within the NHS and the sale of council houses, and to spend more money on the state's schools, medical services and houses, may be justifiable by comparison with some of the things now going on, but they are very conservative – with a small 'c'.

It would be a pity if the left went no further than this. Although some of the steps toward 'privatisation' now being taken are blatantly reactionary in their attempt to restore class privileges and to reduce the quality of public services available to poorer people, they are also, in their more sophisticated forms addressed to some major defects in the state's services. If their opponents do not like the Conservatives' medicine for these defects, they should be prepared to propose alternative remedies. For the defects are real. They include unnecessarily slipshod and wasteful management, and poor quality service, undisciplined by competition or by any other procedures for ensuring accountability to the customers. Too often, co-ordination between different public services is poor and they show insufficient sensitivity to local needs and feelings. The list of complaints is too well known to require illustration. It is true that provision by the private sector is often even worse, but to take refuge in that riposte is an evasion, not a remedy.

Spokesmen of the left have pressing political motives for going further. They must find solutions for these problems if their association with the 'welfare state' is not to become a vote loser instead of a vote winner. They may oppose the sale of council houses, but can scarcely deny that much of the worst public housing – in some places now unlettable – would never have been built if those designing and commissioning it had stopped to ask themselves whether ordinary families would one day be prepared to invest their hard-won earnings in buying it. Those who resist handing public services over to the private sector must nevertheless recognise that the substitution of capital for labour has proceeded more rapidly in the private sector and that many public services are as a result growing steadily more costly in real terms (Gershuny, 1978); if nothing is done about that, these services must eventually suffer cutbacks, whoever is in power. Markets, it is true, respond only to effective demands expressed in terms of money, not necessarily to human needs; but for this reason they do at least place the bus stops, the supermarket, the chemist, the clothing and shoe stores alongside each other in an accessible part of town. Meanwhile the social security office, the unemployment benefit office, the job centre and the social service area team – all of which an unemployed family may have to visit on the same day – are normally placed a long way apart from each other. In a recent study of the east end of Glasgow, one of my colleagues contrasted the travelling times and costs for people going from their homes to the surgeries of local doctors and to the new health centres which are now replacing them. The results suggest that the surgeries were located to suit the patients, while the health centres have been located to suit the dominant professions within the health service. The location of higher education in the same city would produce a more pronounced pattern of the same sort: there is not even a college of further education on the poorer side of town.

These examples remind us that we are not dealing with simple comparisons between the public and private sectors (the GPs and the health centres are both in the public sector; and it was an essentially private sector decision which in the last century moved Glasgow University from the east side of the city to the more affluent west). Nor are we dealing simply with centralisation versus decentralisation. Although that comparison comes nearer to a statement of the issues, the transfer of public security guards, health services and housing to American multinationals, large insurance companies and building societies is in many respects a transfer from one set of large centralised organisations to another.

The problems to be considered are about efficiency and equity, and therefore about accountability – both to the current customers for public services and to the larger communities of voters and taxpayers at local and national scales, now and in future.

NEW DEVELOPMENTS

It is partly because they recognise these problems that reformers in various parts of the political spectrum are taking initiatives which bear some resemblance to 'privatisation' – but in less conservative forms. Although these initiatives cannot be as clearly distinguished as my rather crude simplifications suggest, at least four different developments seem to be under way. They are concerned with: (1) decentralisation of public services; (2) the development of economic opportunities; (3) the creation of new forms of enterprise; and (4) community development.

First, and perhaps least revolutionary in their implications, are the attempts now being made by local authorities – in Walsall, Glasgow and inner London, for example – to decentralise their existing services, to get more of the staff and the work out into more accessible local offices which will, so far as possible, ensure that different departments serve the same areas. These authorities are to varying extents trying to set up local groups which represent the communities living in each area, and to varying extents devolving responsibility for the allocation of resources to them and to officials working at area level. The areas on which these operations are focused operate at about the scale of a local government ward – larger in Glasgow, smaller in Islington. Their central aims are to make existing services more accessible, accountable and acceptable, and to co-ordinate their work more effectively.

A different development, often to be seen in the same places, is concerned with the promotion of new enterprises and the creation or retention of jobs. Something like a standard 'kit' of measures has been worked out to provide small factories, which may be let at subsidised rents; 'enterprise workshops' where new businesses may be nursed into life; loans and grants for small companies; and advice, information and training for entrepreneurs and their workers. Liverpool, Swansea, Greater London, the West Midlands, and the joint agreements negotiated by the Scottish Development Agency with the local authorities in towns like Motherwell, Clydebank and Dundee all provide examples of these developments. The Manpower Services Commission, local or regional Enterprise Trusts and other bodies play major parts in some of these initiatives. The scale of the action is typically city-wide or regional, for these are the scales on which the local economy and its labour market operate. Its central aims are to increase or retain jobs, skills and incomes.

A version of these initiatives which deserves to be distinguished from the general run of local economic development programmes is designed to promote new forms of local enterprise, generally operating on a small scale, which will be more concerned than the conventional capitalist firm with the social value of the product and the welfare of the workers, and less dominated by considerations of profit; the interests of consumers and producers are to bulk larger, those of the money lenders less large, than hitherto. The enterprises supported may be co-operatives or companies distributing no profit to individuals. Sheffield is probably the most articulate example of an authority following these policies, but in many other places there are specific agencies, public or voluntary (co-operative development units and the like), which have objectives of this kind. The scale of these operations is individually very small, although they may extend over a city or region. The aim is to develop new forms of non-capitalist enterprise.

The fourth line of action, least clearly defined in institutional form but potentially most radical in its implications, is the movement for community development. Salaried community workers employed by the state play important parts in this work, but indigenous initiatives by local residents mark the more viable and lasting examples. The Craigmillar and Easterhouse Festival Societies are among them. Although they may demand action from the public services – the reconditioning or demolition of damp housing, more generous discretionary payments from the social security office, and so on – their projects are not confined to this statutory framework. They may begin with drama and the arts, and go on to establish community businesses of various kinds and to set up youth clubs, local women's groups, centres for the unwaged, and so on. They are not so much an organisation as a meeting place and an initiator for many organisations. The activities of these smaller groups are often focused on fairly small numbers of people, not necessarily concentrated in a particular neighbourhood (one-parent families or ethnic minorities, for example). The general, longer-term aim is community development.

These four movements do not exhaust the possibilities, neither are they mutually exclusive. Indeed, some of the most hopeful strategies combine something of all four aspirations. Newcastle is the scene of one such ambitious approach. The city has an enterprise workshop and other projects for assisting small businesses. Priority Area Teams have been set up in each of the most deprived inner wards. These teams consist of local councillors, other representatives chosen by local groups, and officers of the local authority. Each team is allocated a sum of money each year – currently about £50,000 – and is free to propose how this should be spent and to seek additional help from other sources. Although the local authority committees and departments concerned with the action proposed are entitled to comment, the final decision is taken not by them but by a central priority areas committee. The local team normally meets in its ward, often in public. New initiatives launched in this way include the provision of community centres, the setting up of a small farm in the centre of the city (manned by workers funded by the MSC and visited by thousands of school children every year), and the installation of entry-phones for flats. Meanwhile, independently of these officially sponsored projects, the city has a lively range of community-based activities concerned with welfare rights and political education, the establishment of a centre for unemployed workers, the provision of self-help for groups of one-parent families, and so on.

PROBLEMS TO BE RESOLVED

If these new developments are to go forward constructively, a lot of hard thinking and practical experiment will be needed. Here I outline half a dozen related problems standing near the top of the longer agenda that will have to be tackled.

One of the first problems to consider is the question of scale.

Action concerned with economic opportunities has to operate at a large scale because the urban economy works on this scale. Action designed to mobilise and support the community's capacity for developing its own projects and tackling its own problems has to be focused on a very much smaller scale – often covering no more than a few streets. Meanwhile, action designed to devolve power – to spend money, deploy staff or allocate houses, for example – has to operate on a scale large enough to secure resources worth having, yet small enough for representative groups and their staff to get to know the area and its people pretty well. This is probably the scale of a ward, or in Scotland perhaps one of the community councils set up and minimally funded in response to local demand by the district authorities.

I believe action at all three of these scales will be needed. The groups formed at the miniature, 'community' scale should be the building blocks of the system, nominating many of the representatives operating at the middle 'administrative' scale where the work of different services can be co-ordinated and decisions can be taken about the deployment of resources. Meanwhile a programme to extend and preserve economic opportunities, whether in conventional capitalist enterprises or in new public sector or co-operative forms, should range over the whole city and its surrounding region.

Decisions have also to be taken about whether these strategies are to develop 'wall-to-wall' throughout the territory of any authority launching such initiatives, or to be focused selectively on deprived areas needing priority treatment. Walsall and the London boroughs are developing uniform patterns of decentralisation throughout their territory. Newcastle has focused on a minority of priority areas. Glasgow is combining both policies, adding a city-wide decentralisation to a more selective pattern of special initiatives and programmes focused upon areas for priority treatment. Is positive discrimination, designed to concentrate additional resources on areas with special needs, an integral part of the decentralisation programme? If not, what other steps will be taken to achieve some measure of positive discrimination? These are the questions which must be answered.

Thirdly, there is the question of the constitutional structure required to represent the communities concerned – to speak on their behalf to the rest of the world, to provide a forum to which public officials can be made accountable, and a forum too in which local politicians can gain some sort of power base that will help them not to forget the interests of those they represent when playing their parts in their authority's major service-oriented committees. That is not only a political question of elections, representatives, regular meetings, office-holders, and so forth. It is also a matter of devolving parts of the budgets for public services to local areas – the same local areas for each service. People will not enter seriously into this sort of politics unless there are real gains to be made.

Peter Marris (1982), quoting Jan O'Malley's study (1977), has vividly shown how community work which lacks an enforceable constitution and office-bearers with power tends to disintegrate into fragmented campaigns over particular issues defined by the functions and funding powers of statutory services. The 'tyranny of structurelessness' and the lack of any recognised and regular relationship to power lead ultimately to the 'dominance of structures' – very conservative structures.

Some power over the allocation of resources is now being devolved to community-based groups. Glasgow's housing management co-operatives, for example, are beginning to choose tenants for the houses they manage. Such groups will from time to time want to take decisions which run counter to the policies of higher levels of government. Some may even become corrupt or criminal. How much freedom can they be given? Crucial under this heading are questions about the enforcement of national minimum standards as a foundation on which greater variety may be built, and questions about the danger that majorities may tyrannise unpopular minorities – excluding one-parent families, ex-prisoners, ex-mental patients, black people or newcomers, for example. These problems can never be wholly resolved, but they are not insuperable if confronted vigilantly. We should not be panicked by old-style administrators who oppose decentralisation on these grounds. (After all, how many of the unpopular minorities did *they* place in the more popular neighbourhoods? And as for corruption – has Poulson been forgotten? It should be possible to do at least as well as previous regimes.) As for more conventional rules of administrative uniformity, which prompt bureaucrats to say that nothing can be done in one part of town that is not immediately done in all similar cases elsewhere – it is precisely the aim of decentralisation to break with these traditions.

What will these initiatives cost in the short run and in the longer run? In disaster areas of the sort studied by Anne Power and her colleagues (Department of the Environment, 1982), where rent arrears and fuel debts pile up, vandalism is rife and houses become unlettable, the decentralisation of staff and work to local area offices, coupled with a determined attempt to respond to local demands, may actually save money. These areas, fortunately, are not the norm, however. The rather casual accounting procedures encouraged by the

Urban Aid funding that has sustained so many of these programmes will have to give way to more systematic monitoring of expenditure. The public appointments pages of *The Guardian* make it clear each week that authorities like Sheffield, Hackney and Greater London, now pursuing decentralisation programmes of various kinds, are hiring a lot of fairly expensive staff. A realistic assessment of the costs of these programmes and some estimates of their benefits will be needed before too long.

The last of the problems I want to pose here is the most important of all. What, in the longer run, are these developments designed to achieve? What ideology binds them together and carries them forward? The old regime, which has world-class achievements to its credit, had aims and a rhetoric that rightly had political resonance, evoking widespread public support. It was about 'fair shares', 'equal opportunities', 'full employment', 'meeting needs without regard to the ability to pay' and 'giving security from the cradle to the grave'. Those aspirations are to be respected. They should be reinterpreted, not rejected.

The people who built the system of government which was to express those aspirations assumed that the economy would go on generating the jobs and incomes required to sustain the growth of the welfare state. Meanwhile, the social services were designed to operate in what they thought was a businesslike fashion – centralised, professionalised, specialised, uniform, 'top-down' . . . A functional, service-oriented style of government was created. The new movements are creating – tentatively and experimentally – systems that are more economically oriented, more area focused and more community based. Phrases of that sort may serve for the academic seminar and even for administrative committees, but they have little resonance with the electorate. Meanwhile the directions in which they point run counter to long-established trends in British government, which for at least a century has given growing powers to the migrant, specialised professionals at the expense of 'laymen'; has drawn sharper distinctions between the public and the private sectors and between economic and social programmes; and has steadily replaced the varied local friendly societies, local philanthropies and local poor law authorities with uniform, centralised services. There were good reasons for these trends in earlier times, but they have now gained such momentum that it will take a political revolt to reverse them. In their different ways, 'privatisation', the Liberal Party's 'community politics', and the rise of 'the new urban left' all suggest this revolt may be beginning.

CONCLUSION

Equity and efficiency should still be our combined aims; but those words are far too brief to offer sufficient guidance. Community, democracy, enterprise, self-management, open government – these are some of the key concepts inspiring the new trends. They would be more familiar in Yugoslavia and China – and in the Russian workers' soviets before they were put down by Lenin – than they are in some British town halls and Whitehall departments.

We should try to create effective working examples of these developments and think through the principles and implications involved if we are to replace the more brutal forms of 'privatisation' now being imposed with something better, rather than simply reverting to the previous regime and its unsolved problems. The examples of Conservative 'privatisation' which I noted at the start of this chapter may serve as pegs on which to hang some speculations – they are no more – about the more varied responses we should be capable of formulating. Such responses may enable us to create arrangements that would eventually be accepted by most of the governments this country seems likely to form.

Rather than simply terminating the contract of the firm now guarding Bramshill Police College and bringing this work back within the civil service, the possibility should be considered of helping the staff concerned to set up their own co-operative, and helping them to bid for similar contracts elsewhere.

The standards of care provided by the private hospital to be set up in Southampton, and the terms on which it uses the staff and other resources of the NHS, will have to be carefully monitored and regulated by an authority effectively representing the community – not only by the professionals involved. Public resources should not be used to assist the insurance companies on which the profitability of the operation will depend. It is the introduction of profit as a major criterion in the management of medical care and the neglect of patients from whom no profit can be made that are objectionable, not the introduction of private initiatives as such. It would be a pity if supporters of the NHS were led by their antipathy to 'privatisation' to oppose the development of mutual aid, self-management techniques and preventive health education which are now being pioneered by groups up and down the country.

Justifiable hostility to the sale of council housing in areas like inner London, where good, subsidised, rented dwellings will always be needed, should not lead to a complete ban on sales everywhere else, or to the erection of even greater barriers between public and private sectors. Instead, local housing authorities should be encouraged to develop and adapt their stock of dwellings to meet local needs by buying and selling in the market as housing needs and their resources for meeting them change. We shall always require public, rented housing, but we need never again build a council estate. Likewise, helping people to buy, repair or improve a home of their own by lending, building, selling, grant-aiding, homesteading or in other ways should be among the services a housing authority offers its customers.

Cuts in expenditure on education should not simply be restored in their original form. Many would agree that mid-career and second-chance education of various kinds may now be even more urgently needed than an indiscriminate general increase in higher and further education, for example. But funds for adult and continuing education should not be paid without question to universities, local education authorities and other educational institutions to use as they see fit. Individual potential students, along with community groups, trade unions and other bodies, might instead be allocated an entitlement to education resources and enabled to decide for themselves in what forms of learning, secured in what institutions (if any) they will seek these opportunities. If school meals services now being abolished are to be rebuilt in future, this too may be a field in which local co-operative enterprises might be helped to start up, and later to expand into other forms of catering such as meals-on-wheels, cafés, contract catering and so forth – from some of which they would be debarred if they were part of a statutory service.

These are no more than speculative examples of possibilities which might be explored. Their aim, within the limited areas of government concerned, is to contribute to the larger consensus amongst reforming spirits in all parties which now has to be rebuilt: a consensus about the need for more accountable, efficient, innovative, humane services – public or private. Parts of this chapter have been presented in a contentious style. Some features of Britain's present regime leave no other option for citizens with any moral sense. But consensus politics – that much derided practice – is always preferable if the consensus leads in humane, reforming directions. It is preferable not because it is more cosy (trying to keep one's mind open to the facts poses more painful dilemmas than any comfortingly extreme ideology) but because lasting reforms are achieved not through tit-for-tat legislation but in the minds of the people. Government's most important role is to help in creating the culture and the material environment in which progress to a more humane and rational society, built on an evolving consensus, comes about. It would be churlish not to recognise that some of the questions about public services and the state posed by the present regime's actions badly needed to be asked. It is now up to people of goodwill in all parties to formulate more civilised and sensible answers than we have yet been offered.

NOTE

Earlier versions of these arguments were delivered as a John Madge Memorial Lecture in November 1982, and published by the Fabian Society as 'Urban Policies for the Eighties', Tract No. 487, 1983.

4 Is Privatisation Inevitable?

NICK BOSANQUET

The argument about public sector service has raged mainly at the level of general economic and political principle. The old debate used to be about 'cash' and 'kind'. Economists have generally preferred to give assistance in the form that left greatest freedom to the consumer, although some have been prepared to accept that there could be a case for 'specific egalitarianism' – for subsidisation of certain services (Tobin, 1970). There are, however, different ways in which the pattern of output and services could be altered. The aims of specific egalitarianism can be achieved indirectly as well as through direct public provision. The debate now has three options: support through cash; direct public provision; and indirect provision.

There are a number of reasons why the old style of public sector enterprise – which may be defined as a service entirely tax financed and publicly provided by people who are public sector employees with lifetime tenure – will rarely be the free choice at the margin for any new or changed service. These reasons between them may help to explain why there has been a movement away from the old pattern under various administrations of different political colours and why the movement is likely to continue.

This chapter looks at some of the pressures in positive economics for a shift towards indirect provision in the social services. It is concerned with actual performance rather than with ideal types. I begin by setting out the six main reasons for change in detail and then examine which of them are particularly important for particular types of service.

First, levels of taxation have risen, especially on lower incomes, over the past twenty years. The change has particularly affected direct tax payments. Tax money is now a scarcer resource, available only as a result of difficult reductions in other programmes or through increased taxation. That may be possible through inadvertence but will rarely be acceptable as a plan. The scarcity of tax money forces the question of output to the fore. It will be asked more often how much extra service can be derived from a given amount of tax money and the answer to this question will rarely favour old-style public enterprise. It will usually be possible to produce more output for a given amount of tax money by persuading others to come up with an additional finance. Thus interest is bound to grow in hybrid schemes using partly public and partly private finance.

Secondly, new projects require managerial drive. The old-style public sector already has difficulty in managing effectively the assets it has got. A commitment to start a new project on the old orthodox lines implies optimism about whether the public sector can recruit the managerial ability to run it – in the face of evidence that the public sector already has a shortage of this ability. The public sector is most obviously unattractive for people seeking entrepreneurial rewards in terms of profit, but it may also repel people of entrepreneurial disposition looking for rewards in terms of a personal sense of achievement and identification. Such people find difficulties in working for the old public sector, which usually has a complicated network of committees and vested interests. It may be that a more decentralised public enterprise could overcome this problem; if it does so, it is likely to have ceased to be public enterprise in the old style.

Thirdly, forms of organisation intermediate between the orthodox public enterprise and the profit-making firm are still relatively uncommon. In the 1930s, there.was little orthodox public enterprise and it was possible to make a strong case on efficiency grounds for it. Marginal additions could fit to some of the situations where it was most appropriate. They could produce gains in terms of higher output and lower unit costs. Such additions might also be able to draw on management and other resources that had a high productivity in these uses. Similarly in a socialist economy, some diversification towards profit-making firms is likely to bring very high returns, as is being found in Hungary and elsewhere.

In the 1950s and 1960s, the trend of events did not favour non-profit enterprises. Many decisions seemed to reflect an implicit assumption of sharp dualism between the government and the state. In the last ten years there has been some renewed interest, as shown for example by the growth of the housing association movement. It is highly likely that a first wave of expansion would be able to call on specialised resources and to show very good returns. It would be wrong to expect these returns to continue indefinitely, however.

Fourthly, there is an increasing gap between conditions for public employees and the conditions that are considered quite acceptable by employees in smaller voluntary organisations. (The difference between employment conditions in the public sector and those of large primary employers in the private sector may not be great, and is in any case not the important one here.) One major difference is not so much in the immediate salary but in pension contributions and fringe benefits. Local and central government have pension schemes and other fringe benefits that add one-third or more to the hourly wage cost. The most serious difficulties are in hours and flexibility, however. Effective hours in the public sector are often shorter and adhered to more closely. This presents special difficulties in providing twenty-four-hour cover and a seven-day-a-week service. In social services hostels, for example, inflexible patterns of hours make it very hard to provide the continuity of care that would be desirable.

There are also areas in the public sector where unions can exercise strong job control, although differences in the degree of effective control over manning, work output and day-to-day management are probably more important than differences in union membership as such. In the rest of the economy, job control has become less common: in the private sector it has been driven back almost to its old redoubt of Fleet Street. Indeed job control does not exist in many parts of the public sector – for example, there is little evidence of job control among ancillary workers in the National Health Service (Bosanquet, 1982), and it is under siege among dustmen in local government. There are still important bastions, however.

Much more important in its day-to-day effects than union power is the quiet influence of professional demarcation on recruitment. Such demarcations had their origin in the need to protect the public against quack doctors, but they have been extended to a bigger range of professions and of jobs than can easily be defended on such grounds. Particular difficulties arise where the training and approach of a profession have been overtaken by events and where the actual work situation demands change in training, but where established professional power can keep a profession in post and prevent change and adaptation. This has clearly happened in the case of nursing staff working with mentally handicapped people. Rules and custom on the recruitment of professionals with certain forms of training can inhibit a team approach where staff trained on-the-job work with professionals. For example, it is now very uncommon to employ lab assistants in hospital laboratories. Highly trained people must perform simple tasks, such as mixing media, that could be done with perfect safety by people trained on-the-job.

The relative contrast in employment conditions between the old-style public sector and the rest of the economy has grown over the past ten years. The recession has reduced job control and slowed down improvements in fringe benefits in the private sector. It has also had the effect of weakening the drive towards comparability: Employees in new enterprises, whether these are private or semi-public, are less intensely concerned with getting their pay and conditions exactly into line with those in the core public sector. Thus the old public sector now has relatively heavier costs and greater potential embarrassments about efficiency and flexibility.

Fifthly, the old-style public sector now faces severe problems with diseconomies of scale in some activities. This is most clear in the housing field, where the market in every country has shown a retreat from large empires of rented property. This has taken place whether or not there was strong legislation to control rents. The public sector is the only empire left. The difficulty of effective management of estates that may run up to 180,000 dwellings, as in the case of Glasgow, is enormous. Plans for decentralisation are proving difficult to carry through and disappointing in practice.

There is clear evidence from the United States that larger school districts are less effective and there is much public criticism of large schools (Niskanen, 1975). The difficulties with large comprehensive schools may be overcome in principle by a high quality among head teachers, but this will not always be forthcoming. Within local government, there has been an increase in the size of unit that has brought much criticism. For Britain, there are few detailed studies of the effects of scale; but the very great public concern may well have substance to it.

Within the National Health Service, the commitment to large hospitals of 800 beds or more made in the late 1960s has been abandoned in face of the clear evidence that such hospitals experience major problems with diseconomies of scale (Department of Health & Social Security, 1969). The recent reorganisation of the NHS was partly designed to move towards smaller health districts, and plans are now made on the basis of the smaller district hospitals of 400 beds. Unfortunately, however, some very large hospitals had already been built and will be with us for many decades to come.

Thus the trend of decision-making seems to recognise increasing problems of scale, accountability and responsiveness in the old public sector, and the continued advocacy of decentralisation suggests that the action taken so far has not gone far enough to overcome them.

Sixthly, there is an increasing division in terms of standards and acceptability between different kinds of public service. Selective services for the less well off have generally shown a lack of improvement over the years, with services for the single homeless as a notable example. Council housing has moved towards the American model of welfare housing, and that too has shown deterioration in maintenance standards, in public reputation and in the confidence of its own tenants. The more successful services have tended to be those run on a universal basis for all, including the most powerful consumers. Thus, for all its problems, the National Health Service remains popular and acceptable on a day-to-day basis. However, it is just these universal services that run into greatest problems with the great scarcity of tax money.

There is no guarantee that a selective service run on an unorthodox basis will be able to avoid the problems of stigma and declining standards, but it would start with a better chance and a less dismal history behind it.

IMPLICATIONS FOR CHOICE

There are thus certain conditions in which proposals for expansion of the public sector could be made with complete confidence: these should include the availability of tax money – one of those rare periods in which tax burdens are not seen as verging on the intolerable; adequate managerial ability should be available; it should be possible to organise recruitment and the use of manpower in ways that are cost-effective; there should not be major problems with diseconomies of scale; and it should be possible to give the service a reasonable chance of being able to hold its own in society. Such conditions are to be found when expectations of economic growth are high, with benign prospects for tax revenue, and when the public sector is relatively small. Once the expectations of growth falter and once the public sector is very large, then the case for further expansion in the old style must be much weaker. There comes to be more merit in the argument that there are separate decisions to be made about the financing and the production of public services (Buchanan, 1977).

Much previous comment on the issue has suggested that there is a simple dualism between public and private, between the bureaucratic and the profit-seeking form of organisation, and that the only decision rule needed is to bring about the maximum switch from the public sector to the market. This decision rule is not a great help for those types of service – such as the provision of home-help or nursing service to confused or disabled elderly people – where a market does not exist at present, on any scale. There are, moreover, many kinds of activity that are going to be unattractive to risk capital and that are not going to be able to provide the returns required by such capital.

We can list some examples of activities for which there would be a fair consensus across political parties of right, centre and left that a considerable degree of public initiative was required:

- assistance to elderly owner-occupiers with house maintenance;
- places in nursery schools and play groups for children;
- help to very elderly people so that they could continue to live at home;

● places in hostels and small flats for homeless single people.

The right would argue that the main public initiative required would be to stimulate markets for these outputs and services. The new right argues that a market could be stimulated through redistribution in cash. If this is not being done, it is entirely because of political prejudice and vested interest.

There are, however, strong reasons other than those of political prejudice for thinking that the market may be a mirage in these activities. Since the work of Baumol it has been common to make a distinction between the technologically advanced sectors of the economy, where there are rapid improvements in productivity through increases in physical capital, and other areas where the labour input – the quantity and quality of personal attentions – is required for itself (Baumol, 1967). The list above includes both areas where little cheapening through technological progress is to be expected – as with house maintenance – and areas where the quality of attention is vital. Labour costs will be influenced by changes in productivity in the capital-intensive sectors of the economy, which can show both rising earnings and a slower rise in costs; but the 'quality of attention' activities will show rising real costs. Private services such as supermarkets and hotels are more easily able to substitute capital for labour; but even so, many low-cost labour-intensive private services have tended to go out of existence unless heavily subsidised by family labour.

Thus the market will have difficulty in providing certain kinds of personal service at low cost. In an ideal world, redistribution would be through a negative income tax, but such redistribution has not yet taken place and in some lines of vision it never will. What then is the most appropriate public response in cases where the profit-making form of enterprise is not readily available and where a general redistribution through cash is not an option?

This is a very different question from those that concentrate on the simple dualism of the market and the state. It also suggests caution about simple comparisons of efficiency between the private and public sectors. Most of such comparisons relate to activities where a market is readily available – such as the running of airlines (Spann, 1977). Comparison becomes much more difficult where the market is not available. The answers are also likely to change over time. When the public sector was small, as it was when Tawney was writing in the 1930s, the answers would have been very different from today, when the public sector is very large (Tawney, 1964). Nor does the old case for public initiative based on externalities give much help.

We have looked at six points that singly or together may present difficulties for public enterprise in the old style. Their cumulative effect is to suggest that, at the margin, old-style public enterprise will rarely be the first choice. Future public initiatives are going to have to find very different ways of financing and managing public activities. In most cases, a given amount of tax money will produce a higher quantity or quality of output from mixed types of enterprise. Government should see itself as an entrepreneur stimulating action by others. This is already happening to some extent through the force of financial necessity in the short term, but it may have virtue – in lower costs and greater user satisfaction – in the longer term. Above all, it may prevent the social stigma and segregation that affect pure public services administered on a selective basis.

My list of points may also help to explain why the debate about efficiency in the public sector has become a dialogue of the deaf. Certain areas of public work may not suffer from any of these disadvantages. They may also have special advantages in having low capital charges or none at all. As long as they are doing work that does not change very much and that can be contained within the normal working week, they may be able to show lower costs than private enterprise. Hospital laundries and hospital cleaning staff are doing work that has many of these advantages and where additionally there are no capital charges, separate overheads or profit margins. It will hardly be surprising if the public sector is sometimes competitive here. Other areas of the public sector suffer from some or all of the six disadvantages in full measure. Both sides in the debate can make selective quotations of those parts of the public sector that appear most to their case. The left usually quotes the National Health Service as an example of superior public sector efficiency. The right makes great appeal to airlines and more business-oriented parts of the public sector. In a situation where both 'private' and 'public' are faced with professional monopoly, the public route may show up quite well. Where the full advantages of high capital intensity and rapid change in technology are available, however, it will rarely compare so favourably.

NEW 'MIXED' ENTERPRISES: SOME APPLICATIONS

New 'mixed' enterprises are distinguished by some or all of the following features:

- private or voluntary funds are used in capital and revenue funding of the project as well as tax money;

- the managers are not public employees but are accountable to an independent committee or authority;
- the activity is run by an organisation that is independent of the old public sector, and that is legally responsible for the clients or activity;
- the organisation is responsible for setting its own pay and employment conditions and for organising its own recruitment, training and shift systems;
- the organisation is relatively small;
- the managers of the enterprise make their own decisions on service patterns and on the range of clients to be involved.

In each of these respects the new mixed organisation differs from the older type of pure public sector. The latter is entirely tax-financed; the managers are public employees and responsibility is to the civil service or local governments hierarchy; pay conditions and manpower are tightly controlled both by existing formal agreements and by custom. Under such conditions, the organisation is of indeterminate and potentially giant size. There are no strong constraints in terms of funding, manpower and management to set limits to its growth. This affects both central and local government organisations. Some examples would be the drift upwards in the size of local authority housing stocks from 1960 to 1980 and the development of job centres and associated activities by the Department of Employment in the 1970s.

I turn now to some examples of 'mixed' activities already in development and some that are possibilities for the future. Services that rely mainly on family labour, as is the case when foster care replaces care in children's homes, are not included.

Housing associations

The housing association movement has shown remarkable growth under successive governments since 1970. In 1981/2, investment by housing associations accounted for 26 per cent of gross public sector investment in housing, while fifteen years ago it was a negligible amount. Motives ranged from the desire to encourage voluntary effort to the wish to provide more choice in housing. The late Anthony Crosland put particular stress on the need to increase the range of housing providers and to move away from the old public sector's local monopoly in rented housing (Crosland, 1974).

The 'mixed' quality is least in terms of finance. The only independent contribution is by the tenant through payment of rent, which is set on a more individual and independent basis than in the old public sector through the fair rent method. Most of the capital cost is covered by tax finance. In spite of this, the associations have done surprisingly well in maintaining their own identities and management. They set their own employment conditions and pay scales, and are able to exercise greater flexibility. For example, housing associations are able to employ caretakers/handymen to do a range of minor maintenance jobs, whereas union restrictions have made this impossible in local government. Many associations are relatively small, although the expansion has now gone to the point where some of the larger ones are beginning to experience the same diseconomies of scale as have affected the old public sector. Tenants are partly drawn from nominations made by local authorities, which are limited to 50 per cent of vacancies, while the associations make their own decisions about filling the rest. In general, the associations have been a success and have been able to avoid the problems of scale, social segregation and growing unpopularity with the public and with tenants that have affected the old public sector. However, it is wrong to assume that in all localities further expansion in their present form would be equally trouble-free, or that their independence and sense of identity would survive indefinite expansion.

The Youth Training Scheme

Under the 1971 Industrial Training Act much stress was put on the provision of training directly by government in skill centres, which were run as part of the old public sector. Now, policy towards training stresses the greater benefits to be expected from employer-based training. The Youth Training Scheme is a good example of this new approach (Manpower Services Commission, 1982).

Under this scheme most of the formal funding is still public. The trainee is paid an allowance and the managing agent is paid a fee. However, the fee is unlikely to cover all the costs incurred by the managing agent, who will in effect be making an indirect contribution. The managing agent contracts with the trainee to provide a twelve-month programme of training, which must include at least thirteen weeks off-the-job training. The agent has considerable freedom to organise the programme within certain guidelines about content laid down by the Manpower Services Commission. The agent, for example, makes his own arrangements with local further education colleges for the off-the-job part of the training. The trainees have to be paid a minimum allowance, which is set at a fairly low level; the agent can organise work and pay at his own discretion within certain very broad limits. The managing agency is responsible for recruitment and selection.

This is very different from the old type of government training programme. The main government functions are to pay the allowance and to establish standards, but whether these standards are met in practice will depend on the local entrepreneurs or managing agents, who will be carrying the day-to-day responsibility recognised in the contract between them and the trainees. Whatever the scheme's current difficulties, the principle is likely to find wide application in the future.

Hostels for mentally handicapped or mentally ill people

Early plans for community care in the 1960s and 1970s saw the future in terms of hostel places provided in the old style and run by people who were direct public employees. There has been some expansion of this kind of place, but the unexpected development has been in the expansion of informal places in group homes and voluntary hostels (Ritchie *et al.*, 1983).

Although such schemes draw on public funds for the capital expenditure – usually through the standard grants made to housing associations – they are self-supporting in revenue spending. Residents pay rent in the normal way and may either work or claim supplementary benefit. In terms of dependency and need for care, the range of residents in these informal places is similar to that found in local authority hostels. The costs of care, however, are generally lower. In local authority homes, annual direct revenue costs per resident in 1980 were about £3,640 for mentally handicapped people and £3,400 for mentally ill people. For the 'informal' group homes, costs ranged from £286 a year per resident in 1980 for mentally handicapped people to £386 for mentally ill ones. These informal homes are able to draw on volunteer help in a way that is not done by the local authority hostels.

The informal places are often the responsibility of voluntary groups whose organisations are quite small and locally based. They arrange recruitment and make decisions about pay and manpower with a great deal of freedom, and they select their own clients. The high costs of orthodox residential care are creating new interest in this type of solution.

Future applications

There are many ways in which different kinds of mixed enterprise might be developed in the future.

The housing market is a polarised one in which people have either to find the considerable sums required to become owner-occupiers or to find some way of getting access to the public sector. It is also a market in which demand and supply are not in balance and in which prices do not reflect costs because of both implicit and explicit subsidies, especially to owner-occupiers through mortgage interest tax relief. For tenants, even after recent large increases, rents still reflect historic costs rather than realistic replacement costs. It has been been suggested that new types of social housing might be financed as well as managed on a more independent basis. The aim of social housing would be to restore the missing middle of the market, and given the tax constraint this can be done only through attracting private savings. Building societies and other investors searching for fixed-interest investment might lend money to a Social Housing Bank for onward lending to housing associations (Social Democratic Party, 1983). There would be an element of subsidy in the early stages so that rents would be mid-way between fair rents and the full rent required to meet the lending terms. The ownership of the assets would be with the lending institutions, so that they would be able to benefit from the capital appreciation in the long term, but day-to-day management and maintenance would be carried out by the housing association. The subsidy would be required to make for a transition from the current situation to one in which demand and supply was in better balance.

Within education there are some potential applications of the mixed principle to higher education. The London School of Economics has already set an example in finding sources of funds other than the University Grants Committee. Even if the bulk of funds for higher education continues to come from tax money, any growth will increasingly have to be financed from other sources. In the 16–19 age group the training allowance is a kind of voucher scheme, as was the old Training Opportunities programme. This principle could be extended so that the voucher could be exchanged at schools and further education colleges as well as with employers.

The mixed type of enterprise will also become more important in residential care. The high costs of residential social service for more severely handicapped and disabled people will make this an increasingly attractive option.

Some will view the growing move towards mixed forms of initiative with great suspicion, accepting it only under duress and because of lack of alternatives. I would take a rather different view: such schemes have positive virtues in a low-growth economy in which a large, inflexible public sector is faced with many new needs. In such an economy, it may be worth looking for new forms of mixed financing as a first step rather than as an afterthought, and accepting as a basic rule that most new enterprises should be of a mixed type. The only exceptions would be the core of the compulsory stage of education together with the core health services. Here, relatively high levels of 'output' combined with problems of equality and the greater acceptability of these universal services may still give the traditional public sector the edge (Bosanquet, 1983). For many other activities there should be a greater separation of ends and means. The decision to finance publicly should be distinct from the decision to produce publicly. The state will be involved through subsidisation and through helping entrepreneurship by others, rather than through direct public provision. It may well be that public and consumer interests would be better served by the indirect approach.

5 Voluntary Organisations and the Welfare State

ROBERT SUGDEN

Advocates of privatisation usually seem to look favourably on voluntary organisations. Such organisations are private in the sense that they are 'outside the public sector' and it is possible to see in them the self-help motive at work – albeit at a collective rather than individual level. The 1979 Conservative Party manifesto (p. 27) linked these two notions of self-help when it declared:

> In the community, we must do more to help people to help themselves and the family to look after their own. We must also encourage the voluntary movement and self-help groups acting in partnership with the statutory services.

This chapter will discuss the merits of a strategy of encouraging the 'voluntary movement' or 'voluntary sector' – that is, private charitable trusts and reciprocal self-help organisations – to act as a substitute for various statutory welfare services. Throughout the chapter I shall use the word 'privatisation' in this sense. My object is to evaluate the arguments for privatisation in the light of economic theory. To say this, however, is to presuppose that economic theory is adequate for the task; and I am not sure that it is. Much of the chapter will be devoted to showing just how little is known about the economics of the voluntary sector.

VOLUNTARY ORGANISATIONS AS SUPPLIERS OF PUBLIC GOODS

Any economist who tries to investigate the voluntary sector is likely to experience a good deal of embarrassment about the inadequacies of conventional economic theory. The essence of the problem is that the voluntary sector appears to be principally engaged in the provision of public goods, to an extent that is quite inconsistent with standard theory. Yet the standard theory of public goods underlies most economic discussion of the proper role of the state in providing goods and services. The theory predicts that public goods will not be supplied in economically efficient amounts unless individuals are compelled to contribute towards the costs of supplying them; it is because of this prediction that economists can argue that public goods should be provided by the state. In many contexts it is reasonable enough for an economist to ignore the possibility of private provision of public goods, and to treat the voluntary sector as an insignificant exception to his general theory. If, however, the voluntary sector is what is under discussion, one cannot ignore its existence. Nor can one legitimately analyse the arguments for and against privatisation in the framework of a theory that, to all intents and purposes, predicts the non-existence of the voluntary sector.

The claim that conventional theory cannot account for the existence of the voluntary sector is controversial, and I shall begin by trying to substantiate it. My first step will be to argue that the voluntary sector is indeed primarily engaged in the supply of public goods.

In economic theory an activity is a public good if it is a common argument in the utility functions of several individuals, and if each individual's utility increases as the extent of this activity increases (cf. Samuelson, 1954). This definition has some ambiguity because it defines publicness in terms of utility, and utility remains to be defined. In economics, utility is often interpreted in terms of choice, so that it becomes tautologically true that each individual maximises his own utility; but such a 'revealed preference' definition would make the theory of public goods empty. The main conclusion of the theory – that, in the absence of coercion, public goods are undersupplied – depends critically on the proposition that each individual seeks to maximise his own utility and thus takes advantage of any opportunity to enjoy a 'free ride' on other people's contributions to public goods. If the theory is to have any content, this proposition must be an *empirical* one: it must be something that, although (according to the theory) generally true, might conceivably be false.

One cannot, however, simply go back to the original interpretation of utility in terms of psychological experiences of pleasure or satisfaction. The theory of public goods has often been invoked in cases where the publicness of an activity arises out of altruistic interdependencies between individuals: one person's utility is said to increase when another person becomes better cared for in some way. This idea has been used both as an explanation of private charitable activities (e.g. Schwartz, 1970; Becker, 1974; Hood et al., 1977; Collard, 1978, Ch. 10) and as an argument for the provision of welfare services by the state (e.g. Friedman, 1962, pp. 190–1; Arrow, 1963;

Hochman and Rodgers, 1969; Culyer, 1976). Many of these writers seem to interpret altruism to include something more than the propensity to feel pleasure when others receive benefits. There are many other reasons why one person might want another person to receive a benefit – for example, a sense of justice, a disinterested desire to alleviate misery, religious conviction – and such motives seem to be encompassed by the notion of altruism used by economists. At any rate, economists have usually formulated 'wanting another person to receive a benefit' in terms of interdependent utility functions, and they have not thought it their job to enquire into the reasons behind such a want. It would seem, therefore, that if utility cannot (without circularity) be defined in terms of choice, the most appropriate interpretation is in terms of *wants* or *desires*. Then an activity is a public good if each of a group of individuals wants more of that activity to take place. Wants may be 'publicly oriented' as well as 'privately oriented' (cf. Barry, 1965, pp. 38–41). This is the concept of public good that will be used in the rest of this chapter.

Many private charities supply goods that are public in the narrowest sense – goods from which many people simultaneously benefit in a quite direct way. There are many examples in the field of medical research, which is a classic instance of a public good. (Two of the three largest British charities are concerned with cancer research: see Charities Aid Foundation, 1981, p. 32.) Although lying outside most conventional definitions of 'welfare' services, the lifeboat service is an interesting example, for lifeboats are one of the textbook writers' favourite examples of public goods; in Britain, this service is provided in the voluntary sector.

A slightly less obvious kind of public good, and one that is often supplied by voluntary initiative, is the work of a pressure group. If a pressure group works on behalf of a group of people with common *interests*, its activities are clearly a public good to those people. Some pressure groups, however, represent people who share not so much interests as *attitudes*. (Most of the supporters of the Howard League for Penal Reform are not – one presumes – likely to become clients of the prison service; the Child Poverty Action Group is supported by people who are neither children nor poor.) Nevertheless, if public goods are defined by reference to wants, the activities of this latter kind of pressure group are public goods to the groups of people who share the relevant attitudes. It has often been noted that a large, and possibly growing, part of the work of voluntary welfare organisations is pressure group activity.

Another large class of charities is made up of organisations that provide free or subsidised welfare services of an excludable kind. To their recipients, then, these services are private goods. Charities of this kind exist in almost every area of social policy: residential and day centre care for the elderly, for the mentally and physically handicapped and for drug-users; social work among ex-offenders; clubs and hostels for young people; marriage guidance; citizens' advice bureaux; support for people contemplating suicide; sport and recreation; and so on. The extent to which organisations involved in such work are truly *voluntary* is often debatable, since most 'voluntary' organisations of any size receive some income from government (either as subsidies or on a purchase-of-service basis) and many also receive payments from the recipients of their services. Thus the voluntary sector shades gradually into a region inhabited by institutions that are so dependent on public money that their private status is purely formal. (The universities are a good example.) It also shades into another region, inhabited by non-profit-making institutions that derive almost all their income from the sale of goods and services and compete on essentially equal terms with profit-making firms. (Consider retail co-operative societies, building societies, and mutual life assurance societies.) It is, however, possible conceptually to distinguish a voluntary component in all such organisations: the share of the costs of supplying services that is paid by voluntary contributions, whether of money or labour.

If an individual sacrifices some of his own income or leisure for the benefit of an organisation with particular goals, it is not unreasonable to infer that he wants those goals to be achieved. Of course there may be other explanations of individuals' willingness to contribute to voluntary organisations, and I shall consider this issue later in the chapter; but the hypothesis that contributors want the success of the organisation they support seems a particularly obvious one. This hypothesis has been the starting point for most economic studies of charitable behaviour. The significance of this hypothesis is that it makes the activities of a voluntary organisation into a public good: they are public to the group of people who want those activities to be carried out, and this group includes at least all those people who contribute to the organisation in question.

A third important class of |voluntary organisations, overlapping with the two classes I have just described, consists of reciprocal self-help groups. The distinguishing feature of such organisations is that they provide a service for a particular client group, the costs being met by voluntary contributions (typically in the form of labour) of people in the same group. Alcoholics Anonymous, Gingerbread, the Claimants' Unions and the Multiple Sclerosis Society are examples. Many commentators have pointed to the increasing importance of self-help groups in the voluntary sector (e.g. Kramer, 1981, p. 211; Johnson, 1981, pp. 76–7).

There are forms of reciprocal self-help that lie outside the scope of the theory of public goods. If the service provided is excludable, and if potential consumers are in fact excluded unless they bear their share of the costs, then contributions are not voluntary in any useful sense: the arrangement is, in effect, a producer–consumer co-operative. In practice, however, few self-help groups seem to work like this, partly because of a reluctance to establish formal tariffs relating benefits received to costs borne, partly because those members of the client group most in need of the service in question may be those least able to contribute either money or labour, and partly because the service may have elements of publicness (for example, if pressure group activity is involved). In consequence it seems more appropriate to regard the typical contribution to a self-help group as genuinely voluntary. If non-contributors are not excluded from enjoying the benefits of a group's activities – even if exclusion is technically possible – those activities constitute a public good under my definition.

The organisations I have been describing are ones that rely on the contributions of many donors, and it is this more than anything else that gives rise to the presumption that public goods are involved. Not all private charities are of this kind, however. An important exception is the foundation or trust set up by a wealthy philanthropic individual or family – for example, the Carnegie Trust, the Rowntree Trust and the Nuffield Foundation. It is conceivable that the activities of such a trust could be private to the philanthropist who set it up, but in practice this seems improbable. The goals of charitable trusts are usually sufficiently general that they can safely be presumed to reflect the 'publicly oriented' wants of many individuals. This suggestion is made more plausible by the observation that the goals of different trusts often overlap quite considerably.

Thus, I suggest, most voluntary organisations can be regarded as agencies for the supply of public goods. This is not to say that most voluntarily provided welfare services are public goods, because much voluntary activity takes place outside formal organisations. The welfare services provided within the family – for example, in caring for elderly and handicapped people – would, on any sensible measure, far outweigh those provided in the formal voluntary sector. Here, the concept of public goods does not seem particularly appropriate, because although many people are contributing towards, say, the care of the elderly each contributor is seeking to benefit a *particular* elderly person. The proper boundary between statutory welfare services and those provided within the family is an important question, and one that has been raised in many discussions of privatisation, but it lies beyond the scope of this chapter. My concern is with voluntary *organisations*, and it is my contention that an economic theory of voluntary organisations must be a theory of the voluntary supply of public goods.

IS THERE AN ECONOMIC THEORY OF VOLUNTARY ORGANISATIONS?

The economic theory of charitable behaviour has two main strands, which unfortunately are mutually contradictory.

One strand invokes the orthodox theory of public goods to show that charitable activities will be under-supplied if individuals are free to choose how much they contribute towards them; economic efficiency can be achieved, it is argued, only if the free-rider problem is solved through coercion. (Individuals might consent to their being coerced, as part of a kind of social contract; but what they consent to is nonetheless coercion). This argument is often used to justify the provision of welfare services by the state. It has been used to justify both income support schemes (e.g. Friedman, 1962, pp. 190–1; Hochman and Rodgers, 1969) and public provision of particular welfare services, particularly health care (e.g. Arrow, 1963; Lindsay, 1969; Culyer, 1976).

The other strand in the theory attempts to explain private charitable behaviour on the basis of the same assumptions as are used to derive the under-supply result: individuals have altruistic preferences, which can be represented by interdependent utility functions, and each individual maximises his utility, taking the behaviour of all other individuals as given. Variants of this basic model have been presented many times (e.g. Schwartz, 1970; Becker, 1974; Hood *et al.*, 1977; Collard, 1978, Ch. 10; Arrow, 1981), often as the theoretical basis for extensive econometric research into charitable giving. The underlying idea is that charitable giving is a voluntary contribution to a public good; but this is modelled in such a way that free-riding is predicted. (This is why the theory provides a justification for government intervention.) One is bound to ask whether this line of argument is internally consistent: if free-riding is predicted, why are people observed to make voluntary contributions?

The usual answer to this question is that a utility-maximising individual, behaving entirely atomistically (that is, taking everyone else's behaviour as given), may choose to contribute towards a public good; in general, public goods will be *under-supplied*, but they will not necessarily be *unsupplied*. The argument is usually presented by way of a formal model, which I shall try to explain with as few technicalities as possible.

Consider a society of many individuals. Each individual derives utility from two sources – his own consumption of private goods, and some public good. Thus his utility depends on the amount of private consumption that *he* has, and on the amount of the public good that *society* has. It is usual – and, I think, unexceptionable – to take the prices of all goods as given. Because of this assumption it is possible to measure both private consumption and the public good in money units. Each individual's utility can then be said to depend on the money value of his private consumption and on the total amount that the society spends on producing the public good.

If the public good is supplied entirely from voluntary contributions, the amount that society spends on the public good will obviously be equal to the sum of the contributions of all individuals. Each individual's contribution must be equal to his income minus his private consumption. (Assume no saving.) For the purposes of the model, each individual's income is taken as given; the only choice he has to make concerns the allocation of this income between private consumption and voluntary contributions towards the public good.

An individual, it is assumed, will try to maximise his own utility, taking as given the amount that everyone else contributes. An equilibrium state is achieved if everyone is maximising his own utility, given the behaviour of everyone else. The conventional theory of charitable behaviour assumes that equilibrium is achieved and then analyses the properties of equilibrium states. (Under conventional assumptions, an equilibrium can be shown to exist; so the analysis is to this extent internally consistent.)

Figure 5.1 represents the choice problem facing any individual, i. Any combination of private consumption and the public good can be represented by a point in the diagram; the individual's preferences over these combinations can be represented by a family of indifference curves (the *preference map*), of which I_i is one curve. If the individual contributed nothing to the public good, he would be at point A: his private consumption would be equal to his income and the total supply of the public good would be equal to the sum of everyone else's contributions. By making a contribution of his own, he can increase the supply of the public good at the expense of his private consumption. Since he can make any contribution up to the value of his income, he can move to any point on the line AD. (He cannot reach points on the broken line CA, since these correspond with negative contributions – otherwise known as theft.) According to the theory, he will choose the most-preferred point on AD. This is the point B, at which he makes a positive contribution. Figure 5.2 illustrates another possibility. In this case the most-preferred point for the individual concerned (individual j) is A and so nothing is

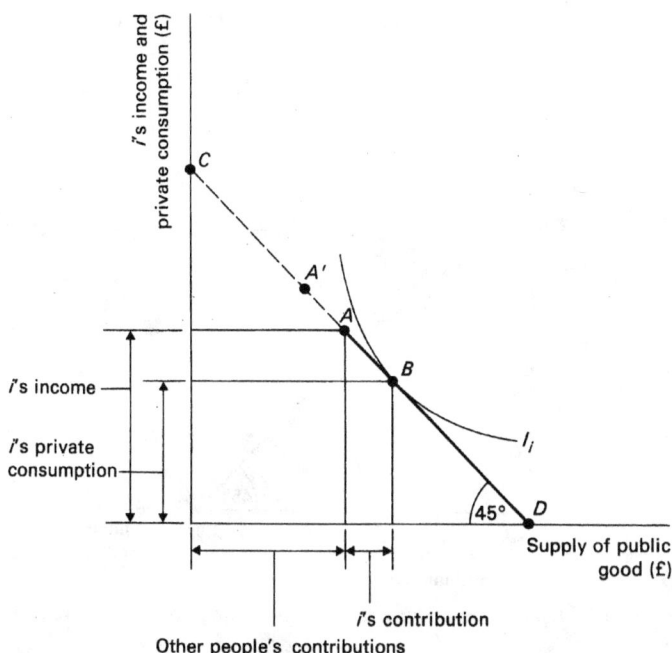

Figure 5.1 *Equilibrium for an individual contributor in the conventional model*

contributed. As far as the internal logic of the theory is concerned, it is quite possible to have an equilibrium, with some people like *i* and some like *j*. It would seem, then, that the theory *is* consistent with an observation that many people contribute towards public goods.

Now suppose that there is a state of equilibrium, and consider how much each individual would be willing to pay for a marginal increase in the supply of the public good – say an increase of 1p worth. Anyone who, like *i* in Figure 5.1, is making a positive contribution, must be willing to pay exactly 1p. This follows from the fact that *i* has chosen a contribution that maximises his utility: the utility that he gets from the last penny he contributes to the public good must be just equal to the utility that he gets from the last penny he spends on private consumption. So, if more than one person is contributing to the public good, there must (according to the theory) be undersupply. Suppose that there are just two contributors. Each is willing to pay an extra 1p to ensure a 1p increase in the supply of the public

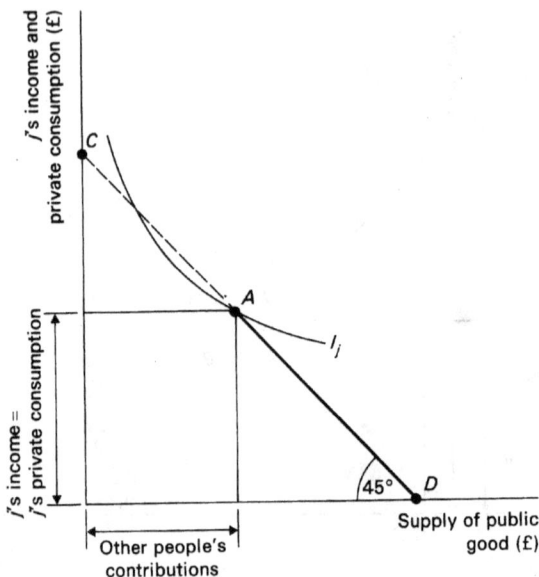

Figure 5.2   *Equilibrium for an individual non-contributor in the conventional model*

good; but that increase could be brought about if each individual contributed only ½p extra. Thus, if both people contributed a little more, both would be better off; yet neither of them has any incentive to do this.

More generally, there is under-supply of a public good if the sum of all individuals' marginal valuations of the good is greater than the good's marginal cost. In equilibrium, however, *each* contributor's marginal valuation is equal to the marginal cost. (Each is willing to pay 1p to increase the supply by 1p worth.) Thus, according to the conventional theory, any public good that is supplied from voluntary contributions must be under-supplied.

One begins to have doubts about this theory when one considers the *degree* of under-supply that it predicts. Imagine a charity with 1,000 voluntary donors – a tiny number on the scale used by charities like Dr Barnardo's, the Spastics Society or the Cancer Research Campaign. Then, according to the theory, the marginal social value of the charity's activity – that is, the sum of all individuals' marginal valuations – is *at least 1,000 times* the marginal cost. For some actual charities, the theory entails that marginal social value is 10,000 or even 100,000 times greater than marginal cost. This is under-supply with a vengeance! Is it really plausible to suggest that each additional £1 of spending by a charity would benefit society by several thousand pounds?

The theory has other problems too. If one looks at it carefully, one can see that it cannot account for some of the most obvious features of charitable behaviour as it is actually observed. I have argued this at length elsewhere (Sugden, 1982), and a similar argument has been put forward independently by Margolis (1982). Here I shall just give an outline of the argument.

Consider again the position of the typical contributor, individual i in Figure 5.1. His contribution is determined by the location of point B, the most-preferred point on AD. The closer B is to A, the smaller is i's contribution relative both to his income and to the total supply of the public good. In reality, there are many charities for which the typical contribution is small in both of these senses – that is, there are many charities that raise large sums of money from many donors, the vast majority of whom contribute quite small amounts. If this observation is to be squared with the theory, it must be possible to envisage an equilibrium in which, for most donors, B is very close to A. In terms of the theory, however, this would be an amazing coincidence.

Notice that preferences are defined over 'bundles' of private consumption and the public good – that is, over all points in a diagram like Figure 5.1. There is no room in the theory for the preference map to shift when the individual's income changes, or when other people's contributions change. Thus the nature of the preference map must be independent of the location of point A. Since it is therefore illegitimate to assume that the indifference curves have any special properties that depend on the location of A, there is absolutely no reason to expect that most people will tend to choose points on AD that are very close to (but not actually at) A.

Essentially the same point can be made another way. We may start from the fact that large charities have many donors and that most donations are small. This implies that most donors, of whatever income group, give only small proportions of their incomes; and this in turn suggests that, for the typical individual, the proportion of any marginal increase in income that is devoted to charity must be quite small. From the viewpoint of any individual, however, the total income of a large charity from sources other than himself is subject to variations that (relative to his own income) are very large. The Cancer Research Campaign, for example, has an income of over £10m. a year, and it is unlikely that its own administrators would be able to predict its next year's income to within, say, £100,000. So if individuals tend to make small donations, we must suppose that the size of an individual's donation is relatively unresponsive to changes in the charity's income from other sources. But now suppose that an individual's income increases by £100 while the charity's income from other sources decreases by £100. We might expect each of these events to induce the individual to give more than he did before, but – if the arguments of this paragraph are right – the increase in his contribution must be quite small, and certainly nowhere near £100. Yet an increase of exactly £100 is predicted by the conventional theory. Figure 5.1 shows why. An increase in the individual's income combined with an equal reduction in the charity's income from other sources can be represented by a movement of the initial endowment point from A to a point such as A'. There is no change in the location of the chosen point B, which means that the individual's private consumption and the total income of the charity must remain unchanged; and this is possible only if the whole of the increase in income is given to the charity.

It seems clear that the conventional theory of charitable behaviour (and, more generally, of the voluntary supply of public goods) is fundamentally wrong. If economics is to contribute anything to the analysis of the voluntary sector – and without such an analysis there is little that can usefully be said about privatisation – it must be on the basis of some other explanation of why people contribute money and labour to the voluntary sector.

SOME ALTERNATIVE EXPLANATIONS OF CHARITABLE BEHAVIOUR

Two main kinds of alternative explanation have been put forward. One kind starts from the idea that individuals derive some kind of *private* benefit when they contribute to charities and other voluntary organisations; since non-contributors are excluded from these benefits, the free-rider problem does not arise. The second kind of explanation accepts the reality of the free-rider problem, but assumes that people are motivated by some principle of morality, duty, public-spiritedness or enlightened self-interest that leads them to behave co-operatively. I shall consider these approaches in turn.

The idea that people derive private benefits from giving to charities is often formulated in a wholly empty fashion: people give because they want to give. This is sometimes dressed up by using the theoretical-sounding notion of 'act utility' – utility that derives from an action independently of its consequences. This amounts to no more than a commitment to the *definition* of utility in terms of choice:

if it is necessarily true that the individual maximises utility, but the individual is observed to behave in what appears to be a non-maximising way, one is obliged to hypothesise some new sort of utility. It may be convenient to give this type of utility a label, but a label is not a theory.

A little more content is given to this approach when it is suggested that act utility is the satisfaction one gets from doing right, or from being seen by others to be doing right. For example, Becker (1974, p. 1083) suggests, as an alternative to his main theory of charitable behaviour, that the act of giving may be only 'apparent "charitable" activity . . . motivated by a desire to avoid the scorn of others or to receive social acclaim'. Similar suggestions have been made by other writers (e.g. Johnson, 1970; Olson, 1971, pp. 60–1). This idea still does not take us very far. In particular, it does not explain why some kinds of activities can attract voluntary contributions much more easily than others. A newspaper or television appeal for donations for children's homes, cancer research, famine relief or lifeboats can raise large sums of money; an appeal for donations to Unilever or to a fund to supplement the incomes of university teachers presumably would not. An appeal to buy a swimming pool or minibus for a particular suburban school can be quite successful in raising money from the parents of children at that school; but the same people would surely be much less willing to contribute towards buying pools or minibuses for schools in other areas. It is no doubt true that if I am seen to donate money to a children's home I shall receive some signs of approval from my friends and associates, and that if I refuse to give anything when asked, I shall be thought mean. On the other hand, it is equally true that if I was seen to donate money to Unilever in response to a television appeal I should be thought a sucker; I should receive scorn rather than acclaim. It may well be that people's *immediate* motives for giving are often a response to various forms of social pressure, but we cannot explain how social pressure works without first understanding the principles of behaviour to which people are expected to conform.

A more concrete version of the 'private benefits' theory rests on the idea that people who contribute to charities receive direct benefits in return – benefits whose value does not depend on any private or social morality, and from which non-contributors are excluded. In the more general context of public goods, Olson (1971) has argued that many pressure groups and trade unions work on this principle: they supply public and private goods as joint products, and the private goods – which are supplied only to paid-up members – are sufficient to induce people to join. For example, trade unions and professional associations often provide specialised information to their members and organise social functions. It is sometimes suggested that the same principle explains how charities and voluntary social service organisations work. This idea gains some plausibility from the wide range of motives that people profess when they engage in voluntary work. (See, for example, Morris, 1969, Ch. 8.) A disinterested desire to serve others, or to redress social injustice, is a common motive; so also is an inability to say 'no' when invited to do voluntary work by a friend or neighbour – in other words, social pressure. But other common motives include a desire to meet people, a desire for some kind of work as an alternative to unemployment or inactivity, and a recognition of the value of voluntary work as 'work experience' – that is, as an intermediate step before taking up paid employment. Similar arguments can be made about a good deal of fund-raising. The fact that social events – garden parties, fetes, dinners, jumble sales, etc. – are so often used to raise money for charities suggests that it is worthwhile for fund-raisers to provide their donors with some private benefits (cf. Obler, 1981).

Clearly, there is something in this version of the 'private benefits' theory, but it cannot provide a self-contained theory of charitable giving. The logic of the theory is that a charitable or public-good supplying organisation has two components. One component works essentially like a private firm, providing some excludable service (information, social functions, work experience, etc.) in return for payments of money or labour. The profits of this 'firm' are then used to finance the other component of the organisation, which supplies some public good or charitable activity. The difficulty with this argument is to explain how the 'firm' succeeds in earning its profit: why is this not eroded by the entry of profit-maximising firms providing the same private services without the public good? For example, if people are willing to work part-time without pay in order to gain experience, why do private firms not poach this labour from the voluntary sector? If garden parties really appeal only to the self-interest of those who attend, why do people not organise garden parties in aid of themselves? The answer must be that voluntary organisations have some advantage over profit-maximising firms in supplying the relevant private goods; and the most obvious advantage would seem to be the ability of voluntary organisations to appeal to charitable and public-spirited motives.

So, I suggest, people's willingness to contribute to the supply of public goods cannot be explained solely in terms of private benefits. If one follows through the logic of this kind of explanation, one finds that something more fundamental is being presupposed: some kind of generally recognised moral rule or social convention that enjoins people to contribute to public goods. It may be that most people, most of the time, are not strongly inclined to follow such a rule for its own sake, and that their resolve is strengthened if compliance with the rule is rewarded in some way. However, the rewards that can be offered by voluntary organisations could not work unless people already accepted that they ought to contribute to them.

If this conclusion is right, the theory of voluntary contributions to public goods should start from an analysis of social conventions. Unfortunately, economics has not made much progress in this direction, although some suggestions have been put forward as possible starting points.

The most common suggestion is probably the so-called 'Kantian' approach (cf. Laffont, 1975; Collard, 1978). This assumes a general adherence to a 'Kantian' rule of behaviour, which is essentially this: behave in the way you would want everyone to behave. Or, more narrowly formulated in the context of game theory: if you are playing in a non-co-operative game in which every player has a choice between two strategies S_1 and S_2, and if you would prefer the outcome of everyone choosing S_1 to the outcome of everyone choosing S_2, then choose S_1. A special case of this rule is that in all n-person prisoner's dilemma games, the co-operative strategy ought to be chosen. Whether or not this principle can properly be attributed to Kant, it has a certain common-sense moral appeal. It would seem to entail that one ought to contribute towards the supply of those public goods that one wants to be supplied.

Harsanyi (1980) presents essentially the same rule, and calls it a principle of 'rational commitment' and 'spontaneous co-ordination'. His point is that there are forms of rational behaviour that cannot be formulated simply as the maximisation of an individual's utility function. It seems, however, that Harsanyi is concerned with how people ought to behave, rather than with how they actually do behave. The moral rule he advocates – rule utilitarianism – entails rational commitment but is far more demanding. (The rule utilitarian must play his part in activities that are socially useful, even if they do not benefit him at all.)

My own hunch is that even 'Kantianism' or 'rational commitment' is too demanding to be generally accepted as a social convention. Notice that this principle requires you to contribute to the supply of a public good even if you have good reason to expect that no one else will contribute anything. In other words, you are not merely required to play your part in co-operative arrangements that benefit everyone; you may be required to pay for other people's free rides – in short, to be a sucker. Most people, I suspect, would reject this demand as unfair. A less objectionable 'principle of fairness' has been put forward by Hart (1955) and developed by Rawls (1972, pp. 108–14) and Arneson (1982). Roughly, this principle requires that if other people contribute towards the costs of providing a public good that you want, they have a right to demand that you contribute too. Thus you must not take a free ride on other people's efforts, but there is no obligation to be a sucker. This principle, with its stress on reciprocity and fair shares, seems to me to come closer than 'rational commitment' to most people's notions of practical morality.

A great deal of work is required to translate a general maxim of behaviour, such as rational commitment, rule utilitarianism or the principle of fairness, into an economic theory of the supply of public goods; and most of this work remains to be done. (I am currently trying to derive a theory of public goods from the principle of fairness; the progress I have made so far is described in Sugden, 1984.) At this stage, only very general conclusions can be drawn. The most important conclusion is that public goods *can* be provided through voluntary initiative; the free-rider problem can be overcome. Unless this is accepted at the theoretical level, no sensible economic analysis of the voluntary sector is possible.

To say that public goods *can* be provided through voluntary initiative is not, of course, to say that they always *will* be – still less to say that they will always be supplied in economically efficient quantities. The theory of the voluntary supply of public goods, when it is eventually worked out, will almost certainly predict a good deal of economic inefficiency of one kind or another; it is too much to expect that unco-ordinated (or spontaneously co-ordinated) individual behaviour should be able to supply public goods in exactly the right quantities. But the theory may also show that voluntary organisations have some important advantages over tax-financed agencies of the state, and that the case for the latter is not so overwhelming as economists have tended to assume.

THE MERITS OF THE VOLUNTARY SECTOR

In discussing the advantages of voluntary organisations as suppliers of public goods, I shall presuppose that income transfers are made through the machinery of the state. This approach is in part justified by the fact that in Britain some form of income maintenance has been a statutory responsibility since the Elizabethan Poor Law, and only the most fanatical libertarians would propose abandoning that policy now. It is further justified by the recognition that voluntary organisations can redistribute income only so far as *donors* choose; the recipients have no say in the matter. At one time this was true of statutory redistribution too, since the recipients of poor relief were disenfranchised, but it is now constitutionally accepted that the votes of gainers and losers should count equally in the democratic procedures that authorise income transfers. I do not propose to get involved in debating the rights and wrongs of this. The arguments that I shall present, like most arguments about economic efficiency, stand independently of the way in which income is distributed.

Almost all commentators seem to agree that there is at least one kind of public good that is best provided by voluntary organisations – pressure group activity (cf. Johnson, 1981, Ch. 4; Kramer, 1981, Ch. 11). Since the purpose of a pressure group is to exert influence on government, this is hardly an activity that can safely be left to government. Although there have been examples of government-sponsored pressure groups – the Community Development Projects initiated in 1969 increasingly took on this role – a pluralist democracy surely requires independent organisations that can criticise the government without any clash of loyalties. (It is significant that the Community Development Projects were eventually closed down by the government.) Pressure group activity is undoubtedly a significant part of the work of the voluntary sector. However, it is not the part that is most relevant to a discussion of privatisation, since it is complementary with, and not a substitute for, statutory welfare services. The more government does, the more work there is for pressure groups.

It is more important, therefore, to consider the role of the voluntary sector in providing welfare services. What advantages do voluntary organisations have over statutory ones in this area?

One suggestion, which appeals to those who believe that the public sector and waste are inseparable, is that voluntary organisations can produce at less cost. However, I cannot see any good reason for supposing voluntary activity to be particularly cost-effective, except in the crude financial sense that volunteers do not have to be paid. Economic theory would suggest that it is *competition*, not private control, that is the best guarantee of cost-effectiveness. This provides a strong argument for purchase-of-service contracting once the state has accepted responsibility for financing and planning a service (cf. Judge, 1982b). Voluntary organisations may supply services for payment on this basis, and one might expect competition for contracts between agencies (whether voluntary, profit-seeking or statutory) to keep down costs. In this context, however, the voluntary organisation is essentially acting as a firm, just as a building society does when it competes with private banks and Giro. It is quite another thing to claim that voluntary provision of public goods is inherently more cost-effective, in real resource terms, than statutory provision.

Another common argument is that the voluntary sector has some special value that is independent of the value of the services it supplies: voluntary activity is, *in itself*, a good thing. This is the central message of Titmuss's (1970) enormously influential study of blood transfusion. For Titmuss, the most important characteristic of the British system of blood donorship is its *voluntarism*: 'the free gift of blood to unnamed strangers' (p. 89). Voluntarism has certain practical advantages (particularly in securing good quality blood) but its main value is intrinsic. In his final chapter, entitled 'The right to give', Titmuss declares (p. 242):

> It is the responsibility of the state ... to reduce or eliminate or control the forces of market coercions which place men in situations in which they have less freedom or little freedom to behave altruistically if they so will.

It is significant that Titmuss sees the market, and not the state, as the enemy of the gift relationship: a belief in the importance of voluntary activity can be as much a part of a socialist ideology as of a libertarian or market-based one.

Titmuss emphasises the *individuality* of altruistic actions – 'They are acts of free will; of the exercise of choice; of conscience without shame' (p. 89) – and sees social pressure as a factor that dilutes true altruism. Given the importance of various kinds of social pressure in maintaining most voluntary organisations, Titmuss's characterisation of the gift relationship seems too idealistic to justify the voluntary sector as we know it. It is perhaps more appropriate to see voluntary activity as a form of social *co-operation* that is independent of the state; it is valuable because it affirms and fosters the idea that people can combine together to solve their own problems. This seems to be the notion of self-help used in the Conservative manifesto; it is what Taylor (1976, p. 134) means when he writes that 'the state is like an addictive drug: the more of it we have, the more we "need" it and the more we "depend" on it'.

These are important ideas, but rather beyond the scope of economic analysis. An economist can say more about another claim that is very often made on behalf of voluntary organisations. This is that they are the pioneers of the welfare state – 'pointing the way', as Herbert Morrison put it (Johnson, 1981, p. 116). This is a deep-rooted part of what might be called the social democratic interpretation of the history of social policy – the idea that there is an inevitable trend of progress towards a more extensive welfare state. The pioneering theory is that, at any time, there will be some welfare services that are not accepted as proper activities for the state; but if far-sighted individuals combine to provide these services voluntarily, the general public will come to recognise their value and eventually the state will be able to take over. Of course, pioneers can make mistakes, and so new ventures must be regarded as experiments. The voluntary sector is seen as an area in which experiments can be made. Ideas that work can then be adopted by the state; those that fail can be abandoned at relatively little cost. There can be no question that nineteenth-century charities pioneered most of the main activities of the twentieth-century welfare state; and there are plenty of examples of more recent pioneering work in the voluntary sector – such as family planning advice, citizens' advice bureaux, the Samaritans, and hostels for battered women (cf. Johnson, 1981, Ch. 3).

This theory has been criticised as an outdated myth by Kramer (1981, Ch. 9), who argues that statutory agencies are just as capable of innovation as voluntary organisations are. But this, I think, misses the point. First, what matters is not so much the rate at which innovations are made, as the process that determines which new ideas are adopted and which rejected. (For example, local authority housing authorities in the 1960s were more innovative than private house-builders when they opted for high-rise flats; but most people would now accept that the forces of the market performed a valuable service in deterring this kind of innovation in the private sector.) Second, the voluntary sector, like the private profit-making sector, provides space for the emergence of new organisations in a way that the public sector does not. The case for the voluntary sector is that it provides an environment in which organisations tend to grow or decline according to the extent of the correspondence between what they do and what individuals want to see done.

To interpret the activities of the voluntary sector solely as *pioneering* or *experimenting* is to presuppose that a consensus can ultimately be achieved about which welfare services should be provided and which should not. If a voluntary organisation's experiment succeeds, this will (it is implied) sooner or later be recognised, and then the state will assume responsibility for the service in question. If the experiment fails, then presumably it will be abandoned. What if there is no consensus about what counts as success? To an economist it seems much more natural to suppose that people's wants are diverse than that they are all much the same. An activity may be a public good to one group of people but not to another; or it may be a public good to everyone but valued very differently by different people. Merely supplying that good for a period of time is not necessarily going to bring about a coincidence of people's wants. A public good that is wanted only by a minority may nevertheless be supplied by the state; but the mechanisms of majority rule offer only an imperfect guarantee that minority wants will be satisfied (Sugden, 1981, Ch. 10; Jones, 1983). The market system offers a much stronger guarantee, but it works only for private goods.

The voluntary sector, I suggest, can be seen as the counterpart of the market in the realm of public goods. Like the market system, the voluntary sector is adapted to supply diverse goods in response to individuals' wants.

It is surprising how little is made of this argument by commentators who are favourably disposed to the voluntary sector. It is conventional to mention religious and racial minorities, who may want to provide certain welfare services for themselves, and unpopular client groups such as drug addicts, vagrants, gipsies and homosexuals, for whom the majority may not be inclined to provide special services (cf Johnson, 1981, p. 140; Kramer, 1981, pp. 193–4); but these are usually presented as marginal issues. The idea that people have different tastes and opinions, that they disagree about which welfare services are most important and about the form that particular services should take, is not an important part of most accounts of the role of the voluntary sector. This is in striking contrast with the way in which economists present the merits of the market system: although it is often claimed that competition favours low-cost producers and that it stimulates innovation, the heart of the conventional justification for the market is that it can satisfy the diverse wants of individual consumers.

CONCLUSION

The economic theory of the voluntary sector is at far too primitive a stage of its development to have much bearing on debates about the practicalities of privatisation. The truth is that economists do not understand how the voluntary sector works; we have been brought up on a theory that tells us it *cannot* work and we are only just beginning to face up to the fact that it nonetheless *does*. If we are to contribute to the debate about privatisation, the first step must be to produce a satisfactory theory of the supply of public goods – one that can explain how voluntary organisations sometimes succeed in supplying them.

All I have been able to provide in this chapter is an artist's impression of what such a theory might look like. If this impression is any guide, there seems to be a case for a public policy that 'encourages the voluntary movement and self-help groups'. The idea that these organisations should be encouraged to act 'in partnership with the statutory services' seems misguided, however. If the virtues of the voluntary sector are connected with diversity and experiment, what is required is not state planning or 'partnership', but rather a policy that supports *all* groups that supply public goods, irrespective of whether they happen to appeal to the government of the day.

ACKNOWLEDGEMENTS

I am grateful for the advice and comments I have received from Tony Culyer, Peter Jones and Ken Judge.

PART II Policy Issues

The debate about privatisation within the social policy area has probably nowhere generated more fierce debate than in connection with the National Health Service (NHS).Attempts to cut NHS budgets as a part of general reductions in public expenditure have encountered fierce opposition from both administrators and medical practitioners. At the same time, social surveys reveal the high level of support for the NHS within the population at large. Not surprisingly, Neil Kinnock, upon becoming leader of the Labour Party, chose the defence of the NHS as the first major issue upon which to attack the Conservative government. In view of the strong emotions raised by this subject, some dispassionate analysis of the issues involved is especially necessary. The first two chapters in this part of the book endeavour to provide just such analysis.

In Chapter 6 Alan Maynard and Alan Williams try to unravel 'the tangled skein of ideological, technical, economic and operational issues involved'. They do this by first contrasting the ideological viewpoints held by libertarian supporters of private health care systems with those held by egalitarian supporters of the NHS. This is followed by a specification of the characteristics of NHS and private health care systems in terms of demand, supply, adjustment mechanisms and success criteria. However, the need to study *actual* systems is emphasised by specifying these characteristics, first, in terms of idealised systems and, secondly, in terms of actual systems. Too much of the privatisation debate, Maynard and Williams argue, is conducted in terms of ideal rather than actual systems. Through an examination of the actual UK scene they ask whether a 'mixed' system of health care, encouraged by privatisation, would assist the NHS in meeting its idealised objectives more fully than the existing imperfect, actual NHS system. Their conclusion is that it is unlikely to do so.

In Chapter 7, Peter West takes as his focus of attention the growth of private health insurance. He argues that it is important to realise that the NHS involves important transfers of resources between age groups: the young, fit and employed finance the health care of the elderly, retired and sick. Transfers under private health insurance, in contrast, are far more restricted. Typically patients receive short-stay, elective surgery under private insurance but still rely upon the NHS for longer-term care in old age. Unless those people (or their employers) who are presently opting for private health insurance recognise that they are almost certain to become users of the NHS in their later life, there is a danger that as voters/taxpayers they will allocate too few resources to the NHS for it to be able to cope with the demands placed upon it by the present elderly generation. It is the resource allocation implications of this intertemporal problem that, West argues, are likely to be more important than any short-term effect of private medicine on NHS resources.

In Chapter 8, Christine Whitehead considers privatisation in the context of housing policy. She starts with a discussion of the special attributes of housing that determine the appropriateness of market versus public sector systems of provision, allocation and distribution. This leads her to conclude that, if people are willing and able to pay for at least a socially defined minimum standard of accommodation, private sector provision is likely to be more suitable; on the other hand, if people lack adequate purchasing power and are likely to be in a weak bargaining position vis-à-vis private landlords, the case for public sector provision is stronger. She goes on to show that measuring comparative efficiency of public and private sector performance is by no means as straightforward as much simplistic, political rhetoric implies. However, available empirical evidence tends to confirm the need to think in terms of a dual market: a private market providing more efficiently for those with the ability to pay, and direct public sector provision and subsidisation performing better for households at the lower end of the market. Finally, in her assessment of current government policy, Whitehead condemns regressive programmes that penalise lower-income council tenants while continuing to award subsidies to better-off owner-occupiers. In this connection, one of the most visible manifestations of privatisation has been the sale of council houses.

Although sales of council houses have taken place for a number of years, the programme received particular impetus from the Housing Act (1980), which made it mandatory for local authorities to sell to tenants who wished to buy their homes and offered discounts of up to 50 per cent of the notional market price depending upon the tenant's length of residence. Despite some misgivings voiced by the Labour Party about the specific form and local consequences of the sales programme, the general encouragement of owner-occupation at the expense of council housing – including sales policy – now has bipartisan support. In Chapter 9. Richard Kirwan discusses the circumstances surrounding the possible demise of council housing. Through a wide-ranging examination of the ideology and practical concerns of the political 'right' and 'left' he shows how the sale of council houses is but one aspect of the reconstitution of public housing in terms of private market principles. While conceding that council housing has in the past suffered from failures of planning, management and financing systems, he argues that there will still be a need for a public rental sector in the future to provide decent accommodation for low-income households and others not catered for in the home-ownership sector. Moreover, on a more general level, Kirwan points out that a continuation of present trends – whereby subsidisation of local authority tenants is withdrawn while assistance to owner-occupiers remains untouched – would represent an insupportable state of affairs.

In 1890, Alfred Marshall wrote: 'There are few practical problems in which the economist has a more direct interest than those relating to the principles on which the expense of education of children should be divided between the state and the parents' (Marshall, 1961, p. 180). Clearly, aspects of the privatisation debate in education have a long history. Indeed, as Maurice Peston points out in Chapter 10, the currently much discussed proposal for education vouchers was advocated as long ago as the eighteenth century by Tom Paine in *The Rights of Man*. Unfortunately, however, the longevity of the debate has not served to clarify the substance of the current dialogue. Too often this lacks precision about the nature of privatised systems of education. Peston remedies this situation by specifying three aspects of privatisation: ownership, finance and control. This examination of a pure privatised system leads him to conclude that there will inevitably be a need for some public finance and, hence, control. Furthermore, given the need for public sector involvement, it may well be that direct public provision is the most efficient means of meeting education objectives. Only by relying upon over-simplified, inappropriate models of perfect competition can the advocates of privatisation predict a more efficient system.

In Chapter 11, Mark Blaug takes a different view. Unlike Peston, he is severely critical of the state education system: 'The stupefying conservatism of the education system and its utter disdain for non-professional opinion is such that nothing less than a radical shake-up of the financing mechanism will do much to promote parent power.' It is through the introduction of education voucher schemes that Blaug believes parental power may be enhanced. He is, however, careful to point out that voucher schemes may take a variety of forms and that only the radical versions will lead to genuine parental freedom of choice, cost-effectiveness, diversity, innovation and other objectives often cited in their support. Through a review of voucher experiments and feasibility studies carried out to date, Blaug shows that radical versions have not so far been tested. Apart from entrenched opposition from educationalists with vested interests, there is the matter of cost. Blaug concludes that the prediction of a half-billion pound annual cost to the Exchequer has no doubt led to the government shelving a national voucher scheme for the present.

Until fairly recently, the subsidisation of public transport would probably not have been considered to be an element of the welfare state, even though it has long been recognised that transport subsidies often fulfil a social function. However the 'Fares Fair' campaign launched by the Greater London Council and similar cheap fare policies operated by other authorities (e.g. South Yorkshire) has focused attention upon the welfare implications of these subsidies. As such, privatisation policies and proposals – in the form of subsidy withdrawal – have generated fierce debate on issues that are common to transport and other more conventional welfare state services. In particular there is the debate about the appropriate level of service and degree of subsidy. In Chapter 12, Stephen Glaister brings some much needed analysis to this contentious issue through a study of the economic returns to different forms of subsidisation. By using an econometric model – the main elements of which are explained in a non-technical fashion – he investigates the economic returns obtainable through different policy options. The results suggest that better returns could be achieved with an unchanged total budget and the simultaneous reduction of fares and service levels than would be achieved by increasing fare subsidies alone. At the moment, there appears to be substantial overprovision of services in many areas with resultant low average-load factors.

Glaister's results are, however, dependent upon constancy in, *inter alia*, households' and firms' location decisions, employment patterns and transport technology, all of which may change in the longer run – possibly as a result of particular simultaneous subsidy decisions. In Chapter 13, Graham Crampton considers the implications such changes may have for predictions based upon short-run economic appraisal. He then goes on to consider a broader set of questions associated with the possible privatisation of provision in the transport sector. He concludes that the scope for privatisation of conventional services is very limited because their lack of profitability is likely to deter private capital, but that innovative services in low-density areas, or for high-quality sectors of the market, provide possible areas for private sector involvement.

6 Privatisation and the National Health Service

ALAN MAYNARD and ALAN WILLIAMS

Before embarking on the daunting task of trying to unravel the tangled skein of ideological, technical, economic and operational issues involved in this subject, it is necessary to define the term 'privatisation' in this context. The National Health Service (NHS) has always been accompanied by some private practice of medicine, largely by practitioners who work mainly for the NHS, but to some extent by practitioners wholly outside the NHS. A sizeable fraction of this private work is for foreigners, an area with which we are not concerned here. The relationship between 'private' practice and 'public' practice has always been an uneasy one, although the tensions have been more acute at some times than at others. Early discussion by economists (e.g. Lees, 1965; Buchanan, 1968) was essentially about this issue.

Lately a different set of issues has been raised under the 'privatisation' heading, namely subcontracting certain NHS activities to the private sector, e.g. laundry services, catering and cleaning. This might be seen as little different from the NHS 'subcontracting' the production of drugs, medical equipment and supplies to the private sector (though understandably we do not use the 'privatisation' terminology in those cases). On the face of it, it is the sort of issue that might be settled purely on efficiency grounds, where it would be virtually devoid of ideological content. There would, of course, still be political tensions about appropriate pricing rules, profit rates and the exploitation of (or vulnerability to) monopoly or monopsony powers for such services, but these are issues that arise with many public sector contracts, and are not then seen as particular 'welfare state' issues.

In the context of the NHS, however, there does seem to be a special sensitivity about contractual arrangements with the private sector – witness the sensitivity about drug pricing. Some of these sensitivities may be generated by special pleading (e.g. NHS employees defending their jobs) or managerial inertia (e.g. resistance to scrutiny or unwillingness to face changes in the status quo). There may also be suspicions that the decision to subcontract may in the event be taken not on the basis of objective evidence about relative cost-effectiveness, but on purely ideological grounds (i.e. an untested presumption that 'the market is always more efficient'). When the subcontracting extends to the buying in of medical care from the private sector on behalf of NHS patients, the distinction between the 'old' debate on private practice versus the NHS and the 'new' debate on the subcontracting issues becomes rather fine.

We share the suspicion that the subcontracting issue will not always be settled on cost-effectiveness grounds and that, from time to time, ideological considerations will prove decisive instead. Nevertheless, we do not believe that this is really the crunch issue concerning the NHS and the private sector. This we take rather to be *the priorities informing decisions about the pattern and volume of health care to be provided, and the principles by which that health care is distributed amongst the population.*

We shall address those matters by distinguishing various 'realms of discourse'. The first of these is the purely ideological. For some, this will be both the beginning and the end of the matter, and they will be ready to stand up and be counted at the end of the first section; the rest of the chapter will be seen as irrelevant sophistry. For others, the discussion of ideology is but a ground-clearing operation before the real work begins. For this latter group we present a highly simplified sketch of a private health service and the NHS in their idealised forms, which will immediately be followed by an equally simplified sketch of the two systems in their actual manifestations. The results should be chastening for the protagonists on both sides. We then offer a brief justification of the proposition that it is impossible to determine 'by inspection' which of these actual systems is best, and still less whether some mix of the two might be better than either in isolation. Finally we look at the UK scene.

IDEOLOGY

The ideological issues in the provision of health care have been admirably dissected by Donabedian (1971). His analysis is summarised in Table 6.1. His 'viewpoint A' may loosely be termed the 'libertarian' approach, under which access to health care is part of society's reward system, and, at the margin at least, people should be permitted to use their income and wealth to gain more or better health care (than their fellow citizens in otherwise identical circumstances) if they so desire. His 'viewpoint B' may loosely be termed the 'egalitarian' approach, under which access to health care is a citizen's right (like access to the ballot box or to the courts of justice), which ought not to be influenced by income and wealth. Under the former view, private practice should predominate, with the NHS providing a minimum standard for the poor. Under the latter view, the NHS should predominate, with little or no role for the private sector. Gallie (1956, in P. Laslett, 1970, p. 128) summarised the alternative ideologies as follows:

> The kernel ideas of liberal morality, commutative justice, the meritorious individual, the moral necessity of free choice and contract (especially in economic life) and the self-limiting character of good government are countered by the ideas of distributive justice, the contributing individual, freedom as essentially freedom to be not to get, and collective action in economic affairs. It is as if the parable of the talents were countered by the parable of the vineyard'.

In Britain, most supporters of the Labour Party adopt viewpoint B. This support had earlier manifestations in the statement of the 1944 coalition (Churchill) government (Ministry of Health, 1944, p. 5):

> the Government . . . want to ensure that in the future every man and woman and child can rely on getting . . . the best medical and other facilities available; that their getting them shall not depend on whether they can pay for them or on any other factor irrelevant to real need.

and in the outline to the 1946 NHS Bill of the Attlee government, which stated that the service would impose 'no limits on availability, e.g. limitations based on financial means, age, sex, employment or vocation, areas of residence or insurance qualification' (Ministry of Health, 1946; p. 3).

Many members of the Conservative Party appear to, and seem to want to, adopt both viewpoints simultaneously, and offer only halfhearted support for viewpoint A. Thus, Margaret Thatcher at the Conservative Party Conference in Brighton on October 8th 1982, said:

> The principle that adequate health care should be provided for all, regardless of their ability to pay, must be the foundation of any arrangements for financing the health service.

Similarly, Lord Trefgarne in a House of Lords debate on the public–private mix for health (Hansard, 27 April 1983, col. 999) stated that:

> The principle should be that good health care should be provided for everyone regardless of ability to pay.

Table 6.1 *Attitudes typically associated with viewpoints A and B*

	Viewpoint A	Viewpoint B
Personal responsibility	Personal responsibility for achievement is very important, and this is weakened if people are offered unearned rewards. Moreover, such unearned rewards weaken the motive force that assures economic well-being, and in so doing they also undermine moral well-being, because of the intimate connection between moral well-being and the personal effort to achieve.	Personal incentives to achieve are desirable, but economic failure is not equated with moral depravity or social worthlessness.
Social concern	Social Darwinism dictates a seemingly cruel indifference to the fate of those who cannot make the grade. A less extreme position is that charity, expressed and effected preferably under private auspices, is the proper vehicle, but it needs to be exercised under carefully prescribed conditions, for example, such that the potential recipient must first mobilise all his own resources and, when helped, must not be in as favourable a position as those who are self-supporting (the principle of 'lesser eligibility').	Private charitable action is not rejected but is seen as potentially dangerous morally (because it is often demeaning to the recipient and corrupting to the donor) and usually inequitable. It seems preferable to establish social mechanisms that create and sustain self-sufficiency and that are accessible according to precise rules concerning entitlement that are applied equitably and explicitly sanctioned by society at large.

Freedom	Freedom is to be sought as a supreme good in itself. Compulsion attenuates both personal responsibility and individualistic and voluntary expressions of social concern. Centralized health planning and a large governmental role in health care financing are seen as an unwarranted abridgement of the freedom of clients as well as of health professionals, and private medicine is thereby viewed as a bulwark against totalitarianism.	Freedom is seen as the presence of real opportunities of choice; although economic constraints are less openly coercive than political constraints, they are nonetheless real, and often the effective limits on choice. Freedom is not indivisible but may be sacrificed in one respect in order to obtain greater freedom in some other. Government is not an external threat to individuals in the society but is the means by which individuals achieve greater scope for action (that is, greater real freedom).
Equality	Equality before the law is the key concept, with clear precedence being given to freedom over equality wherever the two conflict.	Since the only moral justification for using personal achievement as the basis for distributing rewards is that everyone has equal opportunities for such achievement, then the main emphasis is on equality of opportunity; where this cannot be assured, the moral worth of achievement is thereby undermined. Equality is seen as an extension to the many of the freedom actually enjoyed by only the few.

However, such Conservative government statements in support of an 'egalitarian' view of health care (viewpoint B) are usually qualified by strong support for a private sector that would offer choice and a challenge to the monopoly position of the NHS. Thus Lord Trefgarne in the same April 1983 debate (col. 1000) said:

> The private sector has an important role to play. By increasing available health care provision, it relieves some of the pressures on the NHS. But there are other benefits too. There are dangers in being a monopoly supplier or monopoly employer, and the private sector provides a useful alternative to the NHS. It shows that there are different ways of doing things.

This somewhat schizophrenic ideological attitude to health care is due no doubt to the general popularity of the NHS and the mixed feelings many people have about the workings of the private sector.

HEALTH CARE SYSTEMS: PUBLIC AND PRIVATE

In summarising the issues here, we have had to be brutally ruthless with the wealth of subtle material that has been written on the matter. We have divided the discourse into two parts. The first concerns the properties of private and public systems in their idealised forms, dividing their respective key features into: demand, supply, adjustment mechanisms, and criteria of success. Table 6.2 presents this summary. The second concerns the respective properties of the two systems concentrating on the very same features but now in their actual manifestations in this regrettably imperfect world. Table 6.3 presents this summary. It is instructive *both* to compare the left and right columns within each table, *and* to compare each entry in Table 6.3 with the corresponding entry in Table 6.2. Such comparisons speak volumes and have been elaborated elsewhere at length (e.g. Abel-Smith, 1976; Abel-Smith and Maynard, 1979; McLachlan and Maynard, 1982).

We are not going to waste space commenting in detail here, but merely observe that unless you are an ideologue of the most fanatical kind it is not very satisfactory to conduct the debate in terms of Table 6.2 alone, although this is, unfortunately, what frequently happens in much public discourse. A more fruitful debate is possible, however, on two other bases. One would be to investigate why the performance summarised in Table 6.3 is so different from the ideas summarised in Table 6.2, and what could be done to make the former more like the latter (for either or both systems). That is not, however, the principal theme selected for this occasion. Here we shall concentrate on the second possible theme for debate, that is whether, given the actual systems, we still prefer in Table 6.3 the system we preferred in Table 6.2 It is upon this kind of discussion that we now embark.

WELFARE ECONOMICS

The natural first step is to attempt to use welfare economics principles to evaluate this snapshot of reality. Problems immediately arise, however. At a fundamental level, pure Paretian welfare economics is relevant only to those who hold to viewpoint A, and therefore useful only for appraising different ways of organising a system from that standpoint, because it is based on the notion that people are the best judges of their own welfare, and that any change that makes at least one person better off (whoever that may be) and does not make anyone worse off, is an improvement in social welfare. It can, of course, be broadened in the conventional way to embrace *potential* Pareto improvements (so that a change is judged an improvement if potential gainers *could* compensate potential losers and still have some gains left), but, unless the required compensation is actually paid, we are left in a vacuum as regards the distributional consequences. There is no mechanism here for 'social judgements about need' (i.e. communal statements of preference about how improvements in welfare should be distributed), which is an important feature of viewpoint B (under 'social concern' in Table 6.1).

If pure Paretian welfare economics is an inappropriate tool for the job, what tool is there? The best we have at present is recourse to that umbrella concept, the social welfare function, which we could use as a vehicle for conveying whatever we think are (or might be) the appropriate distributional preferences (or equity principles) for appraising alternative systems of health care. In that specific context these preferences or principles might be concerned with inputs, processes or outcomes – e.g. *expenditure per capita*, the *utilisation* of health care, or *access* to health care, or *achieved* health status, or *improvements* in health status – and would manifest themselves in any one of the many variants that have been propounded or used from time to time. The ideal state of this target variable, whichever it is, might be some desired frequency distribution (e.g. absolute equality) or proportionality to some other variable (e.g. risk of illness or death). Furthermore, the equity principle might be held to be not overriding or absolute but moderated by any incentive or disincentive effects it might have (i.e. an efficiency/equity trade-off is envisaged).

Thus it is almost inevitable that we will find that the proponents of

Table 6.2 *Idealised health care systems*

		Private	NHS
Demand	1	Individuals are the best judges of their own welfare.	When ill, individuals are frequently imperfect judges of their own welfare.
	2	Priorities determined by own willingness and ability to pay.	Priorities determined by social judgements about need.
	3	Erratic and potentially catastrophic nature of demand mediated by private insurance.	Erratic and potentially catastrophic nature of demand made irrelevant by provision of free services.
	4	Matters of equity to be dealt with elsewhere (e.g. in the tax and social security systems).	Since the distribution of income and wealth unlikely to be equitable in relation to the need for health care, the NHS must be insulated from its influence.
Supply	1	Profit is the proper and effective way to motivate suppliers to respond to the needs of demanders.	Professional ethics and dedication to public service are the appropriate motivation, focusing on success in curing or caring.
	2	Priorities determined by people's willingness and ability to pay and by the costs of meeting their wishes at the margin.	Priorities determined by where the greatest improvements in caring or curing can be effected at the margin.
	3	Suppliers have strong incentive to adopt least-cost methods of provision.	Predetermined limit on available resources generates a strong incentive for suppliers to adopt least-cost methods of provision.

Adjustment mechanism	1	Many competing suppliers ensure that offer prices are kept low, and reflect costs.	Central review of activities generates efficiency audit of service provision and management pressures keep the system cost-effective.
	2	Well-informed consumers are able to seek out the most cost-effective form of treatment for themselves.	Well-informed clinicians are able to prescribe the most cost-effective form of treatment for each patient.
	3	If, at the price that clears the market, medical practice is profitable, more people will go into medicine, and hence supply will be demand responsive.	If there is resulting pressure on some facilities or specialities, resources will be directed towards extending them.
	4	If, conversely, medical practice is unremunerative, people will leave it, or stop entering it, until the system returns to equilibrium.	Facilities or specialities on which pressure is slack will be slimmed down to release resources for other uses.
Success criteria	1	Consumers will judge the system by their ability to get someone to do what they demand, when, where and how they want it.	Electorate judges the system by the extent to which it improves the health status of the population at large in relation to the resources allocated to it.
	2	Producers will judge the system by how good a living they can make out of it.	Producers judge the system by its ability to enable them to provide the treatments they believe to be cost-effective.

Table 6.3 *Actual health care systems*

		Private	NHS
Demand	1.	Doctors act as agents, mediating demand on behalf of consumers.	Doctors act as agents, identifying need on behalf of patients.
	2.	Priorities determined by the reimbursement rules of insurance funds.	Priorities determined by the doctor's own professional situation, by his assessment of the patient's condition, and the expected trouble-making proclivities of the patient.
	3.	Because private insurance coverage is itself a profit seeking activity, some risk-rating is inevitable, hence coverage is incomplete and uneven, distorting personal willingness and ability to pay.	Freedom from direct financial contributions at the point of service, and absence of risk rating, enables patients to seek treatment for trivial or inappropriate conditions.
	4.	Attempts to change the distribution of income and wealth independently, are resisted as destroying incentives (one of which is the ability to buy better or more medical care if you are rich).	Attempts to correct inequities in the social and economic system by differential compensatory access to health services leads to recourse to health care in circumstances where it is unlikely to be a cost-effective solution to the problem.
Supply	1	What is most profitable to suppliers may not be what is most in the interests of consumers, and since neither consumers nor suppliers may be very clear about what is in the former's interests, this gives suppliers a range of discretion.	Personal professional dedication and public spirited motivation likely to be corroded and degenerate into cynicism if others, who do not share those feelings, are seen to be doing very well for themselves through blatantly self-seeking behaviour.
	2	Priorities determined by the extent to which consumers can be induced to part with their money, and by the costs of satisfying the pattern of 'demand'.	Priorities determined by what gives the greatest professional satisfaction.
	3	Profit motive generates a strong incentive	Since cost-effectiveness is not accepted as a proper

	towards market segmentation and price discrimination, and tie-in agreements with other professionals.	medical responsibility, such pressures merely generate tension between the 'professionals' and the 'managers'.
Adjustment mechanism	1 Professional ethical rules are used to make overt competition difficult.	Because it does not need elaborate cost data for billing purposes, it does not routinely generate much useful information on costs.
	2 Consumers denied information about quality and competence, and, since insured, may collude with doctors (against the insurance carriers) in inflating costs.	Clinicians know little about costs, and have no direct incentive to act on such information as they have, and sometimes even quite perverse incentives (i.e. cutting costs may make life more difficult, or less rewarding for them).
	3 Entry into the profession made difficult and numbers restricted to maintain profitability.	Very little is known about the relative cost-effectiveness of different treatments, and even where it is, doctors are wary of acting on such information until a general professional consensus emerges.
	4 If demand for services falls, doctors extend range of activities and push out neighbouring disciplines.	The phasing out of facilities which have become redundant is difficult because it often threatens the livelihood of some concentrated specialised group and has identifiable people dependent on it, whereas the beneficiaries are dispersed and can only be identified as 'statistics'.
Success criteria	1 Consumers will judge the system by their ability to get someone to do what they need done without making them 'medically indigent' and/or changing their risk-rating too adversely.	Since the easiest aspect of health status to measure is life expectancy, the discussion is dominated by mortality data and mortality risks to the detriment of treatments concerned with non-life-threatening situations.
	2 Producers will judge the system by how good a living they can make out of it.	In the absence of accurate data on cost-effectiveness, producers judge the system by the extent to which it enables them to carry out the treatments which they find the most exciting and satisfying.

private health services subscribe to one social welfare function, while those supporting the NHS subscribe to another, which is merely to say that there is ideological conflict, as indicated at the outset. In this case it is hardly surprising that each group remains convinced that its candidate is best (warts and all), for this would only *not* be so in the unlikely event that it turned out that the NHS proved to be better at meeting the objectives of viewpoint A people than the system that was designed by viewpoint A people to meet viewpoint A objectives! *Mutatis mutandis*, the same goes for private medicine and viewpoint B people.

Is it not then tempting to suggest that there should be two systems, side by side, each serving its own 'supporters'? Unfortunately, this will not work either, for the essence of the viewpoint B position is that we are all one community and there can be no opting out. Giving more freedom of choice for some, by letting their superior purchasing power shift the overall distribution of health care in their direction by more than is regarded as equitable (whether through the NHS or some other system), is still a diminution in social welfare, since there will, by definition, be some other group of beneficiaries with higher social priority for any redeployable resources devoted to health care. So the only compelling argument that is likely to persuade viewpoint B people that a mixed system is better than a purely NHS type solution would be that in practice some achievable mixed system will come closer to satisfying their aims than any achievable 'pure' system would. So the crunch question is whether some *mix* of the two actual systems depicted above would be better than either of them alone, and, if so, what that mix should be. The answer would obviously depend on whether the 'distortions' of one actual system could be used to offset the 'distortions' of the other – e.g. can the 'competitive thrust' of the market lead to the better achievement of NHS goals.

THE UK SCENE

Any analysis of the interaction of the public and private health care sectors in Britain is made difficult by the abundance of rhetoric and the absence of systematic knowledge about the relationships between inputs, processes and outcomes within and between the constituent parts of the sectors. The rhetoric is nicely demonstrated in Lord Wigoder's (Chairman of BUPA) contribution to a House of Lords debate (*Hansard* 27 April 1983, Col. 974):

> The first myth is that in some way, the private sector wants to see the end of or destroy the NHS. Nothing could be further from the

truth. Everyone in the private sector is full of admiration for the work the NHS does. We all recognise it is a cornerstone of the welfare state.

He then went on (col. 976) to argue that the private sector did not harm the NHS, in fact it benefited it:

the existence of the two sectors stimulates competition, competition in the design and building of hospitals, competition in the use of day surgery, developments in preventive medicine and so forth.

Before we attempt to evaluate this assertion, it is perhaps wise to detail some of the characteristics of the private health care sector. It is to be emphasised that this sector is very heterogeneous, with non-profit and profit-making institutions competing for market shares. Inherent in this process is the fact that what is good for the suppliers (high revenues) is not good for the financers (high costs).

At present there are three main non-profit-making provident associations offering private health care insurance (for details of the characteristics of these associations, see Maynard in McLachlan and Maynard, 1982). Between them, the British United Provident Association (BUPA), Private Patient's Plan (PPP) and the Western Provident Association (WPA) cover over 95 per cent of subscribers to private health insurance, and the largest (BUPA) covers 70 per cent of the market. In 1981, expenditure by the big three (BUPA, PPP and WPA) was just over £200 million (less than 2 per cent of NHS expenditure that year) and these associations had 1.8 million subscribers and a total coverage of about 4 million people. The associations finance a relatively narrow range of largely elective (cold) surgical activities: about 60 per cent of their expenditure goes on about thirty such procedures. In 1981, the associations made losses for the first time in their history and in 1982 market growth appears to have been quite small. This follows rapid growth in 1980 – about 25–30 per cent – and seems to be at odds with the government's encouragement of the sector.

There are a variety of reasons for the slump in growth of business. On the demand side, some of the insured groups offered cover in 1979/80 – such as the police and firemen – reacted to the moral hazard inherent in near-full reimbursement policies (i.e. practically zero coinsurance rates) with utilisation patterns in excess of those anticipated by the associations. The impetus to market growth offered by the tax offset arrangements may also have increased cover to lower-income groups with higher utilisation characteristics: in 1982/3 premium payments could be offset against tax only if the subscriber's income was below £8,500 per annum (the tax revenue lost by this was about £4 million). On the supply side, the Conservative government, after an initial large pay increase in 1979, has controlled medical incomes. The new consultant contract introduced by the Thatcher administration made it possible for many doctors to indulge in private work for the first time by allowing full-time consultants to earn up to 10 per cent of their income from private work. At the same time, BUPA (the market leader of the provident associations) initiated, with medical advice, 'generous' (!) fee increases. In sum, these influences have induced more doctors to do private work at higher fees. Moreover, the reversal by the Thatcher administration of Barbara Castle's pay-bed policy is leading to more pay beds being reintroduced into the NHS. However, this is a slow development as private bed stock expansions following on from the introduction of Castle's policy has led to large increases in capacity and problems for providers and associations (financers) about utilisation and fee rates. Thus, after the early boom, the private sector has run into a classic (North American style) cost containment problem. BUPA, WPA and PPP are discovering the differences between the ideals and the actual in terms of Tables 6.2 and 6.3.

At present, there is no systematic evidence to demonstrate that the private provision of such health care is more efficient than the public provision; indeed, such comparisons are inherently difficult to carry out. However, in terms of viewpoint B, such a debate is irrelevant because the egalitarian is seeking to answer the question 'to what extent does the private sector facilitate the achievement of the objectives of the NHS?' Lord Wigoder argues that 350,000 trade unionists are covered by private insurance and that there is clear support for private health care amongst trade unionists who use private (TU-financed) facilities such as the Manor House Hospital. But the fact that it is white- or blue-collar members of the provident associations who acquire access to resources at the expense of (say) NHS geriatric patients in need of care or hip replacements does not alter the fact that, as far as the proponent of viewpoint B is concerned, such activities use resources in a way that is at variance with their objectives, because people with a higher social priority for such resources are denied access to them. The organisation of the health care market is concerned not only with efficiency considerations but also with distributional considerations.

Both the private and public finance and provision of health care have ample scope to use resources inefficiently, as can be seen in terms of Tables 6.2 and 6.3, but is it possible that private sector activity could induce the NHS to achieve at least some of its efficiency and distribution goals better? There is some evidence that, at the margins, the threat of privatisation may have a salutory 'demonstration' effect on NHS decision-makers and, as a consequence, on the achievements of the objectives of the service. The dangers of such demonstration effects are obvious: ideology may override the results of the investment appraisal. Thus, item 76 of the February 1983 Yorkshire Regional Health Authority's minutes shows that the Minister of Health

> had stated that Ministers had concluded that the laundry service for Calderdale should in future be provided by an outside [private] contractor rather than by building a new [NHS] laundry in Halifax. Ministers accepted that the economic appraisal carried out by the RHA/DHA had been undertaken thoroughly and in a way which was broadly consistent with the advice contained in the Department's recently issued draft circular but it was considered that the conclusion reached – of the annual saving indicated by opting for in-house [NHS] service – was well within the range of error which it was reasonable to assume for appraisals of this kind.

The meaning of this NHS jargon is that the ministers wished to opt for private laundry services in Calderdale even though the appraisal had shown them to be more expensive. At the time of writing, this decision is in abeyance: the ministers have given the RHA/DHA two months to revise the in-house option. Clearly the use of demonstration effects has inherent dangers. However, to the extent that they made the NHS more efficient (and this has to be monitored and evaluated), they may make the achievement of egalitarian objectives easier.

It should, however, be possible to introduce efficiency pressures into the NHS by changing the financial regime under which it operates, without going as far as privatisation. Thus a health circular in 1981 (HN(81)30) obliged all authorities to carry out investment appraisal on new capital programmes. Such appraisals have led NHS administrators to develop their management skills and to appraise costs and the quality of services in a novel fashion. In part this novelty is a reflection of the crude basis of past NHS decision-making and of the absence of incentives to be more efficient in resource use (especially with capital), since debt does not have to be serviced and there has in the past been little or no virement between capital allocations and revenue allocations.

The outlook for the NHS is unclear. The efforts by successive governments to persuade decision-makers to shift NHS resources out of acute care into the priority (Cinderella) services will, in the absence of compensating improvements in acute sector efficiency, increase waiting times and generate private sector demand for cold (elective) procedures. Public expenditure on the NHS has increased every year since 1979 in real terms. However, existing Conservative plans for 1984/5 and after (HMSO 1983), indicate the imposition of real resource reductions. Again, unless efficiency can be increased, NHS services will be reduced in an uneven and uncertain manner, thus generating private sector opportunities for growth and outcomes likely to be inconsistent with viewpoint B. Some pressures to increase NHS efficiency are sensible, but it is a nice judgement as to when such pressures in the form of privatisation will generate outcomes at variance with NHS objectives.

From the pure egalitarian point of view, a private health care sector is unnecessary unless it contributes to the achievement of NHS goals. Political pressures from adherents to viewpoint A and producers who benefit from the provision of private health care are likely to cause the maintenance of some private activity. Proponents of viewpoint B will hope that this private activity will not be subsidised by the state with tax offsets or other devices, so that, if the NHS is efficient, the demand for private sector health care will be minimal and will pose only a minor threat to the achievement of egalitarian goals.

CONCLUSION

Throughout this chapter we have put forward the view that the choice between public and private health care should be determined in relation to the priorities informing decisions about the pattern and volume of health care to be provided and in relation to the principles by which that health care is to be distributed amongst the members of our society. The sometimes implicit and sometimes explicit nature of our arguments has indicated that our preference is for the ideals of the NHS as opposed to the ideals of the private sector (Table 6.2), although we admit that these ideals have yet to be achieved (Table 6.3). Some private health care activity seems unavoidable, but there is little reason to believe that it will assist significantly in the achievement of NHS objectives.

7 Private Health Insurance

PETER A. WEST

INTRODUCTION

Chapter 6 has shown that although the private health sector remains small compared with the NHS (which is, after all, one of the world's largest corporate organisations), it has grown rapidly until quite recently. This growth is concentrated in insurance and facilities for acute hospital care, and it is around such facilities that the greatest controversy rages. By comparison, the part of the private sector that caters for the long-term care of the elderly attracts much less interest or hostility. To a degree, this reflects the special category into which acute medical care is placed by critics of the private sector. Health is seen as something whose distribution must be independent of markets and of the distribution of income. Those in favour of the private sector counter that, since health insurance is within the same price range as a drinking or smoking habit, the choice of these or other uses of an individual's income should be left in his own hands. Since the NHS remains to cover emergencies and most other forms of care, a decision to increase well-being by the acquisition of private health insurance is then put in the same class as a choice in favour of beer and skittles.

The debate about private medicine is complicated by the extent to which it is seen as a separable issue or as part of a wider social distribution of income and welfare. Political critics are likely to be in favour of a more progressive distribution of income and welfare, from which standpoint additional health care for middle-income groups is accorded a low social priority. Proponents take the distribution of income and welfare as given and reduce the consumption of private health insurance to an allocative question for those with the means to purchase it. Meanwhile, the efficiency argument developed by economists has been inconclusive.

In the discussion here, the choice of private insurance in Britain, given the existence of the NHS, is examined. The impact of the growth of private insurance on the NHS is then considered, in particular the impact on the distributive characteristics of health services and on the substitutability of private for public health services.

THE GROWTH OF PRIVATE INSURANCE

Private health insurance schemes grew appreciably in the 1970s. This growth in sales, as with any product, could be attributed to changes in taste, changes in income, or changes in price.

Consider first consumer tastes. Why should tastes have changed markedly? Although subject to some redistribution and restraint, the NHS was still at that time protected in public spending decisions. More significant, perhaps, is the group that was recruited and at whom advertising was directed. Health insurance, like any insurance, is most effective when an individual faces a small risk of a large loss. The sales targets for private cover are affluent employees. But since this group is the lowest user of health services, and given that existing medical problems would not be covered in a new policy, dissatisfaction with the NHS seems implausible as an explanation of their involvement.

Rising incomes could influence the decision to purchase health care and insurance against its costs. Aside from the straightforward income effect (assuming the services and cover are not inferior goods), the rise in income could lead consumers to purchase different characteristics of care, or insurance to pay for them. For example, a hospital patient in the NHS will not always have uncongested (and cigarette-smoke-free) access to a television. Use of the telephone and simple privacy are similarly restricted. Nor is the level of comfort always as high as will be found at home. Thus, it would be perfectly consistent for an individual satisfied with the NHS as a potential source of medical intervention to acquire insurance to meet the higher 'hotel' cost of a better environment.

Price is the third factor that changes the purchasing decision. Currently, the price of membership is £30–65 per month for a family all aged under 30, or £35–50 for a family aged up to 50. This is the same cost per day as two–three pints of beer or thirty cigarettes. However, overt price is misleading for large numbers of private scheme members since the price is paid by their employers. Group health insurance schemes, covering a whole stratum of employees, are a major element in the private sector, and, when the employer pays, price has no direct relevance to the employee. The groups scheme has joined the company car as a standard fringe benefit, which in one famous case was extended to a trade union as part of a wage deal. Thus, much of the growth of the private medical sector is bound up with the extension of fringe benefits at a time of wage restraint in the 1970s.

Clearly, the fact that companies rather than individuals are responsible for much of the purchase of private health insurance does not in any way illegitimise its purchase, although it does run counter to the argument that individuals should be left to make their own purchasing decisions. Effectively, individuals are not being left to make a market decision, based on willingness to pay. Rather that decision is made en bloc for a large group of workers and is not the result of private market choices by utility-maximising consumers. It would perhaps be appropriate to give employees covered by groups schemes the choice of insurance or additional income.

THE IMPACT OF THE PRIVATE SECTOR

The growing private medical sector is at times accused of poaching resources from the public sector. In the short run, this argument is difficult to sustain. Staff may be recruited from the NHS but, since NHS budgets are unaffected, there is a change in manpower rather than a diminution. Although, in principle, this could affect the quality and experience of the staff, there is no good evidence on which to assess this.

The NHS embodies a variety of transfers of resources to meet the costs of illness. Employed workers, who finance much of the cost through direct and indirect taxation, are the healthiest sub-group of the population. Thus, one transfer of resources through the NHS is between the healthy worker and the elderly. The average person over 65 years of age uses more than three times the resources of the NHS as do those of working age. This differential rises to a factor of six for those over 75. A further transfer occurs between workers and those unable to work owing to ill-health. While the employed suffer illness and use the NHS from time to time, it is likely that those using most resources as a result of serious illness will drop out of employment more frequently. Finally, there are transfers via the NHS between different social classes. The extent of these has, however, been contested.

It is the transfers directed towards those who have fallen out of work or retired that are of particular concern here. This is the group that is likely to find it difficult to meet private premiums from an income that is almost certainly falling. Where the employer previously paid the cost, continued membership seems less likely. Furthermore, much of the care provided for long-term illness is not covered by private insurance schemes. This in part derives from the lack of impact of much medical care. Fire insurance, for example, can be based on the estimated cost of rebuilding damaged property. Health services, in contrast, may frequently be unable fully to restore health. Thus, the potential expenditure on the sick is not bounded as it is for physical damage to property. To avoid open-ended financial commitments (e.g. for long-term care of the elderly), private health insurance schemes restrict the range, duration or cost of care covered. As a result, private insurance schemes are much more restricted in the transfers that they finance. Transfers are likely to be kept to a substantial degree within the employed group (and family members), to fund care for short-term illness that is followed by return to work.

Since private and public systems are not complete substitutes, the key to the long-run effect of private sector growth on the public sector is the extent to which the differences between the two are perceived. One possibility is that private insurance will be seen as a complete substitute for the NHS by the affluent employees it covers. It is possible that this will reduce their commitment to public expenditure on health services, which imposes a high tax cost upon them while offering little apparent benefit, given their good health and private cover. In consequence, the public sector may contract to a level below that which, with perfect foresight, these insured individuals would prefer, particularly if serious illness or retirement led to the termination of employer-paid premiums. The higher cost of private insurance at a time of falling income is potentially likely to lead to withdrawal from the private system.

The alternative possibility, in which private and public care are correctly seen as distinct services catering for different stages in the patient's life, cannot be excluded *a priori*. This possibility would leave commitments to a large, tax-financed NHS unaffected by the growth of private cover. To the extent that this does not occur, individual voters/taxpayers may find that the intertemporal effects of their choices are not as expected. Hence, just as consumer choices of medical care are argued to be inefficient due to the consumer's ignorance, so, too, defective foresight could lead to similarly inefficient consumption and political choices.

CONCLUSION

The conclusion of this chapter is that the intertemporal impact of the growth of private medicine is likely to be greater than any short-term impact on local NHS resources. Consumers/taxpayers who do not perceive that the NHS is in part an intertemporal redistribution device may make inappropriate choices about the level of commitment of resources to the NHS to be maintained by future governments.

NOTE

All views expressed in this chapter are personal and not those of the Bloomsbury Health Authority.

8 Privatisation and Housing

CHRISTINE M. E. WHITEHEAD

INTRODUCTION

There are three main reasons in a generally market-oriented economy why goods and services may be provided by the public sector: the attributes of the good make it unsuitable for private provision; production and allocation are inherently or practically more efficient in the public sector than in the private; or there is a divergence between private and social objectives that can best be overcome by public provision.

Those who are currently making the case for greater privatisation in housing argue that its attributes, its methods of production and allocation, and its value to the individual and community make it far more suitable for organisation by the market than has been accepted by policy-makers over the last decades. Two main reasons are given for this view:

- that, unlike many of the other services provided by the welfare state, housing is very much a private good, both because most of the benefits go to the individual consumer and because much of this benefit arises from the individual's capacity to choose his own mix, and level, of the wide range of attributes that make up the good housing.
- that one of the most desirable attributes of housing for many people lies in the joint consumption of ownership and occupation – an attribute that cannot be made available through public provision.

Both of these arguments relate to the nature of the housing good. If these are accepted, it is suggested, it is likely to follow that private production and allocation will be more efficient than public and that the satisfaction of private preferences will meet social objectives. If this is the case, privatisation must be desirable.

In order to assess the strengths of this argument, I here examine three questions: first, whether other attributes of housing, not stressed by those pressing for privatisation, make private market provision and allocation unsuitable, at least for some groups of households; second, whether in the light of these attributes, private or public production and allocation are likely to be the more efficient; and, finally, whether the present government's emphasis on privatisation and particularly on subsidising the growth of owner-occupation can be justified in terms of these attributes, relative costs or any divergence between private and social objectives. On the basis of this examination it should be possible to come to some conclusion about the extent to which privatisation in housing can be justified on economic grounds or should be seen more as a reflection of political ideology.

THE ATTRIBUTES OF HOUSING

An important rationale for government provision of any particular commodity is that the market for that commodity is inherently imperfect – because of the public nature of the good, the existence of externalities, problems of information and uncertainty, significant economies of scale in relation to the size of the market, and other causes of market failure (Le Grand and Robinson, 1984). Housing does not obviously fall into this category. The vast majority of benefits above a very low, public health determined minimum standard go to the owner or user of the property; so in the main it is a private good with relatively few externalities. People seem pretty aware of the benefits that come to them from housing; so there is little reason to expect them to make incorrect decisions. There are few economies of scale in production and no obvious barriers to entry into either the construction industry or the provision of existing units; so consumers ought to be able to shop around among many different suppliers. All of these factors suggest that housing is a readily marketable commodity suitable for private provision in a mixed economy (Stafford, 1978; Charles, 1977).

There are, however, a number of important attributes of housing and the way that it is valued that have led people to argue for public intervention. First, a dwelling is a long-lived indivisible investment, the production and purchase of which usually involves borrowed finance. The imperfection of the capital market, which is particularly obvious with respect to individual borrowers, would result in under-investment in housing if government did not intervene to improve the workings of that market and to offset the additional costs (Lansley, 1979).

Secondly, housing jointly provides both an asset and a consumption good. Where it is desired to use them separately, contractual problems are likely to occur. This makes the landlord–tenant relationship inherently imperfect. Although in a free market each has a choice whether or not to contract with the other, once the contract is made there are significant problems arising from opportunistic behaviour, from difficulties in monitoring the contract and from differences in relative information (Williamson, 1975). As such problems are in the nature of the contract, state intervention may be desirable to assist specification and enforcement. Alternatively, and this is the policy of most socialists, the state may take over the role of landlord in order to ensure that the contract is implemented in a socially desirable fashion (Douglas-Mann, 1973). At the limit, all renting would then be provided in the social sector. A more restricted policy would transfer to the social sector all lettings where the tenant was in a relatively weak bargaining position.

Thirdly, new investment can only be a small proportion of the total stock. As a result, supply cannot readily be adjusted to changes in demand. Many factors – such as changes in the location of activity, in income, in the ease of obtaining finance and in expectations of relative rates of returns – can lead to rapid and significant increases or decreases in demand. Changing supply, on the other hand, is necessarily a slow process, while imperfections in the market for construction finance and the risk aversion of builders exacerbate the problems of adjustment (Building Societies Association, 1980). Conditions of excess demand give market power to owners of the existing stock. Inelastic demand, especially at the lower end of the market, pushes up prices and worsens contractual conditions from the point of view of the consumer. Because of the locational specificity of housing, such problems persist in local markets even when there is no overall housing shortage. In these conditions, state intervention is thought desirable to limit market power, to improve supply conditions and to allocate what is available more effectively (Le Grand and Robinson, 1984).

The attributes discussed so far suggest that market failure may reduce the level of private utility obtainable from housing, making state intervention to increase consumption desirable. Other attributes make housing a particularly suitable means of redistributing income and wealth and may cause differences between private and social valuation of the good. In particular, housing is expensive in relation to most people's income. Given the current distribution of income, many households are unable to purchase adequate accommodation and so require state assistance if they are to be reasonably housed (Lansley, 1979). If housing is regarded as purely a private good, this would normally suggest a policy of general income and wealth redistribution (Maclennan, 1982; Grey et al., 1981). However, redistribution based on the provision or subsidy of a socially acceptable good is often politically far easier to implement than general redistributive policies. The provision and subsidy of housing have been a traditional instrument for such redistribution; indeed, the spread of owner-occupation is the most important factor in the widening distribution of wealth ownership that has occurred since 1945 (Royal Commission on the Distribution of Income and Wealth, 1979).

Another attribute, that housing is regarded as a merit good, raises closely related but formally different arguments. Housing is a merit good if society believes that all members of the community should consume housing of at least a given standard whatever the income or other attributes of the individual. In other words, the social utility of housing is seen as being greater than its private value (Robinson in Walden, 1982). Society must therefore provide such housing for all who would otherwise choose to consume less than the acceptable level of housing service, specifically subsidise housing or impose standards that force compliance. On equity grounds, if the standard is imposed to satisfy the community's welfare rather than the individual's, society should pay. It also follows that it is the state's responsibility to determine the extent to which housing is given such social priority and its right to modify that choice (Whitehead, 1983).

Another aspect of the merit good argument occurs if social and private time preference, and particularly that preference in relation to housing, differ (Kay, 1972). It is usually argued in this context that the state is likely to set a higher value than does the individual consumer both on housing investment and on maintaining the existing stock.

All of the factors discussed so far imply state intervention, but none necessarily implies public provision. Investment may be increased by subsidy to the private sector, redistribution can be effected through the tax system, minimum standards may be enforced by decree, and contractual relationships improved through modifying the legal framework. However, one might expect public provision to be the most efficient way of dealing with some of the problems. In particular, minimum standards can be more easily enforced through direct provision and the investment necessary to eradicate shortages relating to need rather than private demand can be more readily undertaken. Further, past housing policies, particularly those affecting the private rented sector, limit the possibility of achieving an adequate level of private provision at the lower end of the market. Finally, public provision inherently removes the difficulties of private contracting that arise in the landlord–tenant relationship – although it may replace them with other, administrative, problems.

On the other hand, private provision is likely to be more responsive to individual preferences and, subject to the problems of capital market imperfections and short-term adjustment, it is likely to be able to provide more effectively the level of output demanded by those with the capacity to pay. Finally, the attribute of ownership, and particularly of joint ownership and occupation, which is highly valued by many consumers, can inherently only be provided in the private sector.

On the basis of these arguments, there appear to be a number of conclusions that can be drawn *a priori* about the relative suitability of public and private provision. These suggest that

- if people are able and willing to demand at least the socially accepted minimum standard (whatever that may turn out to be) and in particular wish to own their own homes, private sector provision is likely to be the more suitable.
- if people lack the capacity to pay for reasonable accommodation and are otherwise in a poor bargaining position, social provision is likely to be preferable.

These points relate mainly to the demand side and to the nature of the rental contract. They say little about which sector is likely to be the more efficient in terms of least-cost production and allocation of housing. Nor do they help determine the extent to which housing should receive special treatment because of its social as opposed to private valuation and the effect any difference might have on the private/public choice. I examine these questions in the next two sections.

COMPARATIVE EFFICIENCY

The present government's ideological viewpoint is that private incentives induce efficiency and consumer orientation, while the public sector tends to be dominated by the interest of suppliers, managers and local politicians. Market discipline, in other words, is likely to be more effective than public influence, and the lack of such discipline is likely to result in significant organisational slack (De Alassi, 1980). Private production and allocation together with state subsidy are therefore| seen as a more effective way of meeting housing requirements than is direct provision. Yet, when one looks at what little evidence there is on the relative efficiency of the two sectors, the position is by no means straightforward.

New building

One comparison is between local authority direct labour and private production. Almost all local authorities employ some direct labour, but over 85 per cent of the housing work undertaken is on repair and maintenance. There is a fairly strongly held belief that private contractors are likely to be more efficient than direct labour in building new dwellings. Yet what limited evidence there is does not confirm this view (Langford, 1982). Rather it shows that productivity is very similar, although it is difficult to adjust for different types and quality.

However, as local authorities generally choose to employ private contractors via open and selected competitive tendering, a more relevant question is whether a private developer produces more efficiently when working for himself than when working for the public sector – i.e. can the public sector organise production as effectively as the private? An unpublished study in Thamesmead in the early 1970s compared the costs of units built by developers for the public sector and those that were built in almost exactly similar conditions for the private market. I understand they found costs to be perhaps 10–15 per cent higher in the public sector. The main reasons for the difference seemed to relate to the complexities of contracting and to the need for detailed accountability. In particular, the public client usually specifies inputs in order to control quality. In so doing, inflexibilities are built in and builders find it difficult to adjust their production methods to changing circumstance. The monitoring process also imposes costs on both the builder and client, which are avoided when the developer sells directly to the public (Hillebrandt, 1974; Short, 1983).

It is clear, however, that many of the more generally observed differences in cost arise from differences in the product and in site conditions rather than from differences in unit costs for the same good. The locations used for public sector provision are often more difficult to build on than private sites, which are chosen by developers to increase profits rather than for overall suitability. Densities used by the public sector similarly may be socially more desirable but lead to higher direct costs. Many public sector developments include special-purpose units for households with specific housing needs, which are more costly than the basic private market product. These and other factors raise unit costs (Merrett, 1979; Short, 1983). The unanswered question is whether social benefits are also increased by enough to offset these costs. Advocates of public provision have often depended simply on assertion rather than attempted detailed evaluation.

Improvement

Conditions appear to be rather different with respect to improvement. Although the majority of small-scale improvement work would seem more suited to private rather than public organisation, even the present government appears to accept that some types of large-scale, particularly external, work are best undertaken by the public sector. It has introduced two main policies that reflect this view: enveloping, and improvement for sale. Under the enveloping scheme, a local authority organises all the external repair necessary for a group of dwellings, which are usually physically attached. The objective is to avoid both the private contracting difficulties of work affecting more than one owner and the problems of individual undervaluation of improvement in these circumstances (Davis and Whinston, 1961; Robinson, 1979). Improvement-for-sale schemes also usually apply to terraced units where the same sort of problems are encountered. (Building-for-sale schemes may be regarded as means of making public sector land available for housing and as demonstration projects for locations and dwelling types traditionally shunned by the private developer. As such they help, with the aid of significant additional subsidy, to improve the operation of the market.) Where there are fewer externality problems and more freedom to express individual preferences, it is arguable that private organisation is better. In these circumstances, schemes such as homesteading, which transfer unfit dwellings to the private sector for improvement with a subsidy, are preferred.

Repair and maintenance

When it comes to repair and maintenance it is usually argued that owner-occupation is more efficient than renting because the owner-occupier has both a stronger incentive to keep depreciation to a minimum and a greater incentive to use some of this leisure time for the upkeep of his property (Merrett and Gray, 1982). This argument relates to two particular aspects of market failure: the interdependence between the value of the house as an asset and its value in consumption, and the difficulties of contractual monitoring and enforcement. Although the arguments seem strong in principle, in practice there is evidence that the standard of repair is as much a function of household income and age as it is of tenure. In particular, there is considerable evidence of maintenance problems among lower-income and elderly owner-occupiers (Kirwan and Martin, 1972).

Adequate accommodation for all

Although it is an over-simplification, it is possible to argue that the UK and other countries (notably Holland, West Germany and Denmark) with large social sectors and with security and rent controls in the private sector are characterised by problems of access and homelessness even where there is no numerical housing shortage. On the other hand, the majority of households that find accommodation obtain adequate space and quality at reasonable prices. Countries that have concentrated on market allocation do not suffer so obviously from these difficulties but instead exhibit extreme variations in housing quality, far higher levels of overcrowding, and poorer value for money at the lower end of the market. These problems of allocation arise mainly as a result of the maldistribution of income and the low capacity to pay of lower-income households; they are exacerbated by conditions of housing shortage in which landlords are able to utilise their market power (Harloe, 1980). If privatisation is to be socially acceptable, these problems must be overcome. This implies that there must be reasonable choice for all at a price the consumer can afford.

Undoubtedly there is no longer an overall housing shortage in the UK. However, there remain areas of housing pressure, notably in London, where lower-income tenants have extremely limited initial choice, let alone bargaining power comparable to their landlords'. The market answer to this would be to free the private rented sector from controls in order to provide incentives for landlords to increase the supply of adequate lower-quality accommodation. For this to be efficient, landlords must be prepared to respond by making supply available wherever a normal rate of return can be predicted. However, because of past policies towards the private rented sector, potential landlords have little confidence in the future and are very unlikely to respond unless the potential rate of return is significantly higher than that obtainable in less risky investments elsewhere. Under current conditions, adequate private rented provision on reasonable terms is not a viable proposition (House of Commons Environment Committee, 1982a).

Even if the problem of supply could be overcome, the lack of capacity of lower-income households to pay for reasonable quality accommodation would remain. In the public sector, accommodation that meets socially accepted standards can be directly allocated to such households together with the necessary subsidy in the form of an income-related rent rebate. These rebates (now called the unified housing benefit) have a take-up rate of well over 80 per cent in the public sector, and those not receiving assistance are often only eligible for small amounts or for short periods (Goss and Lansley, 1981; Cullingworth, 1979). When the system operates in the private rented sector, however, it is far less effective. In the unfurnished sector, take-up is probably over 50 per cent but the vast majority of households that claim housing benefit are also in receipt of supplementary pensions. Those not eligible for other benefits generally do not take up rent allowances. In the furnished sector take-up is probably little more than 10 per cent, and perhaps 30 per cent of all furnished tenants pay more than 20 per cent of their income for housing (House of Commons Environment Committee, 1982a). This is despite very considerable effort by governments of all parties to increase these levels of take-up. While they remain so low, privatisation of housing for lower-income households must involve significant hardship.

Those who argue for market allocation for lower-income rental accommodation usually point to what they regard as the successful experience of the United States, in particular with respect to the housing allowance experiment. This showed a very elastic supply response by private rental suppliers to the increased capacity to pay provided by allowances (Rydell, 1982). As allowances were tied to minimum standards, there was also a significant improvement in housing conditions (Lowry, 1982; Bradbury and Downs, 1981). Yet this experiment produced take-up rates of well below 50 per cent of those eligible and required households to pay at least 30 per cent of their income for housing. In order to make a national scheme financially viable, it has been argued that households would have to pay 35 or even 40 per cent of their income for housing services even with this low level of take-up (Struyk and Bendick, 1981). Such levels of household expenditure and take-up are, one hopes, unacceptable in a UK context, where average expenditure on housing remains about 10 per cent of household income (as measured by the 1981 Family Expenditure Survey and 1979 General Household Survey; House of Commons Environment Committee, 1982a).

Although low-cost home-ownership schemes solve the problem of subsidy take-up and give the household freedom over its own accommodation and from the landlord–tenant contract, they are not a viable solution to the problem. The ownership of an asset is probably not the best use of resources for lower-income households that have many more immediate uses for their limited funds, especially as many of the benefits of owner-occupation appear to be heavily correlated with income and lower-income households therefore obtain lower value for money (Whitehead, 1979). Of more practical importance is that owner-occupation is unlikely to extend much above 60 per cent in the next few years, even with the current government's emphasis on home-ownership. Those who need assistance to meet minimum housing standards are generally among the other 40 per cent and are therefore unaffected by such policies. Public provision together with a rental subsidy would therefore appear to remain the most effective way of providing reasonable accommodation for lower-income households.

Allocation of the available stock

Another relevant question relates to the allocation of the available stock. Evidence on comparative vacancy rates suggests that the administrative sector is able to operate with lower wastage than the private market, given current conditions. A survey carried out in 1977 showed 40 per cent of unoccupied dwellings to have been in the private rented sector (as opposed to 13 per cent of occupied dwellings). Further, over 70 per cent of units vacant in the public sector were being demolished or rehabilitated as against less than half in the private sector. Additional vacancies in the private sector arose from speculative motives, from the effect of rent controls and security legislation and from the problems of financing chains of purchases (Bone and Mason, 1980).

The public sector also distributes the space available more evenly: 80 per cent of all households in the local authority sector have accommodation equal to or one above the bedroom standard, as against 54 per cent among owner-occupiers (General Household Survey, 1981). Overcrowding, measured at more than one person per room, is concentrated in the private rented furnished sector. These differences mainly reflect differences in private preferences and preparedness to pay. However, they also indicate the capacity of the public sector to meet minimum standards and the problems that arise in the private rented sector as a result of rent and security controls and the difficulties of access to the two main tenures. Removing controls and market imperfections would help some groups but would leave those with little market power inadequately housed in terms of socially accepted minimum standards. The difficulties of their position would be exacerbated whenever demand increased relative to existing supply.

Adjustment to change

A final question with respect to relative efficiency therefore relates to the capacity of each sector to adjust supply to changes in demand and need. It is usually argued that the private sector is almost certain to have the advantage because, where profits can be predicted, resources will be made available. The public sector, by contrast, is often constrained by macroeconomic factors, bureaucratic fund allocation is inflexible and cutbacks normally bear heavily on investment programmes (House of Commons Environment Committee, 1980). This is one of the strongest general arguments put by the present government for its emphasis on privatisation – that it gives freedom from its own controls. Yet the private sector in the housing market is not that good at responding to opportunities. In the owner-occupied sector, builders appear to be extremely risk averse and are often heavily constrained by lack of finance. These problems are exacerbated by the cyclical nature of demand (Awan and Whitehead, 1980). Further, as we have already seen, the past history of controls makes it difficult to provide suitable incentives to landlords to adjust supply (House of Commons Environment Committee, 1982a).

Conclusion on comparative efficiency

Evidence on the comparative efficiency of production and allocation achieved by the two sectors is thus not straightforward. To some extent, observed differences reflect the different objectives of those organising the two sectors and so must be assessed in relation to the general acceptability of such objectives. Other differences relate to the comparative strengths and weaknesses of market and administrative allocation when applied to a good with the attributes of housing. On this basis, the evidence would suggest that private production is usually more efficient than public production, but also that public organisation of that production is likely to be better where there are problems of risk and of locational externality. Private allocation works well to meet individual demands where there is capacity to pay, but such allocation, together with income-related subsidies, has proved inadequate as a means of helping lower-income households to obtain reasonable accommodation. Further, additional private provision of adequate accommodation for such households appears impossible given current attitudes to the private rented sector. On the other hand, public sector use and allocation of existing stock appear to be reasonably efficient in meeting socially determined minimum standards. Again, therefore, the analysis would seem to point to private sector provision and allocation at the upper end of the market and direct public sector involvement where there are significant externality and contractual difficulties and to meet reasonable social standards.

THE GOVERNMENT'S HOUSING POLICIES

Such arguments leave open the question of what proportion of households would be better off in the private and what proportion in the public sector. They also imply no positive statement about whether renting or owner-occupation is to be preferred for those with adequate bargaining power. Further, they do not help to define what is to be understood by 'reasonable social standards', for this is mainly a matter of political choice. The present government has taken the position that the proportion of households in the private sector is too small, that policies should concentrate on increasing the extent of privatisation in housing and particularly on increasing the level of owner-occupation, and that additional subsidies should be made available to this end.

Certain of the policies introduced to assist owner-occupation are aimed at overcoming inefficiencies and constraints in the operation of the housing market. Some of the measures taken to increase competition in the mortgage and savings markets can be viewed in this light, as can mortgage guarantee schemes that help overcome the risk-averse attitudes of mortgagees. The momentum behind such schemes as shared ownership, equity mortgages and assistance to elderly owner-occupiers to realise their housing asset while remaining in occupation can also be regarded as an element in developing the market effectively. In the past, a very narrow range of tenures has been available and government policies of this sort could in principle be seen as demonstration projects to show the full spectrum of possibilities and so widen available choice. Such policies do not inherently involve subsidy and should be welcomed on efficiency grounds.

It is not so easy to rationalise the government's emphasis on increasing subsidies for access to owner-occupation via the Right to Buy and other low-cost home-ownership initiatives, particularly as there is little empirical evidence that such privatisation will utilise resources more efficiently. One possible reason for stressing owner-occupation in this way is an extension of the merit good argument. Just as society has accepted that all households should have the right to decent housing at a price they can afford, it could also conclude that the ownership of assets is a similar right. Because housing is particularly important to individual welfare, ownership of that housing should be specifically guaranteed. In this case, society should be prepared to pay for everyone to be provided with owner-occupation. Such a view is in sharp contrast to the traditional socialist view that all assets should be held in common, but it is consistent with the emphasis now placed on owner-occupation by all major political parties. If fully implemented it would suggest a massive commitment to the redistribution of wealth, reaching right down the social scale. Such a commitment is clearly not envisaged by the current government, at least not for the foreseeable future.

Another possible argument for such a policy is that there are social benefits to owner-occupation arising from the different attitudes and commitments of owner-occupiers and therefore that increasing the proportion of owner-occupiers is socially desirable. It is suggested, for instance, that people with a mortgage are less likely to go on strike, feel more committed to the stability of society and are more prepared to work to improve their housing conditions (Kemeny, 1981). This is the obverse of the Marxist view that owner-occupation is an important element in capitalistic control of the economy and its workers (Bassett and Short, 1980). In this context, although there is some evidence that, for instance, owner-occupiers are less likely to be unemployed than council tenants of equivalent socioeconomic groups (Nickell, 1980), there is no evidence on the direction of causality and there has been little detailed study attempted of this type of hypothesis.

The reasons discussed above are not, however, the usual ones given by the present government for its policies to assist owner-occupation. In fact, the main reason given is that 'it is what people want, by and large' (House of Commons Environment Committee, 1981a, q. 180). One can surely argue on the government's own terms that if it is what people want then it should be what people are prepared to pay for (Whitehead, 1983). Yet the government argues that 'as a matter of policy [they] want to encourage owner-occupation and give very substantial fiscal incentives to do that', and further that mortgage interest relief provides 'an expensive incentive at the beginning in order to jump from the rental situation to the owning situation' (House of Commons Environment Committee, 1981a, q. 180). (This begs the question of whether it is mortgage interest relief or the lack of imputed income tax and capital gains tax that is the subsidy – Grey et al., 1981; King and Atkinson, 1980; Whitehead, 1977.)

In addition to these incentives, the government provides large-scale capital subsidies in the form of discounts of up to 50 per cent of valuation when households exercise the right to buy their council houses and the provision of land at below current cost for building-for-sale and similar schemes. Given these special subsidies, it is extremely difficult to avoid the conclusion that owner-occupation is being stimulated for ideological rather than economic or financial reasons, neither of which suggest that the case for owner-occupation is overwhelming (see Chapter 9).

Clearly the government has the right to make such decisions, and indeed the sale of council houses has been one of its most popular policies, endorsed by large sections of the community that are not themselves direct beneficiaries. Yet such policies also have adverse effects, some of which go directly against many of the government's other objectives. In particular although assisting marginal owner-occupation improves the overall distribution of wealth by making a larger proportion of the population asset-holders, it mainly helps the reasonably well-off at the expense of the poor. On the whole, those able to buy as a result of these policies are either already well housed or are young people who are helped to become owner-occupiers a little earlier. The extent of the subsidy given to owner-occupiers is positively correlated with the value of their property and with household expenditure on housing, both of which are positively correlated with income (Robinson, 1981; Hughes, 1979).

The sale of council houses also reduces the range and suitability of dwellings available in the public sector and so reduces choice for existing and potential tenants. It probably increases the average costs of maintenance and administration of those units that remain, partly because sales are patchy and so economies of scale are lost, partly because it is the better-built units that are the more desirable and therefore the more likely to be sold (Malpass and Murie, 1982; House of Commons Environment Committee, 1981a). Because sales are at prices below replacement cost and only 50 per cent of the price is available for reinvestment, they reduce the capacity of local authorities to keep up their existing levels of provision. In some areas this may be unimportant, but in areas where there are continuing queues for rented accommodation potential tenants are disadvantaged. Further, especially where older dwellings are sold, the policy increases the rent burden for existing tenants necessary to achieve either break-even or the required surplus on the Housing Revenue Account. The overall result is that a relatively small number of reasonably well-off gain at the expense of the poorer, less well accommodated households (House of Commons Environment Committee, 1981a).

In this context, perhaps the most important factor is that such policies, although they involve significant additional subsidy, do almost nothing to expand the total supply of accommodation made available. Low-cost home-ownership initiatives other than the sale of council houses (which simply transfers units from one tenure to another) have added fewer than 10,000 units to the owner-occupied stock, and some of these would have been made available anyway by other means (House of Commons Environment Committee, 1983).

Because total supply remains almost unchanged, the policy does little to help those further down the housing scale who need assistance to obtain adequate housing. The sale of council houses could in the longer term free funds to expand the supply of public sector accommodation. So far, however, such increases have been insignificant in comparison with the cutbacks in main programme housing funds, and planned output levels are well below those existing before 1979. Moreover, any such expansion imposes significant costs on existing tenants because their rents will have to take account of the high cost of new housing in comparison with those sold (House of Commons Environment Committee, 1981a; Webster, 1980).

The obvious private sector response to this problem is to introduce policies that improve the workings of the private rented market and provide additional assistance to tenants in that market, who are the only group who receive no general government housing subsidy. A range of policies has been introduced for this purpose, including in particular assured tenancies, where the tenant has security of tenure but pays a market rent, and shorthold, where he need pay only a fair rent but has security on a limited contractual basis. So far, the total effect of these policies has been negligible – with about 5,000 tenancies created in the first two years, many of which were probably simply transferred from other more controlled parts of the private rented sector (House of Commons Environment Committee, 1982a). Income-related benefits have at the same time been made available to additional groups (although overall take-up has not been effectively increased) and rent determination procedures have been modified to a limited extent to help landlords cover costs and cope with general inflation more easily. The changes made to the private rented sector are, however, little more than cosmetic. All the underlying problems remain and cannot be cured without fundamental changes in the subsidy and control systems – changes that the present government is not prepared to implement (House of Commons Environment Committee, 1982a,b).

As a result of the continuing problems of the private rented sector, privatisation policies not based on owner-occupation are generally accepted to be infeasible. Privatisation policies based on owner-occupation clearly are able to transfer large numbers of households into the private sector, but apparently only with a significant additional element of subsidy, the justification for which remains unclear.

CONCLUSIONS

The benefit claimed for privatisation is that it allows individual preferences and values to speak for themselves in the market place. It is argued that there has been too much paternalism in the past and that people should instead have the right to consume what they want but should have to earn the necessary money with which to exercise that right. Housing policy has been seen as a particularly important example of government paternalism, with the state providing what it thinks is best for the individual and allocating the available stock in line with the community's rather than the individual's preference function. In this sense, it is argued the consumption of housing has been treated as a merit good that has a higher value to society than to the individual.

What the present government has done by its policies is not to remove paternalism but to change its nature. Those in the public sector (while being given some greater control over their own property once they are in occupation) have had their choice of accommodation reduced and, through increased rents, have been required to pay more for what they already have. In this way the government appears to have reduced its social valuation of the consumption of housing. One would therefore expect to find that it was prepared to reduce all housing subsidies and concentrate its efforts on improving the operation of the market – including allowing the transfer of units from one tenure to another. Instead, it has provided a substantial additional subsidy to assist individual tenants to transfer to owner-occupation. At the same time, it has left general subsidies to owner-occupation unchanged. Overall, therefore, it has significantly increased the relative subsidy given to owner-occupation as opposed to renting. Implicitly it has increased the social valuation of ownership; i.e. it has treated the attribute of ownership of housing as a merit good while reducing the subsidy to provision of reasonable minimum standards of consumption. Moreover, as currently operated, the effects of this policy are mainly to redistribute wealth by luck. Households that happen to be living in desirable public sector accommodation or are allocated such accommodation under low-cost home-ownership schemes are able to purchase their homes at a large discount. Many such households would anyway have been able to buy. Most are not better housed as a result. Those unable to take up their option to buy, who live in less suitable public sector accommodation or who have not yet gained access to that sector lose out.

A more consistent approach to housing policy would recognise that, although there are undoubted benefits to owner-occupation, these are in the main private benefits that people should be free to purchase if they value them highly enough. To this end the operation of the market should certainly be improved and supply made available – but at resource cost. There is no obvious rationale for additional subsidy. Such a policy would also recognise that public sector provision has significant benefits relative to private provision in the rented sector, particularly because of the contractual difficulties inherent in the private landlord–tenant relationship, because the past history of the private rented sector makes it a very inefficient source of supply, and because income-related rent assistance, when separated from provision, has not been effective in reaching all those in need. Finally, while accepting that housing is far more a private good for which people should be prepared to pay than has been implied by the policies of either the Conservative Party or the Labour Party in the past, such a policy would recognise that significant state assistance continues to be necessary if everyone is to be able to obtain a decent home at a price they can afford. It would then attempt to concentrate this assistance on those in real housing need in whichever tenure they were located.

9 The Demise of Public Housing?

R. M. KIRWAN

INTRODUCTION

Public housing in Britain is under attack on many fronts. Indeed, one may well ask whether the conception of a directly subsidised supply of family housing, owned and managed by local authorities, is likely to survive to the end of the century. The present Conservative government's introduction of a statutory 'right to buy' for council tenants is in fact only the latest and most head-on assault in a series of developments that have served to undermine the established post-war conception of public housing. True, the attempt by a previous Conservative administration in 1972 to prise the public housing sector free from the stranglehold of historic cost financing, by establishing an independent rent-fixing mechanism based on the established 'fair rent' principles, was unsuccessful. But the failure of the subsequent Labour governments to face up to the problem of the reform of public housing finance left the sector vulnerable to further right-wing measures. The new approach to the sale of council houses is one among a series of radical changes in traditional public housing policy that has included also the determination of national targets for rent increases and the progressive withdrawal of central government subsidy.

In the context of housing policy therefore, the transfer of publicly owned housing to private owners, which is the aspect of privatisation on which I have chosen to focus in this chapter, must be seen as only one component of a more general trend towards the reconstitution of public housing as market or economic rent housing. The transfer of ownership may in fact turn out to be the least important element in the package.

SOME ARGUMENTS FOR PRIVATISATION

The present Conservative government's concern with extending the potential for the privatisation of public housing arises from two quite different sources. One is completely general: the belief, on the one hand, that it is necessary to reduce the size of the public sector and the burden of public expenditure for the good of the economy at large, and the commitment, on the other hand, to restoring opportunities for private profit and capital accumulation. In this connection, the pursuit of privatisation is not always motivated by the direct needs of the field of activity in question. It is interesting to note, however, both that there are legitimate grounds for arguing that the constraints of public finance do create real problems for public sector investment in housing and that (apart from a small, London-based luxury sector) rental housing currently offers virtually no opportunities for profitable investment. Since privatisation in this instance is mainly focused on owner-occupation, the main change in the scope for private profit that would result from a transfer of ownership (other things being equal) must arise predominantly in the provision of finance. Whether or not the curtailment of public investment in rental housing could lead to the regeneration of a profitable rental sector in the foreseeable future must be regarded as at least dubious.

The other main justification for privatisation draws on arguments that are specific to housing. There is both an ideological strand and a pragmatic strand. The ideological arguments tend to stress the virtues of home-ownership on the one hand – the encouragement to thrift and the work ethic and the relationships between property ownership and political stability – and the virtues of the market system of provision and allocation on the other hand – the scope for choice and the expression of individual preferences, efficiency in the matching of supply and demand, and so on. The pragmatic arguments stress more immediate concerns: the barriers to mobility and migration in the public housing system; the unrealistic rents and heavy burden of subsidy that has to be met by taxpayers for public housing; and the poor quality of public sector management.

These are powerful arguments. What then are the arguments for the continuation of the traditional conception of public housing?

THE IDEOLOGICAL BASIS FOR PUBLIC HOUSING

It is arguable whether council housing was ever fully conceived as an integral part of the welfare state. At the end of World War II, the firm establishment of the twin principles of 'housing as of right' (which was embodied in the concept of the waiting list and permanent tenure irrespective of changes in household need), and of 'non-profit provision' (embodied in the historic cost financing system) was certainly an assertion of a clear break with the ideology of private landlordism. None the less, unlike the social security and national health systems, housing lacked the dimension of universality. Rent control in the private rented sector was a poor second-best. The approach to the socialisation of responsibility for basic shelter and supportive environment was essentially incremental. There was no attempt, for example, to nationalise private rental housing. This incrementalism brought with it difficult choices: about 'standards' and the allocation of resources to meeting present and future needs; about equity between those in private rental housing and those in council housing; and about criteria for the selection of tenants. As the conflicts over the establishment of explicit criteria of need in the 1960s indicated, the effective conception of the role of public housing as working-class and family housing that many local authorities adopted in practice had little in common with the universalist tenets that underlay national policy in such fields as health, education and social insurance. Just as most rural authorities saw council housing as a means of reinforcing established class relations in the countryside, so the larger Labour-controlled municipalities eagerly grasped the new opportunity to reify the privileged position of one sector of the organised working class.

The ideological commitment on the left to the responsibility of the state for basic needs is focused more these days in relation to housing onto the issue of homelessness. What has been demonstrated is that the existence of a publicly owned housing stock is neither a necessary nor a sufficient condition for a solution to this problem. (Indeed, local authority bias in favour of families has been blamed in part for the growing problem of single-person homelessness.) So the ideological presumptions of those who favour publicly owned housing at the present time tend to stress three main arguments. The first is the continuing commitment to 'non-profit'. The second is abhorrence of the class relations, and the individual relations, implied by private landlordism. And the third is the belief that renting is preferable to home-ownership and that home-ownership may indeed be a barrier to the achievement of other progressive goals. The pragmatic arguments, by contrast, tend to focus more directly on the cost and availability of housing. In inner-city areas, for example, where there is still strong competition for space between different land-users and households of different income levels, a return to private market provision for lower-income groups would be bound to entail higher rents and lower standards. The corollary, moreover, of tight housing market conditions and limited resources to meet the housing needs of these lower-income groups is the absolute necessity for social control over the allocation of available housing. In the final analysis, the essential role of the public sector in housing provision arises from the dual impossibility, on the one hand, of re-creating the conditions for private investment in rental housing and, on the other hand, of extending home-ownership further down the income scale.

The interesting thing in practice about the current views on the right and on the left is the ambivalence both sides display towards the issue. For example, while Conservative policy has made great play with its support for home-ownership through the scale of council houses, little has been said about privatising the residual rental stock. The contrast here with the government's commitment to the re-creation of opportunities for profitable asset-ownership in other fields is marked. At the same time, Labour has indicated clearly, when it was last in power and subsequently, that it recognises the strength of working-class demand for home-ownership. The perceived loss of benefit to the marginal trade unionist home-buyer from the abolition of mortgage interest tax deductability has been a far more potent influence in policy thinking than the general arguments about income redistribution. This type of thinking has extended also to the sale of council houses in areas where there is no great pressure of unsatisfied housing need.

Where left and right have increasingly come to a measure of agreement (albeit somewhat reluctantly on the left, and truculently on the right) is on the poor record of much of the existing public housing provision in the larger cities. Few can deny the low quality of a large part of the inner-city and overspill stock of public housing, especially the high-rise units constructed mainly between 1960 and 1975. A commitment to public housing cannot be a commitment to the replication of the unsuitable living environments and low design standards that were foisted onto public housing tenants by the unholy alliance of greedy builders, opinionated architects and narrow-minded housing committees. What is unfair, however, is to represent these units as characteristic of the total numbers of reasonably attractive units that have always been much sought after by council tenants. It is, of course, exactly this supply that is most vulnerable to privatisation. There is, too, some agreement over the problems of immobility and the lack of adequate choice (though housing associations have played a role in improving conditions).

THE DIVERGENCE BETWEEN THEORY AND PRACTICE

More problematical for the left has been the need to come to terms with criticisms directed at the poor quality of bureaucratic management and the alienation it has produced. (It is not accidental that the strongest movement among radical urban sociologists at the present time is a renewed interest in Weber.) The fact that some of the same management problems are now emerging also in the larger housing associations only seems to underline their general significance. A crucial issue is the allocation of housing to tenants. Much of the present-day disquiet has its roots in the experiences of the 1960s when concern was increasingly focused on the treatment of three groups: ethnic minorities; so-called difficult or disruptive tenants; and 'alternative' households. While the debate about the first two groups crystallised around the issue of 'ghettos' in the housing stock, the experience of groups of mainly young people, with a propensity to form unconventional households, many of them single yet unable to compete successfully in the increasingly tight private rental market, was probably much more critical to the reformulation of ideas about public housing on the left. The political battles between squatters and short-life tenants, on the one hand, and the representatives of established council tenants, on the other, which have on occasion continued even after members of the 'excluded' groups have made successful bids to win control of local Labour Party organisations, typified the emergence of a potentially divisive anxiety about the role of bureaucracy as a manager of scarce resources. The tentative steps towards tenant self-management and the decentralisation of responsibility for such matters as estate maintenance have provided only a partial answer. The issue of power and choice remains central to the definition of the future role of public housing; and here the prescriptions of right and left are certainly not in agreement.

The current emphasis on the transfer of council housing into owner-occupation inevitably also raises in an acute form the question of the relative merits of owning and renting. It is a question that causes great difficulty for those concerned with the formulation of an ideology for 'evolutionary socialism'. On the one hand, it seems plausible to argue that home-ownership provides labour with a means of increasing its sphere of action and its control over the conditions affecting its own reproduction (cf. Stretton, 1974). On the other hand, home-ownership is accused of fragmenting working-class solidarity, reducing militancy and shifting loyalties away from the traditional concern with the distribution of income flows to a concern with the maintenance of the value of property (cf. Kemeny, 1981; Thorns, 1981). Public housing in these terms offers the ideal solution, since it allows for political control of living conditions without redirecting labour's attention from the essential and continuing struggle over wages and working conditions.

The difficulty with these arguments is clear. On the one hand, experience has shown that neither home-ownership nor public housing permit labour such a straightforward assumption of control over the conditions of its reproduction. Home-owners are at the least still heavily dependent on sources of financial capital; while control over local public housing policy may pass out of labour's control, either through the failure to gain political control of the local authority or because local housing autonomy is severely constrained by central government. On the other hand, public housing itself has been a cause of fragmentation in the working class, as the damaging splits between council tenants and others in housing need over local housing policies have demonstrated. However, the frequent reference in the press coverage of recent industrial disputes to the influence of mortgage payments on the willingness of better-paid groups, such as the coal miners or car workers, to participate in or continue strike action suggests that there may well be substance to the argument about militancy. It is also worth noting that the contrast between the low rate of mortgage foreclosure and the high incidence of local authority rent arrears seems only in part to be explained by the social composition of the council tenantry, the poorest of whom are likely to be in receipt of housing benefit. Although in the recent past inflation has quickly reduced the burden of mortgage payments, that is much less true now. The building societies also (from purely self-interested motives) are keen to assist borrowers over financially difficult periods in order to avoid foreclosure. But the evidence supports the view that house purchase brings with it a greater exercise of financial self-discipline, if only because there is more at stake.

'Non-profit' too is a concept that turns out to be not so straightforward. The notion of eliminating private landlords' profit seems clear enough. But are we talking about short-run 'excess' profits or long-run 'normal' profit? It is an elusive concept. Profit can be shifted forwards and backwards – to financiers, to the construction industry and to landowners. In practice, public housing has been able to insulate itself from the economic logic of the market economy more by accident than as the deliberate expression of a socialist approach to value. If the price of land turned out to be favourable, this has had more to do in most cases (New Towns and similar expansions excepted) with the failure of the market to anticipate future development value and with quirks of the planning and compensation systems than with the principled rejection of the concept of opportunity cost in cases where the alternative development is seen to be 'anti-social'. Similarly, the relatively favourable terms on which local authorities have been able to raise capital for housing have been due in the main to the general failure of the capital markets to anticipate correctly the changing rate of monetary inflation.

So the ideological case for public housing has found itself weakened as a consequence of the changing political and economic realities of the world in which it must operate. Theoretical strands in the discussion turn out to have been formulated insufficiently rigorously; practical evidence does not always lend credence to the underlying assumptions. For some, of course, this is good reason for restating the case in fundamental socialist terms. Others, however, have pointed to more straightforward and practical reasons for resisting the privatisation of public housing.

THE FINANCE OF PUBLIC HOUSING

A major component of this more pragmatic debate is inevitably centred on the issues of finance and subsidy. Are public housing tenants too heavily subsidised and an unreasonable burden on taxpayers? Doesn't the system encourage inefficient use of the housing stock and lack appropriate financial discipline when it comes to new investment?

Broadly speaking, one can say that a review of these issues leads to two clear conclusions. The first is that, to the extent that some of the criticisms are justified, this is the product not of public ownership of housing *per se* but of the failure on the part of successive governments to place the system of housing finance and subsidy on a rational and defensible footing. Only if one takes a very strong view of the constraints on political action would one be justified in concluding that a public housing system must be such a messy animal in financial and economic terms. The second conclusion, of course, is that at least in relation to the volume of subsidy involved, both on average and at the margin, there is no evidence for the claim that public housing tenants are more heavily subsidised than owner-occupiers. Without entering the debate about the best method of establishing comparability between housing tenures, one may note that a succession of studies of the overall incidence of subsidy have reached broadly the same conclusion (cf. Hughes, 1980; Robinson, 1981; King and Atkinson, 1980). Marginal calculations have to depend on extremely specific assumptions, which cannot easily be related to the general experience but point generally to the same answer.

That public rents have been low – and were allowed to fall to exceptionally low levels in the period 1976–80 – and that subsidies have been an unwelcome burden on the taxpayers is undeniable. With few exceptions, however, low rents for public housing have been the product not of the policies of local housing authorities but of the 'over-generous' subsidies allocated by central government. The outstanding shortcoming of government policy during the years of high and rising inflation was in fact the failure to come up with a system of subsidy that was not either insufficiently generous to accommodate the front-loading cash flow problems of the local authorities as fixed-interest borrowers in an inflationary market, or over-generous because of its failure to recognise the built-in cost reduction brought about by the effects of inflation on historic debt. Taxpayers were the unfortunate fall-guys. In this financial climate the arguments about subsidy have been overshadowed by the issue of unanticipated capital appreciation. Here, owner-occupiers, as the majority tenure, have come to represent a bench-mark against whose advantages the lot of other groups is measured.

All this is unfortunate. It is easy to point out that, in general, the real source of the 'subsidy' enjoyed by council tenants has been the inflation that was unanticipated by the capital markets, to the disadvantage of lenders, and the real rises in value of housing over time (which itself may have incorporated an element due to the capitalisation of unexpected untaxed capital appreciation); that a system of long-run marginal cost pricing, based on the real rate of return on the current replacement cost (or market worth) of the housing stock, would remove this type of anomaly; and that in this context there might well be little justification for a general subsidy to public housing tenants, apart from those explicitly designed to overcome the income deficiencies of individual households or the unwanted spatial effects of land prices (cf. Grey *et al.*, 1981). Unfortunately, this line of argument is very unreal in a world in which owner-occupiers have also been the beneficiaries of the inefficiency of the capital market and of large-scale government tax expenditures. Ironically, the present *ad hoc* method of reducing government subsidies to public housing and increasing rents is steadily undermining the argument for privatisation based upon the burdens borne by central and local taxpayers. Indeed, we already face the prospect in some areas of local services for the more affluent residents being financed in part from the 'surplus' rents of their council tenants. There is almost certainly less interpersonal and intergenerational equity in the new situation than in the former.

I am bound to admit, however, that the anomalies of the finance and subsidy systems have led in some areas to sizeable over-investment in public housing. Individual units were unnecessarily expensive; poor-quality units were constructed that turned out not to be attractive, even at relatively low rents, to households in need. It does not follow, of course, that the privatisation of the 'surplus' stock is obviously the best course of action. Indeed, in some cases, very large additional subsidies are being made available (under the Urban Development Grant Scheme) to convert such units for sale. This involves such things as the conversion of four-storey maisonettes into two-storey town houses, the replacement of flat roofs with 'more attractive' sloping roofs, and the construction of new access so that prospective purchasers will not have to pass through an existing council estate. This last point is perhaps the most serious indictment of the destructively class-bound way in which public housing policy has developed in many areas – for which the blame would have to be distributed very widely. More subsidy may be justified to compensate for past mistakes; and this may be better than writing off the investment of resources altogether. In a growing number of areas, the least desirable public housing units are simply being demolished, after even as little as fifteen years' use. The lesson is surely that this type of limited privatisation is as likely to deepen the rifts in the housing system (as the last example illustrated) as it is to even out the great variance that has emerged in the housing conditions of moderate and lower-income groups over the last twenty-five years.

Over-investment is not of course confined to public housing. Until recently, the limited range of alternative investment opportunities and the structure of tax advantages have almost certainly encouraged over-investment in owner-occupied housing. In some parts of the country, notably the South East, the effects of planning may have converted a large part of this into a price effect; elsewhere there has probably been a real resource effect. None the less, owner-occupation does offer the real advantage of the transferability of accrued benefits. By contrast, the council tenant is locked into one form of tenure and one geographical area, although the geographical effect is probably the stronger of the two. (King, 1980, for example, estimated a lower price elasticity of demand for council tenants at the average rent than for owner-occupiers.) A 'generous' capital market might allow the tenant to make up for some of the deficiencies in this system, but, given the age and employment composition of council tenure, a generous interpretation of risk is not what one can expect of money-lenders.

THE GAINS AND LOSSES FROM COUNCIL HOUSE SALES

The scale of the transfer of ownership effected by the present Conservative government's 'right to buy' legislation – approximately half a million sales of council houses – is almost certainly less than it anticipated or would have hoped for. It is none the less large enough for one to ask who has gained or lost by the transfer (cf. Murie, 1975, 1982; Charles 1982a). Unfortunately, the answer is not straightforward. In the unpriced sectors of social consumption like education and health it is reasonable to make general assumptions about the cost or benefit and to compare these with hypothetical systems of pricing or private provision. The public housing system, by contrast, is so fraught with current and prospective financial anomalies that the general case is virtually non-existent. The problem arises mainly from the uncertainty about the future rent and tenure conditions that tenants would face if they remain, or had remained, a council tenant; the one thing one cannot assume is that these conditions will continue unchanged, since the housing finance system has an in-built dynamic. The present specification and the future incidence of these conditions depend not merely on assumptions about central government policy but on the specification of local circumstances. For example, if one uses the current replacement cost of housing as a bench-mark, it is clear both that tenants in different local authorities, in different types of housing and even in different income groups may currently be in receipt of very different levels of 'cost' reduction and that there are no grounds for expecting a consistent pattern of movement over time from one area or group to another, even if one assumes that the current government subsidy and rent regimes remain in force. (This assumption itself is problematical as more and more local authority housing accounts are expected to move into surplus.)

The important point is that the uncertainty that invalidates a simple notion of a typical case is the same uncertainty that must be faced by individual households attempting to make rational decisions about purchasing their dwelling. The substantial rebate (up to 50 per cent after five years of residence) on the official estimate of its current market value – how much uncertainty is attached to that, one may wonder – provides substantial protection for the buyer. But the complexities demonstrate clearly the impossibility of avoiding essentially politicised decisions: the surest defence against being worsted is to vote for the party that guarantees to make sure you are not the one to lose out. There has, of course, been no barrier to voluntary transfer into owner-occupation up to now, except the inability to realise any of the accumulated benefits of remaining in a council tenancy and the difficulty of qualifying for a mortgage. For those with a strong investment motive, owner-occupation would until recently certainly have offered a better option than remaining a tenant and investing elsewhere. That is probably less true now because, although council rents are rising in real terms, owner-occupation has a much higher real cost, and positive real post-tax returns can be earned quite easily by the small saver. For those who want to borrow, owner-occupation offers better security than the expectation of relatively low rents. Moreover, the combination of the rebate on market value and the potential tax benefits almost certainly represents a higher rate of subsidy than would be enjoyed by staying put. None the less, owner-occupation does carry with it the fear of less protection against changes in individual and household circumstances. With low and unstable income prospects, an aversion to risk is scarcely surprising. There is also legitimate scope for concern about the medium-term resale prospects for many former council dwellings.

Much of the debate over the sale of council housing has focused on the impact of individual local authorities' finances and hence on those who remain local authority tenants and those who might hope or expect to gain access to the sector (cf. Edwards and Posnett, 1980; Posnett and Edwards, 1982; Foreman-Peck, 1982; Charles, 1982b). Here, once again, there has been no agreement over the definition of a typical case. The elements of the relevant equation are not simply whether or not the local authority's capital receipts will generate a surplus or a deficit over the attributable historic debt – ignoring the cash flow implications of the requirement to provide a self-financing mortgage to the purchaser – but whether the effect on the prospective combination of real and inflationary rental growth and on the entitlement to subsidy will be greater than the effect on the monetary amortisation costs of the historic debt. The arithmetic is mind-boggling, since interest rates, inflation, real rental prospects and future rates of subsidy are all unknowns. The most disadvantaged of the remaining or prospective tenants should in any event be protected by the rent rebate system from substantial increases in net costs as a consequence of sales. Moreover, under the current central government subsidy system, a rise in costs per dwelling on current account, in excess of that deemed appropriate for rent increases, entitles a local authority to additional subsidy.

The immediate change in prospect is that the most attractive and sought-after dwellings are those most likely to be transferred to private ownership (together with the grant-aided 'unlettable' stock mentioned above). This will reduce the range of choice available to existing and prospective tenants – and given the anomalies of the rent-fixing system one cannot assume that they will be proportionately compensated – and reduce the rental growth potential for the local authority. The significance of this for those tenants able and willing to pay (albeit at subsidised rents) for better accommodation but not willing or able to move into owner-occupation, and for prospective tenants, will depend on the freedom local authorities have to make good the loss of dwellings by new investment or by upgrading their residual stock. This is currently outside the control of local authorities. In addition, the burden of subsidy is likely to rise in the short run (*ceteris paribus*), although the rise will be disguised as tax expenditure. And, as Sutton and Whitehead (1982) have suggested, there is some risk that the requirement for local authorities to provide mortgage finance for council house sales may increase the costs of private housing finance.

Present Conservative policy towards the privatisation of council housing has stressed the unfairness of preventing council tenants from enjoying the benefits of home-ownership. The argument is perverse. If owner-occupiers do indeed enjoy disproportionate advantages – and the evidence seems clearly to be that they enjoy no less benefits from the tax and subsidy systems than council tenants – how can it contribute to overall equity to assist a privileged minority of tenants to convert their tenancy to ownership, leaving the most disadvantaged majority trapped in the less preferred tenure? Certainly it would not be progress either to defend the *status quo*. There remains a desperate need for the establishment of a finance and subsidy system that is, on the one hand, proof against the vagaries of inflation and the capital markets, and, on the other hand, equitable in its treatment of households irrespective of their tenure. It is an old cry, and one that we seem to be no nearer satisfying.

CONCLUSION

In the unreal world of theory, many of the legitimate concerns about public housing could be set to rest by appropriate economic reforms. Unrealistic rent levels, excessive subsidisation, lack of financial discipline, unreasonable burdens on taxpayers, over-investment, geographical immobility and tenants' inability to encash the value of accrued benefits could all be solved through integrated reconstitution of the housing finance system. Public housing would none the less remain vulnerable to attack for the nature and quality of its political and bureaucratic management. Even the most committed adversaries of privatisation should admit there still remains a great need for improvement in this connection. Home-ownership may entail new responsibilities and hence new costs for prospective purchasers, but the reduction in alienation is a tangible offset. The target for public housing managers is certainly not an easy one. However, none of these arguments is central to the real case for public housing in future, which will remain the critical need for a continuing supply of reasonable-quality rental housing, given the relatively small proportion of existing council tenants, and of those who in future with the expected decline of private renting will look to the sector, who could not reasonably be expected to assume the responsibilities and risks of home-ownership. Given the impossibility and undesirability of reconstituting low-income housing as a profit-making rental sector in private ownership – which appears to be accepted even by most Conservatives – there is no alternative but for the maintenance of a sizeable rental sector under local authority and housing association control.

The privatisation of council housing may thus turn out to be a mixed blessing for its advocates. As rents are increased, more tenants will be encouraged to buy; and there is a serious likelihood that the total public expenditure cost will rise, as the main subsidy to new owners occurs in the early years of a mortgage and as more of the remaining tenants become eligible for housing benefit. Provided local authorities and housing associations are free to allocate resources to replacing their stock where there is a genuinely unsatisfied need and to improving conditions in their existing stock to bring living conditions into line with those of equivalent owner-occupiers, the direct economic impact of council house sales on local authorities may not be so severe. However, there is a real danger of creating even worse ghettos of poor-quality housing and of increasing the stigma of public sector tenancy if public housing is allowed to sink, as in the United States, to a residual welfare sector. The hope is that, with a smaller stock to manage, local authorities will be able to improve the responsiveness and efficiency of their management. The American example, though, illustrates dramatically the high long-run cost of this strategy taken to its extreme, as unit management and maintenance costs rise and eventually even more of the stock has to be written off before the end of its theoretically useful life.

The limited privatisation in prospect will with luck not create such an extreme outcome. Even if it manages to avoid greatly exacerbating the divisions that presently exist in the British housing system, however, it will certainly do nothing to increase equity. For that one must look to a long-overdue reform of housing finance and taxation that seems increasingly unlikely, the larger the proportion of the electorate who, as owner-occupiers, have a vested interest in the perpetuation of the current system. The more worrying prospect is that the conditions affecting owner-occupiers will be left untouched, while public housing finance will be steered increasingly towards market rents and minimum cash transfers. That really would be an unfair and insupportable state of affairs.

10 Privatisation of Education

MAURICE PESTON

INTRODUCTION

My main purpose in this chapter is to clarify the meaning of 'privatisation' as it relates to education, and to indicate the sort of questions that an economist would ask about a privatised system. In doing so, I would not wish to suggest that the central issues are economic, or that the chief problems are technical. Rather I see the subject as arising for ideological reasons. Most of the contributions economists are likely to make will therefore be on the periphery of the political debate. It is as well to add that, although for academic reasons I try to take an even-handed approach to the subject, I am against privatisation of education. I believe that the chief policy needs in education are the strengthening and extension of the public sector. Having said that, there are reforms of financing and the encouragement of community initiatives that are sometimes included under the heading of privatisation that I would strongly support.

For simplicity I shall concentrate on the school system. As a curiosum, the universities are treated as part of the private sector for national accounts purposes, and their finance is a transfer payment from the government. (Their capital expenditure is treated as part of 'capital grants to private expenditure'. and their current expenditure as 'current grants to personal sector'. 'The personal sector . . . includes private non-profit-making bodies serving persons, such as universities . . .' – Maurice, 1968, pp. 22 and 35.) There is thus a genuine sense (pace Buckingham) that the universities are already privatised. The lesson to be learned is that wheresoever ownership lies, if the main source of finance is the government, there will be official interference, the Comptroller and Auditor General will have a right and duty to examine the accounts, and Members of Parliament will wish to investigate and ask questions. (There is an interesting contrast to be noted here. Judging from the published statements in recent years of leading figures in universities, they regard themselves as subject to growing and excessive governmental interference. Ministers and officials, however, tend to emphasise how little they get involved, and, indeed, might well say that the universities have been, if anything, out of control. It has been hypothesised that the universities, guided by the University Grants Committee, are a form of cartel, maximising their own utility subject to minimum constraints to do with student satisfaction and vague governmental interpretations of national needs.)

A PURELY PRIVATISED SCHOOL SYSTEM

I shall return to the question of monitoring later when I ask what is the point of privatisation. For the moment let me list the obvious meanings of the word as applied to schools:

- private ownership,
- private finance,
- private control.

Moreover, these may refer to

- some or all levels of schools,
- some or all types of schooling,
- examining bodies.

Within ownership it will be relevant to distinguish profit-making from non-profit-making bodies. On finance, a relevant distinction may be made between pure private finance and various modified forms. In the former case, no government money would be involved directly in the payment of fees and meeting other costs, and there would be no subsidies, even by implication. (There would be no such thing as charitable status.) On this definition, few if any schools now are purely privately financed, although plenty of secretarial and language colleges are. Modified private finance would allow for tax concessions and, perhaps, for government loans (or guarantees of loans) to the proprietors.

Purely private control would still mean that the schools are subject to the law of the land. Company law would be relevant to them as firms and charity law as charities. The relevant distinction is between that state of affairs and additional legislation directed specifically at education. It is worth noting that much of the private sector is subject to specific legislation, examples being food manufacturing, drugs and transport. The purist may ask whether recognition of the school as achieving charitable ends and giving it corresponding tax advantages is not already to concede an externality and, therefore, to open the way for further public intervention.

I would thus define a purely privatised school system as one that was fully privately owned, privately financed and privately controlled. All examining bodies would be similarly owned, financed and controlled. As a matter of pure principle, it is difficult to see what would be the case for compulsory education within such a system. Essentially, education would be a matter of household choice, the nature and extent of what would be provided being determined by market forces.

It has been suggested to me that this pure case is too pure in that a considerable degree of compulsion is regarded as compatible with private enterprise – typical of this are traffic regulations, licensing of drivers, MOT tests and compulsory motor insurance. This, however, is to miss the point. The public interest in motoring arises from the recognition that it involves externalities. Driving on the left-hand side is desirable because everybody gains by following the same rule, which itself is enforced by a public authority, the police. Compulsory education may also be justified to some extent because an externality is involved, but it is surely much more a matter of paternalism. However, it is perhaps worth pointing out that few people have espoused this pure case. Adam Smith surely preferred private to public provision, but still allowed for the latter together with local subsidies (*Wealth of Nations* vol. v). Equally, Mill limited public intervention to the setting of a school-leaving age.

A pure private educational system would reflect the strengths and weaknesses of the market system. It would be responsive to demand, so that the dominant pressure would derive from income, and to a lesser extent from preferences. Another way of putting this is that, within any income group, those with a stronger disposition in favour of education would demand relatively more of it, and that there is a high income elasticity of demand for education. (Income here refers, of course, to the actual income of the household rather than the expected income of its children.)

It is idle to speculate on what would actually be demanded. Suffice it to say that within such a purely private system no preferences would automatically be ruled out. Schools that did not admit certain types of pupil would be permitted and would exist if demand were sufficient to cover their costs. Equally, any school unable to cover its costs would not survive. Presumably, whatever the type of education offered, there would be a great range of quality. In addition, of course, some households would not purchase any schooling at all.

On the supply side, the cost curve of a school would presumably, have the usual U shape. Given the fixed capital of the building and the site and the indivisibility of the individual teachers, it must be assumed that there will be some range of increasing returns to scale. A large enough school, however, will experience diminishing returns from organisation problems and congestion. Similarly, the scope and variety of the curriculum will increase with size. In particular, very small schools will be narrow and expensive. Thus, the costs of non-boarding education will be higher in more sparsely populated areas. On the usual assumptions, therefore, the actual demand for education in such areas will be less then elsewhere.

More generally, in terms of market theory each school will have its unique characteristics including its location. All schools, therefore, will have some monopoly potential, and a few schools may have a great deal of monopoly power. The relevant model is, therefore, monopolistic competition, or even pure monopoly.

How will schools compete? Mostly, this question is about how schools will compete with each other, but, in addition, they are competing with other demands on the household's purse. In a free choice, purely private enterprise world, there are many alternatives to education. Within education, there are also alternatives to schooling – for example, being self-taught by purchases of books, audio-video tapes, etc.

Competition among schools in the sense of new entry is by definition impossible along at least one dimension – the dimension of age and tradition. The supply of schools over a hundred years old cannot be increased, and there are obvious limits to the number of places that their owners will wish to offer. It is worth making the trivial point that privatisation does not mean that everybody can go to Eton if they can afford the fees. It does not even mean that everyone can go to the local grammar school or something similar. (The position is not symmetric. There is no limit to the number of new schools that can be opened.)

On a related theme, the schools are limited in the nature of what they offer by both their teachers and their pupils. The quality of the output is a function of the nature of certain inputs and certain demanders. (A school is, therefore, similar to a club.) It will also be a function of size, i.e. the nature of the product is a function of the supplying unit. The purchase of a motor car, by comparison, is not concerned with precisely who made it or the identity of who else has bought it. (Even here, one cannot totally rule out snob, bandwagon and Veblen effects.)

Since the nature of what is supplied is closely connected with the identity of the supplier, establishing this identity and convincing demanders of its worth will be an important part of any competitive strategy. In other words, we shall have not merely a Chamberlinian model of the market, but something much closer to Galbraith's view of oligopoly. What this means in its simplest terms is that advertising and the provision of information and misinformation will have a significant role to play. More to the point, the perfectly competitive model of price takers responding to externally given demand (itself a reflection of 'true' preferences) will be singularly inappropriate.

This is not to say that schools will or could totally ignore whatever preferences exist, or that the service they offer will be quite arbitrary. Instead, there will be an interaction between a demand that is there, in some sense, and a demand that the schools will attempt to create. It follows that whatever welfare consequences are alleged to be associated with the perfectly competitive model will not carry over *a priori* to an actual privatised system. The theoretical merits of such a system will have to be established directly, and they will then have to be proved in practice.

There are two additional points with which we must concern ourselves here. One is to note that many of the consequences of education are long term and of a qualitative kind; they are, therefore, difficult to express or test objectively. The second, which is complementary to the first, is that many other consequences are short term and easily discernible. The inculcation of skills of the 3Rs type and the obtaining of diplomas are the best examples of the latter. Personal development and an ability to cope with society are examples of the former. Most people agree that both are important, but opinion has fluctuated on the correct balance between the two. In professional circles, the first was dominant up to the beginning of the 1970s. Since then the pendulum has swung rather the other way. It is important to ask whether a fully privatised system will itself be biased in favour of the immediate and clearly discernible. Will it generate diploma factories? And will that tendency be assisted by the emergence of private testing and validating bodies. In addition, will private examining bodies themselves be susceptible of objective scrutiny? I make no attempt to answer these questions here, but it is worth noting that, although the private sector at the present time tries to produce an immediately recognisable product, it is also much concerned with so-called character building for the longer term.

In helping to discern value for money in schooling, there will be those who place their faith on 'Which?' reports. Within a privatised system in which information is so important, there will obviously be a market for independent analysis of schools and of validating and testing bodies. However, excessive optimists must bear the following points in mind. First, to offset existing consumer reports there is the massive array of producers' marketing methods, including pseudo-objective studies. Second, the main market for consumer reports is the middle class, which leaves the working class not as well protected as might be thought desirable. And third, in the case of schools, access will be much harder, than (say) for motor cars or washing machines; therefore, testing will be extremely difficult.

Now, difficulties of this kind arise with any type of economic activity. Those who favour privatisation would argue, no doubt, that to place too great an emphasis on them is unfair, for, if the same approach were adopted generally, there would be no private enterprise at all. More generally, they would say that these difficulties have always been recognised, and that virtually no one has ever advocated such a fully privatised system. I would agree that it is perhaps not unreasonable to suggest that a fully privatised system does not represent an ideal model. Nobody doubts that any scheme likely to be introduced would be modified in many ways, not merely as a matter of practical first steps but also as a long-run objective. The difficulty is that, once one moves away from the pure milk of privatisation, it is not at all easy to see where one should stop. This is especially so if education is regarded as intrinsically different from most other services.

MODIFYING THE PURELY PRIVATE SCHOOL SYSTEM

If one wants to modify the purely private system, the topics one needs to consider are:

- the role of public subsidy,
- the role of public control,
- the role of public provision.

All of these must be placed within the context of a broadly privatised school system.

Public subsidy

The case for public subsidy is partly a matter of externalities, and goes back to the earliest debates on public involvement in education. It is made up of two parts. One is that people other than the individual concerned gain from his education. (Incidentally, the gain here is usually regarded as a generalised one, and not connected with the identity of the individual.) The nature of the gain may be to do with better social behaviour, involving such things as better health, less crime, an ability to communicate and to participate in democratic processes. It may be of a more direct kind, amounting to little more than that some people feel it right that the population as a whole should be educated. Given such externalities, it may be questioned why they require public subsidy. The answer is that subsidies may be easier to organise universally rather than on a decentralised, voluntary basis. This will be essentially the case if universality itself is part of the externality. It may also happen that people's utility functions are of the sort that justifies taxation – namely, X is happy to contribute if everyone else does, but not otherwise (see Peston, 1966; Blaug, 1970).

Without doubting the existence of potential externalities, it is difficult to believe that they represent the whole case for public subsidy, or actually account for its history. Obviously, voluntary subsidy of a charitable nature existed long before state subsidy. Moreover, as a matter of record, state subsidy was at least as much connected with a paternalistic view of the problem as it was based on externalities pure and simple. Government expenditure on education has always been closely connected with a political view of the need for the populace to be educated, whether or not they wished to be. The government has also not been indifferent to the nature of that education. Of course, paternalism can always be expressed as a form of externality, but in my opinion that rather trivialises the matter (Peston, 1966). To a large degree, externality as an argument has been invented *post hoc* to justify intervention. In practice, it is rarely used to determine whether intervention should continue or its scale be varied.

The other aspect of public subsidy is to do with income distribution. Households left to themselves may choose too little education because of externalities or because their preferences are incorrect, and thus need to be overruled. (On the latter, there is the usual paradox – people would choose to be educated if only they were educated.) Demand may also be too low because households are too poor. Public subsidy, therefore, allows for redistribution without full freedom of choice.

The question that must be answered, therefore, is whether public subsidy of education, whatever the case for it used to be, continues to be justifiable today. Would households left to themselves choose correctly, whatever that may mean? If they would not choose correctly, can they simply be compelled to choose in a certain way, but also be obliged to meet the cost directly. (It may be remarked that compulsion to spend privately is hard to distinguish from taxation anyway.) On the question of choice in general, it is worth bearing in mind that we are discussing parental choice rather than pupil choice. If the interventionist argument is that some parents undervalue education for their children, it may be asked why this state of affairs persists through the generations. Why has not a century of compulsory education done away with the need for compulsion, or, at least, not made it a formality? On pupil choice, it is hard to accept that those who opt for less education are necessarily acting against their own best interests. Thus, truancy in the inner city could well be regarded as a rational response to schools that fail their pupils rather than simply as an undervaluation of education as such. E. G. West (1965, p. 100) has said

> The argument seems to assume that if the government did not spend on education but returned the money to ordinary people (e.g. through reduced taxes) they would not buy in the long run at least the same quantity of education privately. There is no evidence the author knows of that supports this assumption.

My own view is that the case based on paternalism still holds for too many households to allow compulsion to be abandoned, but I agree that this does not reflect at all well on the overall achievement of the education service.

If the case based on externality and paternalism continues to be made, and is thought to justify public subsidy, economists would still point out that matters are far from settled. The subsidy might take many forms, including tax concessions, school fees supplements and direct support for schools. Logically, it does not follow that there must be public provision. The state could rely on private enterprise to provide the schools, but could finance them directly or help households to meet their fees. (Indeed, as is well known, economists have always made heavy weather of the question of public provision of almost any service. For the most part they tend to assume that there is little or no economic case for public provision; they say it must be explained in social or political terms.)

Public control

If the state were to finance private enterprise schools, whether directly or indirectly, it is difficult to believe that ministers would be indifferent to how the money was being spent, or that Parliament would allow them to be. As was indicated at the outset, there is a public responsibility to see that public monies are not wasted and that tax concessions achieve the desired ends. This suggests that, even setting paternalism on one side, a privatised system would of necessity be subject to some measure of public scrutiny and control if it were the recipient of public money. The schools would not be left indefinitely uninspected, and the bodies awarding certificates and diplomas would not be allowed untrammelled freedom solely to meet a market test. As far as causation is concerned, a desire to intervene may precede the use of public finance in education, but the introduction of public finance will certainly act as an incentive to intervention.

In present circumstances, in which most young people attend schools in the maintained sector, the private sector is left largely to itself. The various examining boards together with the universities are thought to be sufficient to maintain academic standards, and for the most part there is no need for inspection. (I am not certain whether it is proposed to have an inspection procedure in association with the assisted places scheme.) If, however, a more fully privatised system emerged based on public money, it is likely that those schools would be rather less free of state interference. This would be especially the case if the examining boards were abolished to be replaced by pure private sector counterparts, and higher education were to be made more genuinely private. (One consequence of a loans system is that universities would, for better or worse, become more accountable to students, who might themselves insist on greater government efforts to see that their demands are met.)

A particular aspect of control concerns freedom of entry into the schooling business. Although a combination of local monopoly power, compulsory attendance up to some age and state subsidy will reduce market risks, these will still be there to some degree. (The fact that the state can spread such risk may lower the costs of maintained schools compared with privatised ones.) The problem arises, therefore, of the source of capital for investment in free enterprise schools. To the extent that there are increasing returns to scale, there will be a minimum size for new entry. In addition, schools will be the sort of business in which the most important asset is goodwill (actual or potential), which may not be sufficient collateral for the banks and other participants in the capital market. Privatisation, therefore, may also have to be based on the state as a supplier of capital. Here again the problem of control emerges. How are funds to be allocated? What are the criteria of choice between different proposed schools in the same neighbourhood? How is the capital advanced to be protected? There is no suggestion here that these problems are insuperable. The point is the much simpler one that privatisation with state finance implies a remarkably high degree of state interference.

Central to many discussions of the public–private issue in education are educational vouchers. Essentially, they consist of a direct subsidy to education that could be used in either the private or public sector. In principle, a voucher scheme could be progressive if the subsidy were varied inversely to parental income. In addition, if charitable status and other tax concessions were ended, there need be no net subsidy to those households that would anyway be sending their children to private schools. In practice, however, the advocates of vouchers have for the most part seen them as ways of encouraging the private sector, and have not been unduly worried about helping those who are already helping themselves, so to speak. In my view, a voucher scheme would lead to an expansion of the private sector, and, if that is the only objective desired it is worth considering. I am extremely doubtful whether there would be any gains in the state system. I agree with Blaug when he says 'We have too little experience with market provision of education to predict the precise effect of enhanced choice backed up by purchasing power, and to argue that competition will necessarily improve education as it has improved the quality of automobiles is mere dogma' (Blaug, 1970, p. 316; see also Blaug's discussion of vouchers in Chapter 11 of this book).

I must stress further that vouchers, together with other forms of public subsidy, leave open the question of what is education and what is a school. Do the proponents intend to allow literally anybody to set up something called a school and to allow vouchers to be valid for it? What about political and religious extremists and the various cults of the present day? In terms of education narrowly defined they may set up and run perfectly admirable institutions and meet public demand. Unless they are to be rejected *ad hoc*, which goes totally against the principle of freedom of choice, it is not obvious that they are not fully as worthy as any other schools. After all, one man's extreme is another's moderation. (It is a commonplace that Tom Paine advocated vouchers in *The Rights of Man*. More recently, some of those on the American left have favoured vouchers to enhance the political power of the poor in education.)

Public provision

I have remarked already that economists have always tended to find the issue of provision rather a difficult subject, and have often argued that it has little or nothing to do with economics. Nonetheless, if we are to discuss privatisation, the dual problem, so to speak, of public provision becomes unavoidable.

The case for and against public provision revolves fairly obviously around the following issues:

• Which is the cheaper form to operate in achieving what might be called the private or individual ends of education?

- Which is the cheaper form to operate in achieving what might be called the public or community ends of education?
- Which ends does the one serve that the other cannot?

In broadest terms, one is, naturally enough, simply comparing cost and benefits. It seems useful, however, to break these down, in particular to distinguish the goals of schooling in a narrow 3Rs sense from broader educational goals, some of which are themselves by-products of academic pursuits. In other words, education is about techniques (e.g. can the pupil read?), about academic outlook and standard (e.g. what does the pupil want to read?), and about broader values (e.g. what role will the adult play in the economy and society and what will be his relationships to other people?).

The question is partly whether or not privatisation leads to this being done more cheaply, but it is at least as much about what a private school actually does as compared with a maintained school. If in some essential ways each does a different job, the cost comparison becomes irrelevant. It is simply an issue of evaluating different benefits. Moreover, these benefits may not be comparable or compatible with one another, which is a long-hand way of saying that the central question is, after all, ideological.

In suggesting that costs in this case may be irrelevant, I mean merely that to ask what it would cost for the private sector to do what the public sector does is without meaning. It cannot do the same job and, therefore, the cost is infinite. I am not suggesting that costs are unimportant. If private schools are cheaper than state schools *for what they do*, this may outweigh in the minds of some the fact that the benefits they provide are different; or, of course, the reverse may be true. We must agree, however, that costs on their own can never answer the key questions. As economists we are also aware of the pitfalls of cost–benefit studies that focus chiefly on what is measurable or most easily observable.

To digress from my main theme for a moment, I understand that Buckingham University claims to bring students to full graduate standard in two calendar years rather than three academic years. In the case of economics, I have little doubt that any department could do the same if its concern were solely with giving the students an acquaintance with the subject and appropriate drill in using it. We could get the academic material over to them in less time and, perhaps, with less effort on our part. Most of us would then go on to argue that that is too narrow a view of what we are doing, and that education implies more than academic training; it is to do with maturation and the development of values. Let me hasten to add that we may be mistaken. There is nothing sacrosanct about the three-year honours degree. Indeed, it has always been my view that we need a much wider range of undergraduate possibilities, and that the system of university financing and student support should be adapted to encourage that. But my point here is a much simpler one: productivity measured as academic performance per unit of staff time is not the only measure of university performance (if it is a relevant measure at all).

Returning to the main argument, there is one additional aspect of cost and benefit that needs to be mentioned. Assuming that we do not fall into the trap of crude cost-effectiveness comparisons, it is still necessary to compare like with like as far as possible after a move is made towards privatisation. (Obviously, we can never standardise to such a degree that we are always comparing exactly like with like. None the less, if costs are different, it is vitally important to ensure that benefit differences do not wholly account for this.) There are two points to note in this comparison. Firstly, private enterprise will wish to move initially into those areas that are likely to prove to be most profitable. Secondly, in attracting certain pupils they may raise the costs of educating the remainder. Neither of these is a necessary consequence of privatisation, in that the state may subsidise certain difficult activities to a degree that makes their provision most attractive to the private sector. It is simply a matter of bearing them in mind both in deciding what state finance is to be made available and in comparing the performance of private and maintained schools. (This consideration is also fundamental when it comes to comparing different maintained schools. The fact that the achievements of one school are superior to another tells you nothing about efficiency unless the pupils the schools have to deal with are sufficiently similar. A fortiori a high-spending, low-achieving school may be the more effective educationally if it has more difficult pupils and an adverse environment in which to operate. Education authorities may direct funds to more difficult areas, which gives a simultaneous equation bias to simple cost-effectiveness comparisons. Unhappily, existing education ministers are ignorant of this, wilfully or otherwise.)

To summarise so far, one can describe a system of pure privatisation of finance, control and provision. Doing so leads almost inevitably to arguments in favour of the need for some public finance and control. These in turn suggest that a maintained system may be cheaper to finance and easier to inspect and keep up to standard. Apart from that, there is a case for public provision in its own right that stands on all fours with the case for private provision. (It might be thought remarkable that, whereas there are people who advocate wholly state provision and finance, virtually nobody advocates wholly private provision and finance.)

Where then does that leave us? One possibility is to say it is all ideological, and that, apart from the sorts of points I have already made, there is no other contribution the economist can make. The second possibility is at the other extreme, and amounts to the view that, setting ideology on one side, each case can be judged on its merits. Between privatisation and the maintained system the optimum decision would not be a cornerpoint, but some mixture of the two. It is impossible to say *a priori* what the optimum mix would be. Some would judge that it would involve a smaller private sector than we currently have, some, including Conservative ministers, a larger one, and a third group would be less concerned with size and more concerned with the nature of provision in each sector.

This leads me to the question of the nature of non-state enterprise within education. I use 'non-state' advisedly to indicate that one needs to talk about a wider range of institutions than monopolistically competitive profit-seeking ones. Privatisation may occur by means of the encouragement of charities and voluntary groups. Beyond that a private school may be thought of as a workers' (chiefly teachers') co-operative in which the objective function to be maximised is not pecuniary revenue minus cost. Any economic analysis of such schools involves consideration of what their objectives will be, how they will set about competing and marketing their product, and what their attitude to risk taking will be. To the extent that their source of capital will, directly or indirectly, be the state, the last of these will be extremely important. In particular, it is not clear that, coupled with limited liability, funds will be used correctly, whatever that is deemed to mean. On the one hand, it is not certain that consumer demand will be satisfied; on the other, it is not obvious that it should be. But, if consumers are to be overruled, whose preferences should be given greater weight? (We may recall Tawney's 'wise parent' – Tawney 1964, p. 146 – as well as Vaizey in his left-wing phase seeing education 'as in substantial degree . . . an intervention to save the individual from the family' – Vaizey, 1962, p. 29.)

Is the objective of privatisation to give more power to teachers or to local community leaders? The economist has no difficulty constructing an appropriate taxonomy, but the resulting boxes are likely to be empty. There are, however, three negative conclusions that are worth mentioning. First, it is impossible to demonstrate that a policy of privatisation will increase consumer satisfaction. Secondly, such a policy will not necessarily be more efficient, in the sense of using fewer resources to achieve given ends. Thirdly, privatisation will not necessarily raise total educational expenditure. In other words, at the level of pure theory, about the only definite prediction that can be made is that no definite prediction can be made.

CONCLUSION

My opening remarks referred to the point of privatisation. I have commented already that the debate is largely ideological, but it is one in which economics will be used and misused. Attempts will be made to fit the subject into a perfectly competitive model in which preferences are given and utility is maximised relative to a resource constraint. The practical manifestation of that theory, in which competing firms survive and maximise profits by responding to consumer demand and keeping costs down, will be presented as relevant to the prediction of what will actually happen.

The main purpose of this chapter is to emphasise how mistaken such an analysis would be. The relevant models are monopolistic competition and oligopoly, and the relevant marketing strategy is not limited to price and the provision of information. Moreover, those who see the great merit of privatisation as one of little or no state intervention either have to postulate an extreme degree of free enterprise or may be disappointed to discover little or no diminution of government involvement. (Its form may change, but not necessarily for the better.)

None of this is to say that experiments are not worth encouraging. There is no reason to believe that the existing structure of education in the UK is the only one possible. In particular, attention might be paid to three areas:

- the consequence of greater parental control of maintained schools,
- the encouragement of state-financed schools organised by the local community,
- policies to reduce the monopoly power of existing institutions and taxing away their rents.

11 Education Vouchers – It All Depends on What You Mean

MARK BLAUG

INTRODUCTION

Despite considerable international differences in the pattern of educational finance, it is true to say that the bulk of educational expenditure the world over is financed out of general tax receipts, so that there is little if any connection for most families between the taxes they pay and the education their children receive. The idea of establishing a direct link between taxation and educational choice by giving all parents an education voucher – a coupon of prescribed purchasing power that can be 'cashed' at any school whatever and that can be topped up like a book token or a luncheon voucher – was put forward by a number of British and American economists in the 1960s. It was thought to have been invented by Milton Friedman (1962), but an earlier version is found in Wiseman (1959; Horobin and Smyth, 1960). Actually, the concept of education vouchers is a much older idea that goes back to Thomas Paine in the eighteenth century (West, 1967). Moreover, it was debated as a serious proposal in the French parliament in the 1870s (Van Fliet and Smyth, 1982). The Institute of Economic Affairs in Britain published a number of books and pamphlets in the 1960s and 1970s advocating education vouchers in both compulsory and post-compulsory schooling (Peacock and Wiseman, 1964; West, 1967, 1968; Beales et al., 1970; Maynard, 1975; Crew and Young, 1977); the notion nevertheless remained a taboo subject in Britain among both politicians and educators. Since the election of 1979, however, the question has been repeatedly mooted by Tory ministers, encouraged in part by the publication of a voucher feasibility study for the Ashford area of Kent by the Kent County Council (1978). The concept of education vouchers fits remarkably well into the Tory programme of 'privatisation' of the social services and one might have expected the Conservative Party to move quickly towards a practical scheme of education vouchers. It is not even clear that a voucher system would require a new act of Parliament since the 1980 Education Bill appears to give Local Education Authorities (LEAs) the necessary legal powers to implement such a scheme. Nevertheless, the idea of education vouchers is, rightly or wrongly, regarded as so politically explosive that even the Tory government has moved very cautiously on the voucher front, constantly taking away with one hand what it has just promised to deliver with the other. Thus, nothing is said about education vouchers in the Tory manifesto of 1983 and Sir Keith Joseph, the Secretary of State for Education, claims that open enrolments, under which LEAs would be encouraged to expand and contract schools in response to parental demand, would raise fewer difficulties than a voucher scheme while reaping many of its advantages.

In point of fact, an open enrolment policy would fall far short of the objectives of a voucher scheme. But, of course, everything depends on what is meant by a voucher scheme. Although the possible advantages and disadvantages of vouchers have been thoroughly aired by both advocates and critics, the debate has been confused by a bewildering variety of interpretations of the concept of education vouchers. It is difficult enough to assess the possible effects of a new, untried method of financing education, but when its proponents differ among themselves about the precise details of the scheme, the task of evaluation becomes virtually impossible. I shall begin, therefore, by sorting out the types of voucher schemes that are possible, at least in principle, after which I shall return to the kind of education voucher that has been recently proposed for Britain.

A GLOSSARY OF VOUCHER TERMINOLOGY

Imagine a typical country with, say, ten years of compulsory education and a mixed system of public and private schools; state education is financed out of general taxes but parents may opt out of the state system by sending their children to private schools, thus paying 'twice', so to speak, for education. We now introduce a system of education vouchers, that is, we issue every parent with children of school-going ages with a 'coupon' whose value is just sufficient on average to 'buy' a place in a state primary or secondary school. If we have done our sums correctly, and if parents do not switch between public and private schools as a result of the issue of education vouchers, the tax bill for education will be exactly the same as before.

We can guarantee that parents will not switch between the public and private sector of education by confining our vouchers to state schools. I shall call such vouchers 'limited vouchers'. In that case, however, education vouchers have only a modest effect because they amount simply to the 'de-zoning' of schools, that is, the elimination of the legal provision that gives parents a right to send their children to state schools but only in the catchment area in which they reside. The 'zoning' of schools has been an emotive issue in the educational history of the United States. It has been considerably undermined in recent years by a series of Supreme Court decisions that have forced American schools to draw their pupils from distant neighbourhoods even if this entails 'bussing' children from home to school at public expense. Similarly, secondary schools have been effectively 'de-zoned' in Britain by the Education Act of 1981. Thus, if 'limited vouchers' are all we mean by education vouchers, they are virtually in operation under another name in both the United States and the United Kingdom.

Suppose, however, that such vouchers were made 'unlimited' by permitting parents to cash them at any school whatever, public or private. Most private schools, however, charge fees that exceed the current-plus-capital costs per place in a state school. It would be necessary, therefore, to allow parents who opt for private education to supplement the value of a voucher out of their own pocket. I shall call such vouchers 'supplementable vouchers' in contrast to 'fixed-value vouchers'. Thus, a system of 'unlimited vouchers' would have to include the notion of 'supplementable vouchers'.

So far, I have gone along with the cosy belief that all state schools at a given level of education have equal costs, being the simple quotient of total public education expenditure on a given level of education and the number of children enrolled at that level. This is clearly not the case. State schools differ in the age of their buildings, in the size of their plant, in the mix of their teachers in terms of sex, age and qualifications, and sometimes even in their course offerings. In short, there are cheap and expensive state primary and state secondary schools. Suppose we now allow state schools to charge cost-covering rather than uniform fees in a world of unlimited, supplementable vouchers. The value of the voucher is sufficient, or more than sufficient, to buy a place in a cheap state school, but parents can top up the voucher and thus choose expensive state schools as well as private schools. I label such a system one of 'cost-fees vouchers', taking it for granted that such vouchers are also unlimited and supplementable.

It is tempting to think that such an arrangement would maximise parental choice, but we have forgotten the major constraint on parental choice of schools, which is distance and the implied cost of transportation. To underwrite a system of cost-fees, unlimited and supplementable vouchers, we need to include transport costs (up to some limit) in the value of the vouchers. I label such vouchers 'transport-included vouchers'.

Nothing I have said so far has addressed itself to the issue of equity:

rich parents can normally afford to buy more expensive education for their children than poor parents and a system of cost-fees, unlimited, supplementable and transport-included vouchers merely increases the scope of their superior position in the education market. It is easy to deal with this problem, however, under a voucher scheme: we simply make the value of the voucher a declining function of parental income. The obvious way to do this is to make the voucher part of taxable income to the full extent of its value; the existence of the progressive income tax will then guarantee that the voucher will be worth less to rich than to poor parents. If this fails to reduce its nominal value sufficiently to the well-to-do, we can stipulate that it be taxed at twice or three times its value. In other words, we can scale down the value of a voucher in relation to income to any extent we like. If, on the other hand, the income tax base in a given country fails to reach down to all parents with children of school-going ages, we can reduce the value of the education voucher in direct proportion to declared income. Whichever of these two variants is adopted, I shall call any such voucher an 'income-related voucher'.

I have assumed that the government sets minimum educational standards that must be observed by all private and public schools. Some advocates of vouchers have gone further and argued that no school in receipt of vouchers ought to be permitted to deny access to pupils on racial or ethnic grounds. However, what is true of the racial or ethnic characteristics of students might also be held to be true of their religious characteristics. In other words, education vouchers could be used to break down the entry barriers of parochial schools. And to go still further, schools in receipt of vouchers might be required to practise an open door policy by having to admit all students who apply, regardless of their educational qualifications. Be that as it may, I shall label vouchers that deny schools the right to bar admission on grounds other than strictly educational ones as 'restricted vouchers' and vouchers that leave schools free to exclude potential students on any grounds whatsoever as 'unrestricted vouchers'.

To sum up, I have constructed a tree of possible vouchers, running from the most modest to the most ambitious versions of the concept (see Figure 11.1).

The reader is warned that the particular labels I have adopted have no general currency. The first practical scheme for vouchers was devised in America by Christopher Jencks and his associates (1970) and implemented in a pilot project in Northern California, the so-called Alum Rock experiment. Jencks called his vouchers 'regulated compensatory vouchers'. Other authors (for example, Maynard, 1975) proliferate yet another set of labels.

```
┌─────────────────┐
│    Limited –    │
│  fixed-value –  │
│   uniform fees  │
└─────────────────┘
         │
┌──────────────────────────────┐
│ Unlimited – supplementable –  │
│         uniform fees          │
└──────────────────────────────┘
         │
┌──────────────────────────────────────┐
│ Unlimited – supplementable – cost-fees – │
│           transport-included           │
└──────────────────────────────────────┘
         │
┌────────────────────────────────────────────────┐
│ Unlimited – supplementable – cost-fees – transport- │
│     included – income-related – restricted      │
└────────────────────────────────────────────────┘
         │
┌──────────────────────────────────────────────────────┐
│ Unlimited – supplementable – cost-fees – transport-included – │
│         income-related – unrestricted          │
└──────────────────────────────────────────────────────┘
```

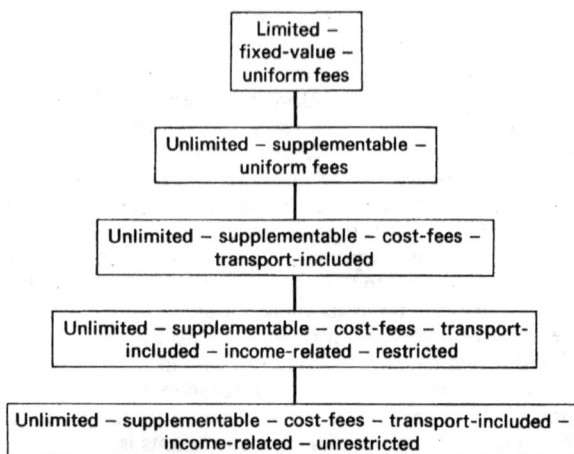

Figure 11.1   *The voucher tree*

Even my extensive glossary does not capture all the nuances that may be conveyed by a particular interpretation of the concept of education vouchers. A much-discussed question is what to do about popular, over-subscribed and unpopular, under-subscribed schools. In the case of over-subscribed schools, the usual notion is that parents should be given choice of second-preference schools, third-preference schools, etc. Should educational authorities, however, be required to provide mobile classrooms to supplement the places of an over-subscribed school? Similarly, should an under-subscribed school be given a period of grace before it is closed down, and how long should this period of grace last? These remain open questions to which various advocates of vouchers have, as we shall see, their own particular answers.

The voucher model that Friedman originally proposed was in my language an unlimited, supplementable, cost-fees, unrestricted voucher whose value did not vary with income. On the other hand, the Jencks voucher that was used in the Alum Rock experiment was a limited, fixed-value, uniform fees, transport-included, restricted voucher with an income-related feature in the form of a 'compensatory' voucher issued to low-income families. Income-related features are also built into the so-called 'effort voucher' of the influential American team of Clune, Coons and Sugarman (1971), in which the fees charged by schools, rather than the value of the voucher, are scaled inversely to income. Finally, Peacock and Wiseman (1964) and West

(1967, 1968) propose the exact equivalent for the United Kingdom of my most ambitious voucher model, the unlimited, supplementable, cost-fees, transport-included, income-related, unrestricted voucher.

The voucher scheme that the Department of Education and Science was said to be considering in 1982 for primary and lower secondary schools falls roughly halfway between the most modest and the most ambitious voucher model. Parents were to be given means-tested vouchers worth the annual cost of an average place in a maintained school (£800 for primary schools, £1,100 for secondary schools, and £1,600 for a sixth form college), which would then be cashable at any school, maintained or independent, provided they were used only to buy day places. Maintained schools would continue to charge uniform fees but would adopt an open enrolment policy: popular schools would be assisted with loans to expand and unpopular schools would be encouraged to contract and eventually to close. Maintained schools would have to admit all students applying to them, exactly as under the present system, and independent schools would presumably be allowed to refuse students as they do now. It is not clear whether transport costs to distant maintained schools would be paid for under public funds, as is now the case, but at any rate nothing was said about financing transport to private day schools. So, in my terminology, the DES scheme was one of unlimited, supplementable, uniform fees, partly transport-included, income-related, partly unrestricted vouchers.

THE EFFECTS OF VOUCHERS

I have already dismissed the limited, fixed-value voucher as being of little interest, since it amounts in effect to the de-zoning of schools, which is perfectly feasible without the introduction of voucher schemes. The moment a voucher is made unlimited, however, the total fiscal cost of the scheme must exceed the public costs of the present educational system by virtue of the vouchers issued to families with children in private schools. Such families are better off under an unlimited voucher scheme than they now are, despite the fact that they will have to share the higher tax burdens of the voucher scheme with all other families. The long-term effect of an unlimited voucher on total education expenditure is difficult to predict. A number of families might switch out of the state sector into the private sector, thus increasing private expenditure on education. Since the level of taxation would vary directly with the face value of the unlimited voucher, there might well be broader electoral support for increased public expenditure on education under a voucher scheme than exists at present: parents with children in private schools have little reason under the present system to press for increased public expenditure on education because they share the burden of increased taxation but receive none of its benefits.

Once we allow state schools to charge different fees in accordance with their different cost structures – unlimited, supplementable, cost-fees vouchers – we begin to get the efficiency effects so frequently invoked by the advocates of education vouchers: vouchers would be the principal source of income for schools, which would therefore have to compete for clientele, in the course of which waste and slack would be eliminated. Moreover, competition would generate a much greater diversity of educational services because parents have radically different tastes for schooling: some schools would specialise in expensive, academic-type education; others would specialise in cheap, vocational-type education; some schools would offer a narrow, carefully chosen curriculum; others would offer a broad, comprehensive curriculum; some schools would invest heavily in facilities; others would instead devote their resources to teachers and paraprofessional assistants; but whatever the choice, each school would be forced to provide the best possible service at the lowest possible resource cost. Competition would also generate the incentive to search for, and experiment with, new teaching methods. Private schools in Britain were among the first to introduce computer-based language laboratories and do-it-yourself computer workshops, and this is only a small indication of the stimulus to educational innovations that a voucher scheme would promote. The fact that the basic technology of education has altered little over the past two or three centuries is due, not to any inherent features of the learning process, but to the existing state monopoly of education.

Such are the claims of voucher enthusiasts: vouchers would increase efficiency, promote diversity and encourage technical dynamism (Blaug, 1970; Richter, 1976; Cohen and Farrar, 1977; Greenaway, 1979; Friedman, 1980). The critics of vouchers, however, point to the danger that competition would force schools to advertise themselves (Horobin and Smyth, 1960; Woodhall, 1977). In the effort to gain a particular brand image, much of the advertising might be misleading: schools would appeal to their opulent buildings, their fancy equipment and their examination results (even if these were obtained only by an extremely selective admission policy). Education being a difficult process to evaluate, parents might be forgiven if they judged quality by price. Thus, high-fee schools would attract the wealthier parents, while the higher fees would at the same time allow such schools to hire better teachers and to purchase the most up-to-date equipment. Poorer parents would be driven to choose low-fee state schools, which would then become educational 'ghettos' for children with deprived backgrounds. The division into high-fee and low-fee schools would soon become a self-perpetuating vicious circle, thus exacerbating the segregation between public and private schools that already exists under the present system. In short, vouchers would be socially divisive.

Although such criticisms raise serious objections to a voucher scheme, they seem to be based on a number of implicit assumptions derived from the existing state monopoly of education. Even the friends of vouchers agree that the quantity and quality of information in the education market is critical to the operation of any voucher scheme. The great merit of educational vouchers is that they generate a demand for information that is irrelevant to parents under the present system of education finance. Because education vouchers will force parents to choose between schools, they will create a market for advisory services that will assist parents to interpret the information provided by schools. Moreover, the state may regulate school advertisements to, say, provide information about the activities of schools in a common format so as to facilitate comparisons between schools. The very existence of vouchers will constitute, as it were, an education in choice, and educational choices will naturally improve with practice. Finally, vouchers and the pressure to advertise will force schools to be clearer about their own objectives and more eager to determine the degree to which they succeed in achieving these objectives. In consequence, vouchers would almost certainly make schools more cost-effective and more willing to be seen to be cost-effective.

I say 'cost-effective' and not 'efficient' because the notion of efficiency makes little sense if we are talking about non-profit-maximising institutions. It is perfectly true, of course, that an ambitious voucher scheme would force all schools to operate like profit-maximising firms. Even in these circumstances, the inherited endowment income of certain private schools might allow them to escape the penalties of the market place, in effect operating schools at a loss for all sorts of paternal reasons. Furthermore, in order to capture all the classic efficiency effects of free competition by means of a voucher scheme, we would have to allow popular state schools to borrow in the private capital market to finance their expansion; this stretches the ambitious interpretation of education vouchers even further than most voucher advocates would allow. Finally, to the extent that vouchers stimulate greater diversity of educational offerings, it becomes increasingly difficult to define what is meant by more efficiency in education. Schools that pursue different objectives can be compared not in efficiency terms but only in terms of the costs that they incur to achieve identical objectives at lower or higher levels of effectiveness.

Suffice it to say that 'cost-effectiveness' is a less question-begging term than 'efficiency' in educational matters.

The notion that vouchers would create a dual system of education, condemning the children of the poor to attend slum schools, presupposes that poor parents are indifferent about education and that only well-to-do parents are willing to make financial sacrifices to send their children to better, more expensive schools. There is little reason to believe that parental attitudes to education are so tightly linked to family income even under present circumstances, and, under the greater diversification of schooling promoted by a voucher system, parental attitudes would likewise become more heterogeneous. In other words, vouchers may promote the polarisation of schools into 'good' and 'bad' schools, but there is no necessity for them to have this effect.

In any case, any such tendency towards educational 'apartheid' can be offset by making vouchers income-related. Indeed, an extreme version of the income-related voucher reduces the after-tax value of the voucher to zero at a median family income level; in that case, only 'poor' families receive effective vouchers, which is to say that they are given an advantage over 'rich' families that they totally lack under the present system of financing education. It is difficult to imagine a better demonstration of the extraordinary flexibility of the voucher mechanism than this: educational vouchers can be adjusted to achieve almost any objective that is deemed desirable. However, perhaps this apparent strength of vouchers is actually its principal weakness: any government wishing to enact a voucher scheme is faced with almost endless controversy about the specific features of the scheme. As a consequence, a voucher scheme may never get off the ground.

Of all these specific features of vouchers, the most divisive are those pertaining to the admission criteria of schools eligible for vouchers. Some British advocates of vouchers (Peacock and Wiseman, 1964, p. 55) agree that a heterogeneous society like that of the United States, with a large immigrant population and sizeable coloured minority, would be justified in preventing voucher-approved schools from barring students on racial and ethnic grounds; what they deny, however, is that such considerations are applicable to a more homogeneous society like that of Great Britain. Milton Friedman (1962, p. 8), on the other hand, is convinced that forcible desegregation of schools increases rather than decreases political tensions and he is therefore in favour of unrestricted vouchers. The American ideal of the comprehensive high school was clearly based on the notion that immigrant populations are more easily assimilated if all children are made to go to the same kinds of schools. Nevertheless,

American educators were forced to tolerate private parochial schools in which children are segregated on religious grounds. Similarly, the British movement towards the comprehensive reorganisation of secondary schools was predicated on the theory that schools mixing children of different home backgrounds would work to break down traditional class barriers in Britain. We see, therefore, that the 'melting-pot' theory of schooling has had wide support in both countries. Moreover, the concept of the melting-pot has always been extended in the state sector to admission standards based on purely educational achievements: state schools have had to accept all children, regardless of their educability. There is an argument, therefore, for extending the same restriction to private schools that enter the voucher scheme. Why should public money be used to subsidise schools that claim the right to select children on any grounds other than financial ones?

However, restricted vouchers would have very different social effects from unrestricted vouchers and, moreover, they would also have different efficiency effects. It is one thing to talk about cost-effectiveness in a high-fee school that selects its children to be of outstanding quality and quite another to talk about it in a high-fee school with children of mixed abilities. A completely unrestricted voucher takes us into hitherto untried areas without any historical precedence. No wonder then that its consequences invite almost unlimited speculation.

PRACTICAL EXPERIENCE WITH VOUCHERS

As I noted earlier, there has been one practical experiment with education vouchers in Alum Rock, California, and a number of feasibility studies have been conducted in both America and Britain. What, if anything, do these have to teach us?

The Alum Rock experiment was based on the 'regulated compensatory voucher' model of Jencks and his associates (1970). Jencks' voucher sought to give parents a greater range of choice over educational alternatives without permitting increased segregation by race, ethnic origins, social class or educational ability, while at the same time providing low-income families with additional purchasing power over education. Its main features were:

- the creation of an Education Voucher Agency, which received all government funds for education and paid them to schools in return for vouchers;

- the issue of a basic voucher to every family with a child of school-going age 6–14 equal in value to the average recurrent costs of schooling in the area; this voucher could not be supplemented, but low-income families were furnished with a second 'compensatory' voucher whose value varied inversely to their declared income;
- any school, public or private, was eligible to receive a voucher provided it charged the uniform fee equal to the face value of the voucher and accepted all students who applied to fill vacant places; if demand exceeded the supply of places, at least half of the available places had to be allocated randomly (in practice, these provisions limited the voucher scheme to state schools);
- all voucher-approved schools were required to cover their own expenses out of voucher income, to maintain an adequate accounting system, to provide standard information about themselves to parents, to conform to certain broad curricula and staffing standards, and to submit their advertising claims to the Education Voucher Agency; and
- free transport was provided for children enrolled at schools distant from their home within the entire area of jurisdiction of the local school board.

The Alum Rock School District in East San Jose, California, consists of nineteen elementary schools (age range 6–11) and six middle schools (age range 12–14), serving some 15,000 pupils. The area is relatively poor, urbanised, predominantly Mexican-American in ethnic composition (53 per cent of the population) and has a high rate of residential turnover. The voucher experiment started in September 1972 with the participation of six state schools serving 4,000 pupils; no private schools joined the experiment. The school district provided the basic voucher but the federal government provided the funds for transport and administration as well as all the finance for compensatory vouchers. During the five-year period of the experiment, the number of voluntarily participating schools rose from six to fourteen state schools and from 4,000 to 9,000 pupils.

The degree of parental choice that the Alum Rock experiment provided was, however, greater than these figures imply. In order to offer parents a wider range of educational alternatives, each voucher school had to provide two or more educational programmes within the same building. These 'mini-schools' were given autonomy over budgets, curricula and staff appointments under the overall authority of the school's principal. By the end of the experiment in 1977, there were fifty-one mini-schools in operation within the fourteen voucher-approved institutions, ranging from the traditional, academic curriculum through various versions of informal, individual-ised learning programmes. At first, every effort was made to expand popular schools and mini-schools by means of mobile classrooms and the use of satellite space in less popular schools with empty places. However, teachers in voucher schools had been promised security of tenure and seniority rights at the outset of the experiment and this made it impossible effectively to contract unpopular schools. In time, mobile classrooms and satellite schools were abandoned as being unmanageable, maximum school and class sizes were reimposed, and thus mini-school programmes came to be fitted into the previous structure of local schools, including the previous distribution of teachers among schools.

The voucher experiment at Alum Rock came to an end in Sep-tember 1977. What survived the experiment were not vouchers but a limited range of mini-school programmes in six schools, an increased volume of school information to parents, a network of parent advis-ory committees, and a system of open enrolment by parental choice backed up by the provision of free transport within the school district. The experiment proved that state schools can provide a greater range of alternative educational options than was thought practical hitherto. Apart from this result, however, the experiment demon-strated once again how difficult it is to take power away from teachers and administrators and to give it to parents. Counselling and informa-tion programmes for parents were slow to take effect and parents continued to think of the neighbourhood school as a unit rather than a bundle of mini-schools. Even if a particular set of mini-school pro-grammes proved popular, they were only allowed to expand within definite limits. Contrariwise, if they were unpopular, they were only allowed to contract if this did not endanger the employment of teachers. In these circumstances, it is hardly surprising that vouchers at Alum Rock failed to produce the dramatic effects hailed by advo-cates of vouchers (Mecklenburger and Hostrop, 1972; Weiler et al., 1974; Levinson, 1976; Cohen and Farrar, 1977).

One needs to keep in mind, however, the severely limited nature of the Alum Rock experiment, which involved what was in effect a limited, fixed-value, uniform fees, transport-included, partly income-related and restricted voucher. Even if it had proved success-ful, it would have told us nothing about the effects of a really ambiti-ous unlimited, supplementable, cost-fees, transport-included, fully income-related, unrestricted voucher.

Six voucher feasibility studies have been conducted in various American cities, none of which however reached the stage of being implemented. In Seattle, the experiment was defeated by the attempt to include the participation of private schools (US Office of

Economic Opportunity, 1971). In Gary, Indiana, teachers threatened to take strike action over the voucher issue, which killed off the proposal. In San Francisco, the community at large showed little interest in vouchers, their attention being taken up instead with the issue of bussing consequent on a court-ordered desegregation plan. In Rochester, New York, teacher opposition once again proved decisive (US Office of Economic Opportunity, 1973). In New Hampshire and in East Hartford, Connecticut, frequent changes in the proposed voucher model and the vexed issue of parochial schools proved to be the principal stumbling block (Milne, 1975; Esposito and Thomson, 1976). Although the education voucher as an instrument of parent power is no longer a vital political issue in the United States, some school districts have used the experience to develop systems of open enrolment, greater scope for parent–teacher associations, and methods of presenting comparable information about local schools to parents.

Britain has witnessed only one feasibility study, in the Ashford educational division of Kent County. The Kent study, carried out in 1977, surveyed parents, pupils, teachers and headmasters in an effort to discover their reactions to a hypothetical unlimited, supplementable, uniform fees, transport-included voucher with income-related features on Alum Rock lines, the value of the voucher being set equal to the average recurrent costs of state primary and state secondary education in the county (supplements only being required for private schools). Surprisingly enough, most parents, while dissatisfied with the amount of information about local schools they were currently receiving, asserted that they already obtained a place in their first-preference school. Thus a voucher scheme would cause only 10 per cent of Ashford parents with children in a maintained school to transfer their child to another maintained school and only 9 per cent to transfer their child from a maintained school to an independent school; needless to say, a large proportion of that 9 per cent turned out to be parents from social class I. Not so surprisingly, three-quarters of the surveyed teachers opposed the idea of vouchers and half went as far as to say that they would refuse to teach in a voucher-eligible school. Even headmasters of private schools were not particularly keen on vouchers, doubting apparently that the voucher subsidy (about one-quarter to one-third of private school fees) would greatly increase the demand for private schooling (Kent County Council, 1978, pp. 30–9).

There is some excess capacity in maintained schools in Kent, which meant that the costs of mobile classrooms to facilitate school transfer would have been small. If one adds transport and administration costs, however, and if furthermore one adds the costs of supplementary vouchers for disadvantaged children, sums of £0.9–1.3m. a year are reached in Ashford alone, one of fourteen divisions in a county whose total education budget is £172m. (in 1977). In other words, a voucher scheme such as the one contemplated by the Kent authorities might increase public expenditure on education in the county by 10 per cent, suggesting that it is a perfectly practical but by no means insignificant proposal.

After the submission of the report, the Kent authorities announced the introduction of a pilot voucher scheme in the county to be financed from funds outside the normal county budget. However, little more has been heard of this pilot scheme since then. More recently, they have been experimenting with a system of open enrolments in Tonbridge and Tunbridge Wells secondary schools.

The evidence from Alum Rock and the American and British feasibility studies cannot support or refute the extensive claims made for education vouchers. There has never been a full practical trial of unlimited, cost-fees, income-related, unrestricted vouchers and yet many of the arguments in the voucher debate are precisely about their effects on the size of the private sector, the fate of different state schools with different cost structures, the demand for schooling when poor parents are given an inherent advantage in the education market, and the proliferation of schools segregated by race, religion and ethnic origins. On all these controversial questions, one gains little insight from Alum Rock and the feasibility studies to date.

CONCLUSIONS

Let us recapitulate. Education vouchers have been assessed in terms of six criteria: parental freedom of choice, cost-effectiveness, diversity, innovation-mindedness, the level of total educational expenditure, and equality of educational opportunities. On all these criteria, the debate has failed to come down decisively on one side or the other. But that is the nature of the case. For one thing, the participants in the debate cannot even agree on what is meant by freedom of choice, efficiency, diversity, equity, etc. The criterion of parental freedom to choose, for example, is frequently trivialised to mean being able to choose any school within hailing distance. It is obvious, however, that one does not need education vouchers to secure wider access to schools. Provided there is surplus capacity in schools and provided the community is willing to be taxed to finance bussing across school boundaries, freedom to choose among available schools can be achieved by the simple expedient of abolishing 'zoning'. The de-zoning of schools and the provision of free transportation, however, will not secure parental sovereignty in educational matters, which depends critically on a direct rather than an indirect connection between choosing a school and paying for education in that school. Similarly, there is much loose talk about vouchers promoting efficiency, diversity and educational innovation in schools, as if these were achievable at zero cost. Obviously, however, the disappearance of inefficient schools imposes definite resource costs on the educational system. Finally, equity questions have been similarly vulgarised to imply equality of access to a uniform pattern of educational provision, as if greater income were the only advantage that rich parents have over poor parents. The present state monopoly of education – subordinating parents to educational professionals, disguising the true cost of education, repressing the diversity of tastes for educational services – has had such a powerful hold on our minds that even the friends of vouchers, and certainly its critics, have been unable to think through the radical implications of an unlimited, supplementable, cost-fees, income-related, and possibly unrestricted voucher.

The educational system is a formalised, bureaucratic organisational structure and, like any bureaucratic organisational structure, it strives for maximum autonomy from external pressures as its cardinal principle of survival. While ostensibly devoted to the education of children, teachers, school administrators and local education officers must nevertheless regard parents acting on behalf of children as a force to be kept at bay because parental pressures in effect threaten the autonomy of the educational system. Education vouchers are therefore to be resisted, not because they might increase parental choice, promote efficiency, stimulate innovations, etc. but because they tend to undermine the locus of power in the educational system.

It is sometimes argued (Woodhall, 1977) that all the so-called advantages of vouchers could be achieved more effectively and cheaply by a piecemeal approach: if the chief aim is to encourage cost-effectiveness in schools, this might be accomplished under the present system by greater accountability and superior auditing; likewise, if the aim is to encourage diversity and innovation in schools, this might be achieved by the creation of mini-schools on the lines of Alum Rock; similarly, if equity is the ruling objective, schools in poor neighbourhoods might be provided with additional finance; and so on. In short, there is no need for a radical change of the financing mechanism for education because all our educational objectives can be achieved by a one-at-a-time approach. But this is, surely, an illusion of the first order. The present educational system is firmly in the hands of educational administrators, headmasters, principals and teachers and, if the Alum Rock experiment has anything to tell us, it is that no half-way measures have the least chance of giving real power to parents. Of course, something could be done under the present system to reduce waste, to increase diversity, to promote innovation and to widen the range of choice of parents. In my view, however, this remains icing on a largely inedible cake. I would hold that the stupefying conservatism of the educational system and its utter disdain of non-professional opinion is such that nothing less than a radical shake-up of the financing mechanism will do much to promote parent power. And, in the final analysis, parent power is what the entire debate is all about.

However, the sort of voucher plan that has been under discussion in Britain – unlimited, supplementable, uniform fees, partly transport-included, income-related, partly unrestricted vouchers – is a far cry from the ambitious cost-fees vouchers that Friedman, Peacock and Wiseman, and West originally had in mind. It would do nothing as such to spur competition between maintained schools, and it amounts quite simply to an additional subsidy for independent schools. Independent schools already enjoy a subsidy of about £200m. per annum as a result of various tax exemptions, as well as school places purchased out of public funds (Blaug, 1981). These subsidies are usually regarded as a *quid pro quo* for the 'double' taxation imposed on parents who opt out of the state system. But most of the 40,000 teachers in private schools have been trained for a year at taxpayers' expense, which dilutes, at least to some extent, the force of the argument of 'double taxation'. At any rate, even if one defended more competition between maintained and independent schools on grounds of 'efficiency', one might have doubts about increased subsidies to independent schools on grounds of 'equity'. Besides, it is a little perverse to argue for 'privatisation' in education by means of greater subsidies to private schools, while leaving maintained schools largely as they are. An open enrolment policy was said to be an integral feature of the DES voucher scheme, so that maintained schools would not be left as they are; but an open enrolment policy is to be welcomed on its own merits and is not a necessary feature of a voucher plan. The fact remains that, so long as the fiction is upheld that the costs of education are the same in all maintained schools, many if not most of the acclaimed virtues of education vouchers fall to the ground.

It is not difficult to understand why the Tory government has, at least for the present, abandoned its plans to introduce vouchers in education. The biggest cost of any unlimited voucher would be the subsidy to children already going to independent schools, not to mention the subsidy to additional children switching from maintained to independent schools. Even if the full value of the voucher were added to taxable income, as Peacock (1983) has proposed, the additional cost to the Exchequer of a national voucher scheme might be as much as half a billion pounds. To a government committed to cutting public expenditure, this is clearly what took the steam out of the voucher movement in Britain.

12 The Allocation of Urban Public Transport Subsidy

STEPHEN GLAISTER

Local public transport in England has been in decline since the mid 1950s and in the 1970s it ran into progressively serious deficit. It was a topic of dispute in Parliament with the Transport Act (1980), which abolished the severe quantity licensing restrictions on express (long-distance) coach services and made it somewhat easier for new operators to obtain licences to compete with established operators on stage carriage (local) bus services. At about that time, some of the metropolitan counties and the Greater London Council (GLC) formulated explicit policies of increasing subsidies to their services. This precipitated a bitter and continuing dispute over the powers and responsibilities of local and central government, the criteria by which subsidy should be judged and the extent and method by which services should be given financial assistance. The realities of the escalating cost of financing deficits (currently of the order of £500m. per annum on a turnover of about £1500m. per annum in the metropolitan counties), the progressive breakdown of the industry's ability to sustain the extensive system of cross subsidy that was codified in the Acts of 1930 and 1933, and the provisions of the Transport Act (1983) have created a new interest in alternative ways in which the industry might be analysed, financed, controlled and organised.

In this chapter I present a technique that estimates and compares the economic benefits, narrowly defined, of subsidy to public transport in the English metropolitan areas. The Transport Act (1983) introduced a requirement to measure benefits from subsidy as a part of the planning process. I raise for discussion the extent to which developments of the aggregate techniques presented here are useful for this purpose, as against alternatives such as analysis of specific candidate services for subsidy and the greater use of competitive forces.

THE BACKGROUND

The 1983 Transport Act (HMSO, 1983b) was a response to the confusion surrounding the legality of the payment of subsidy to public transport services in the English metropolitan authorities, which followed the House of Lords' ruling against the 'Fares Fair' scheme in London and similar cases in the provinces. The Act allows the Secretary of State to issue each year a protected expenditure level or 'guideline' for the GLC and each of the six metropolitan authorities, and 'To the extent to which the amount of the revenue grants made in each year by [a Passenger Transport] Authority . . . does not exceed the amount specified . . . the making of those grants shall . . . be regarded for all purposes as a proper exercise of that power' (clause 5(2)). The intention is that a case brought against an authority that was spending within its guideline would be unlikely to succeed.

This chapter reports on research carried out before the Bill was drafted. It investigates the extent to which it might be possible and useful to incorporate the measurement of economic benefits and costs of revenue support in the annual process of determining the guidelines. By way of illustration, results are presented that bear on (a) the balance that has been struck between fares and levels of service within each of the metropolitan authorities; (b) the balance of revenue support levels between them, assuming a fixed overall budget; and (c) the marginal rate of return to the total revenue support budget.

The work was carried out between April and June 1982 with the assistance of Peter Gist, and with guidance and practical help from the officials of the Department of Transport. We had to carry out the work entirely on the basis of information either published or immediately available within the Department. We also had to analyse the six metropolitan authorities in addition to London within a short space of time. These factors placed severe constraints on the realism and sophistication that we could achieve. We were in any case concerned that the computation should remain well within the capabilities of the microcomputers that are readily available to those who might be interested to experiment with the model for themselves. Versions of the program now exist in BASIC, PASCAL and FORTRAN, the latter having been especially developed for release to the general user in a standard form. In this way we have been able to keep computing costs very low and we have reduced the obstacles to an understanding of the economics of the problem to a minimum.

Fortunately we had the benefit of information and advice that we had received while carrying out an earlier piece of work for the London Transport Executive (Beesley, Gist and Glaister, 1983). Had it not been for the outstanding quality of London Transport's published and unpublished research, the present study would not have been possible.

It should be emphasised that, although I do quote below the first set of guidelines, published in the White Paper (HMSO, 1982), the results shown in this paper do not relate to them directly: after the initial study was completed there were significant developments in information and techniques. Circumstances and policies in some of the metropolitan authorities have also changed. I mention some of the technical developments in the final section, where I also give some details of the content of the Act that was eventually passed.

The mathematical relationships in the model and the data used are fully specified in two volumes published by the Department of Transport (1982). The intention in the following section is to give a general impression of the nature of the model. I then give some results; list the various economic phenomena that play a part in producing them, and end with a discussion.

THE RELATIONSHIPS IN THE MODEL

The model traces the effects of changes in public transport fares and service levels on the transport system in each of the major urban areas. Table 12.1 is presented by way of a general introduction to the kinds of quantities with which the model deals. The figures in the first column of the table relate to London after the March 1982 fares increase. It will be noted that there are five modes: commercial vehicles (CV), private cars (including taxis and motorcyclists) (CAR), bus (BUS), London Transport rail (in London only) (LT) and British Rail (BR). A set of changes is specified to fares and service levels, the latter being represented by vehicle miles run. In the example given in Table 12.1, bus and LT rail fares are reduced by 25 per cent and services are unchanged. In response to this, the model estimates a new set of vehicle and passenger flows. These values appear in the second column of the table. The changes as a percentage of the initial position appear in the third column.

The effects on revenues, costs and hence overall (LT) subsidy are estimated, and there is an account of the assessed gross benefits to each mode – both in financial terms excluding time savings and in terms of financial savings and valued time savings – and of the total savings net of the cost of the additional subsidy. In the example, the grand total of net benefit from the 25 per cent fares reduction is shown as £40.6m. per annum and the extra net benefit per pound of extra subsidy is shown as 40.6/98.8 or £0.41.

Table 12.1   *The effects on the transport system in London of a 25 per cent reduction in LT bus and rail fares*

	Initial position	Position after reduction in fares	Change as % of initial position
Passenger miles p.a. (million):			
CV	2,172.0	2,172.0	0
CAR	10,891.4	10,779.6	−1.03
BUS	2,131.68	2,365.32	10.96
LT(rail)	2,360.52	2,496.2	5.74
BR	2,081.82	2,013.05	−3.31
Total LT	4,492.2	4,861.52	8.22
Change in LT passenger miles		369.32	
Fare (£ per passenger mile):			
CV	0.263286	0.262764	−0.2
CAR	0.0819693	0.0817026	−0.33
BUS	0.127648	0.095736	−25.0
LT(rail)	0.141385	0.106039	−25.0
BR	0.0884	0.0884	0
Vehicle miles per annum (millions):			
CV	1,738.0	1,738.0	0
CAR	7,780.63	7,700.76	−1.03
BUS	167.0	167.0	0
LT(rail)	28.8	28.8	0
BR (index)	100.0	100.0	0
Wait time (mins per passenger mile):			
CV	0	0	0
CAR	0	0	0
BUS	3.66234	3.71864	1.53
LT(rail)	1.5246	1.63956	7.54
BR	1.008	1.008	0
Passengers per vehicle:			
CV	1.24971	1.24971	0
CAR	1.39981	1.39981	0
BUS	12.7646	14.1636	10.96
LT(rail)	81.9625	86.6736	5.74
BR (index)	100.0	96.69	−3.31
Revenues (£m. p.a.):			
CV	571.856	570.723	−0.2
CAR	892.761	880.722	−1.35
BUS	211.887	181.609	−14.29
LT(rail)	333.742	264.694	−20.69
BR	184.033	177.954	−3.31

Table 12.1—*continued*

	Initial position	*Position after reduction in fares*	*Change as % of initial position*
Costs (£m. p.a.):			
CV	571.856	570.723	−0.2
CAR	892.761	880.722	−1.35
BUS	435.666	435.151	−0.12
LT(rail)	383.647	383.647	0
BR (index)	100.0	100.0	0
Revenues minus costs (£m. p.a.):			
CV	0	0	0
CAR	0	0	0
BUS	−223.78	−253.543	13.3
LT(rail)	−49.9048	−118.953	138.36
BR (index)	100.0	96.69	−3.31
LT subsidy	−273.684	−372.496	36.1
Change in subsidy		98.8111	
Benefits (gross):	*Money*	*Money and time*	
CV	1.13317	6.32418	
CAR	2.9079	10.0577	
BUS	58.3888	55.8181	
LT(rail)	83.2506	73.2842	
BR	0	0	
Change in net social benefit (£m. p.a.):			
CV	6.32418		
CAR	10.0577		
BUS	26.0553		
LT(rail)	4.23584		
BR	−6.07918		
Total	40.5938		
Extra net social benefit/£ extra subsidy:			
		0.410822	

To give an indication of how these results were generated there follows a brief summary of the main relationships in the model.

(1) The demand for each of the modes is assumed to be dependent on the money cost of the mode (the 'fare'), on the money costs of using competing modes and on the other costs of use of all modes (the user costs). Money costs for commercial vehicle and car users are calculated from the standard Department of Transport operating cost formulae, which relate costs to road speeds.

The demand relationships used take the functional form favoured by LT in much of their research work: the demand on any one mode depends upon the generalised cost of travel on each of the other modes, generalised cost being defined as the sum of money costs and other user costs represented in monetary units. The formulation used (semi-log linear) has the property that own price elasticities of demand are directly proportional to fares levels. There is also a simple implied relationship between fares elasticities, values of time and service quality elasticities. This is convenient since the evidence on fares effects is quite good, but that on service effects is very much poorer. The exceptions to these general principles are that total commercial vehicle miles are assumed to be constant – although their occupants do, of course, benefit from any time savings due to improvements in traffic speeds; the own price and service elasticities for private car users are assumed to be zero; and those who do not pay full fares (usually the elderly benefiting from concessionary fares) only respond to, and benefit from, the part of a fares change that they actually face (if any).

(2) The user costs comprise the sum of waiting time, time spent in the vehicle whilst stationary and time spent in the vehicle whilst moving, each converted into money units through a respective value of time. The time values used are those used in other transport evaluations by the Department of Transport.

(3) Waiting times (for the public transport modes only) comprise a simple function of service level through the vehicle headways, and a factor to represent the increasing probability that users waiting at stops will encounter full vehicles as the average load factor increases: the 'load factor effect'. A further penalty for increasing levels of discomfort is also included here.

(4) Times spent in vehicles are determined by general road traffic speeds (except rail). Stopped times are determined by passenger boarding times and the number of boardings that occur, which, in turn, are related to the vehicle load.

(5) Traffic speeds are determined as a function of traffic flows through speed/flow relationships. Four road types are identified: in the case of London these are central, inner, outer and primary roads.

(6) Finally, traffic flows are determined by commercial vehicle flows, private car flows and bus vehicle flows, using the system of 'passenger car unit' equivalent weights.

It will be noted that (1)–(6) represent a simultaneous set of relationships. An equilibrium is a set of values for the variables that is mutually consistent with all of the relationships. If any policy variable is changed, then a new equilibrium is calculated by means of a search procedure. Having found the equilibrium, the following calculations are performed.

(7) Revenues are calculated from demands and fare levels.

(8) Costs are calculated from service levels, wage rates and achieved vehicle speeds (because, if vehicles move faster, a given annual total of vehicle miles can be provided at lower cost). Speeds depend upon the considerations already listed at (4), (5) and (6).

(9) Subsidy is calculated as cost net of revenue. Being a claim on public funds, changes in grant in respect of concessionary fares is treated as being a component of change in total subsidy (although the results could also be produced on the alternative convention that they constitute fares revenues).

(10) In principle, wage rates can be calculated on the assumption that there is an upward sloping supply of labour – that higher wage rates would have to be paid if more drivers were required in order to run more services. This had been the experience of many operators until relatively recently, but they can now recruit as much labour as they require at the going wage. The results quoted in this chapter assume this to be the situation; that is, they assume an infinitely elastic labour supply.

(11) In general, any policy change will cause the set of money costs and service qualities on all modes facing the user of any given mode to change. This will cause a general redistribution of demand between modes and this causes some difficulties of principle in estimating the economic benefits of the change. This is a technical matter that is discussed in the Department of Transport (1982) report. The resolution of the difficulties adopted in the study is founded on the principles first suggested by Hotelling (1938) and Hicks (1956).

(12) A calculation is performed (not shown in Table 12.1) to find the extra net social benefit that would be earned at the margin by using £1 extra subsidy to change each one of the policy variables in turn, holding the others constant. These 'shadow prices' on the policy variables are central to the assessment of the optimality of the balance between fares and services, the balance of expenditure levels between authorities and the rate of return to subsidy in general. The shadow prices at the 1980/1 levels (1982/3 in London), which are shown in column 2 of Table 12.3 below, illustrate the principle. They indicate that, at the margin, £1 of subsidy spent on reducing bus fares in London is estimated to yield £2.12 gross benefit or £1.12 net of the extra subsidy. But using it to reduce tube fares would yield a net benefit of only £0.26, and using it to improve bus services would produce a gross benefit of only £0.37 and hence a net disbenefit of £0.63. The fact that the four shadow prices are not equal suggests that the fares and service levels are out of balance, in the sense that benefits could be created by, say, cutting bus services and using the funds saved to finance cuts in bus fares in such a way as to keep the

total subsidy level unchanged. If the four shadow prices have not been equated, then it will always be possible to do better within the same total budget.

(13) Work by the Greater London Council and London Transport indicates that the effect on accidents may be an important consideration because of the diversion from public transport to cycles and motor cycles (particularly by young people). We investigated the possibilities of including accident benefits in the model. There would have been no particular difficulty in doing this, in principle, but we found that the information that we would have required was so poor that we decided to omit accidents from the formal modelling. It is not possible to give a firm estimate of the magnitude of the accident benefits, but one rough calculation that we made suggested that in the case of London, if subsidy were to be increased by, say, 10 per cent above the current level, the inclusion of accident benefits would increase the net benefit of this extra subsidy by a factor of 1.1. (The GLC estimated that the inclusion of accident benefits might add 50 per cent to congestion benefits; see London Transport Executive, 1982.)

RESULTS

Table 12.2 gives some of the characteristics of the areas. Note that Tables 12.2, 12.3 and 12.5 list the authorities in increasing levels of subsidy per capita (Table 12.5, col. 1), and that the Tyne and Wear Passenger Transport Authority is not included in the results because the Metro was opened during the year to which the study relates.

Columns 3 and 4 of Table 12.3 give the calculated marginal net benefit per pound of extra subsidy spent on each of the policy variables at the base levels (post March 1982 in London and 1980/1 elsewhere). There is wide variation between the areas, with particularly good returns obtainable from reducing London bus fares (fares had been doubled in March 1982) and improving London underground services. Service cuts would be beneficial in W. Yorkshire, Manchester and London. Reference to Table 12.2 shows that in each of these three cases average bus load factors are relatively low at 11 or 12 people per bus. Thus the economic benefit calculus reflects the elementary observation that service provision is relatively generous in the three cases. Note also that the shadow price on fares reductions in these three cases is generally high because if services are to be provided at this level one may as well reduce fares so as to improve the load factors. In S. Yorkshire, where the subsidy per capita is the

Table 12.2 Area characteristics

Area	Population (million)	'Density' (population per road mile)	Bus fare (£ per mile)	Rail fare (£ per mile)	Bus miles (vehicle miles per capita p.a.)	Rail miles (vehicle miles per capita p.a.)	Bus load	Subsidy/cost (%)	Bus passenger miles (per capita p.a.)	Commercial vehicles (million vehicle miles per road mile p.a.)	Car trips (million passenger miles per road mile p.a.)	Car trips (passenger miles per capita p.a.)
W. Midlands	2.645	686	0.063	0.05	74	2.0	19	12	532	0.25	2.2	3,206
W. Yorkshire	2.038	461	0.101	0.042	34	1.0	11	30	363	0.11	1.56	3,394
Greater Manchester	2.595	564	0.107	0.061	31	1.7	11	36	338	0.13	1.92	3,397
Merseyside	1.513	599	0.077	0.056	48	3.3	14	46	436	0.12	2.21	3,687
S. Yorkshire	1.302	446	0.027	0.031	38	0.9	16	72	608	0.12	1.72	3,848
London	6.696	5,038	0.128	0.141	25	4.3 (LT)	12	33	{319 (LT bus) / 353 (LT rail)	1.31	8.20	1,627

Table 12.3 Returns at the margin and changes required to equate them

Area	(1) Passenger miles per £ of subsidy Fares	(2) Passenger miles per £ of subsidy Services	(3) Net benefit per £ of subsidy Fares	(4) Net benefit per £ of subsidy Services	(5) % changes to equate returns Fares	(6) % changes to equate returns Services	(7) Marginal net benefits if equated
W. Midlands	5.93	7.10	0.21	0.41	+5	+4	0.24
W. Yorkshire	3.17	2.85	0.29	-0.19	-24	-13	0.18
Greater Manchester	3.59	2.28	0.33	-0.29	-23	-17	0.19
Merseyside	5.64	4.82	0.31	0.15	-6	-3	0.26
S. Yorkshire	5.79	5.83	0.03	0.03	0	0	0.03
London { Bus	6.29	2.92	1.12	-0.63	-28	-31	0.28
London { Tube	3.26	4.08	0.26	0.79	-11	+19	

highest outside London (Table 12.5, col. 1), the return at the margin is close to zero.

For comparison, columns 1 and 2 of Table 12.3 give rates at which public transport passenger miles could be generated by extra subsidy, passenger miles per pound having been promoted by some as a more comprehensible criterion than economic benefit. There is a relationship with the economic returns, but it is by no means perfect. For instance, S. Yorkshire shows a relatively high return on the passenger miles per pound criterion.

For each authority the fact that the shadow price on fares is not generally equal to that on services suggests that benefits could be secured within the same overall level of subsidy by juggling fares and services until the shadow prices are equated. This is illustrated in Table 12.4, which presents an alternative to the simple 25 per cent fares cut of Table 12.1; bus services are simultaneously cut back by about 37 per cent. It will be noted that this policy generates a benefit of £38m. per annum at almost no extra cost in subsidy, whereas the pure fares cut required an increase in subsidy of £99m. per annum in order to generate net benefits only £3m. per annum higher. Although there is little to choose between the policies in aggregate cost–benefit terms, they are, of course, very different in their impacts on the different groups involved.

The percentage changes required to achieve a balance in each of the areas is shown in columns 5 and 6 of Table 12.3. Column 7 shows the rate of economic return to subsidy at the margin once this balance has been achieved. At this point one can more sensibly compare the rates of return across authorities and hence address the question of whether a redistribution of expenditures would be indicated. Until the fares and service balance has been struck, it is difficult to analyse whether there would be a net advantage in reducing expenditures by £1 in, say, S. Yorkshire and increasing them by the same amount in Manchester, because the result would depend crucially on whether it would be spent on fares reduction or service improvements.

The shadow prices for each authority are represented graphically in Figures 12.1–12.6, which plot subsidy per capita against marginal benefits per pound of subsidy. The base level of subsidy is indicated by the horizontal straight line, and the shadow prices on the policy variables at the base (Table 12.3, columns 3 and 4) are indicated by the small circles. The lines in the graphs show how these shadow prices would change if subsidies were changed either by changing fares while holding services constant (the thinner lines) or by changing services while holding fares constant (the thicker lines). The line marked 'balance' shows how the return at the margin varies with subsidy level, if fares and services have been brought into balance at

Table 12.4   *The effects on the transport system in London of a 25 per cent reduction in LT bus and rail fares and a 37 per cent reduction in bus services*

	Initial position	Position after reduction in fares and services	Change as % of initial position
Passenger miles p.a. (million):			
CV	2,172.0	2,172.0	0
CAR	10,891.4	10,931.8	0.37
BUS	2,131.68	1,659.91	−22.14
LT(rail)	2,360.52	2,707.9	14.71
BR	2,081.82	2,117.13	1.69
Total LT	4,492.2	4,367.81	−2.77
Change in LT passenger miles		−124.389	
Fare (£ per passenger mile):			
CV	0.263286	0.261891	−0.53
CAR	0.0819693	0.0812316	−0.91
BUS	0.127648	0.095736	−25.00
LT(rail)	0.141385	0.106039	−25.00
BR	0.0884	0.0884	0
Vehicle miles per annum (millions):			
CV	1,738.0	1,738.0	0
CAR	7,780.63	7,809.51	0.37
BUS	167.0	106.0	−36.53
LT(rail)	28.8	28.8	0
BR (index)	100.0	100.0	0
Wait time (mins per passenger mile):			
CV	0	0	0
CAR	0	0	0
BUS	3.66234	5.9744	63.13
LT(rail)	1.5246	1.81902	19.31
BR	1.008	1.008	0
Passengers per vehicle:			
CV	1.24971	1.24971	0
CAR	1.39981	1.39981	0
BUS	12.7646	15.6595	22.67
LT(rail)	81.9625	94.0243	14.71
BR (index)	100.0	101.69	1.69
Revenues (£m. p.a.):			
CV	571.856	568.828	−0.53
CAR	892.761	888.009	−0.54
BUS	211.887	127.72	−39.73
LT(rail)	333.742	287.142	−13.97
BR	184.033	187.154	1.69

Table 12.4—*continued*

	Initial position	*Position after reduction in fares and services*	*Change as % of initial position*
Costs (£m. p.a.):			
CV	571.856	568.828	−0.53
CAR	892.761	888.009	−0.54
BUS	435.666	305.621	−29.85
LT(rail)	383.647	383.647	0
BR (index)	100.0	100.0	0
Revenues minus costs (£m. p.a.):			
CV	0	0	0
CAR	0	0	0
BUS	−223.78	−177.901	−20.51
LT(rail)	−49.9048	−96.5046	93.37
BR (index)	100.0	101.69	1.69
LT subsidy	−237.684	−274.405	0.26
Change in subsidy	0.720734		
Benefits (gross):	*Money*	*Money and time*	
CV	3.02784	16.6171	
CAR	8.15624	26.8496	
BUS	41.0564	−69.7486	
LT(rail)	90.2876	62.3374	
BR	0	0	
Change in net social benefit (£m. p.a.):			
CV	1o.6171		
CAR	26.8496		
BUS	−23.8695		
LT(rail)	15.7376		
BR	3.12102		
Total	38.4558		
Extra net social benefit/£ extra subsidy:		53.3565	

each subsidy level. (The figures are all drawn on the same axes, except that the vertical axis for S. Yorkshire is translated by £10 per capita and both of the London axes are at half the scale of the others).

Some of the more important features of these graphs are as follows. First, the 'balance' curves are moderately steep, indicating that, in general, moderate changes in subsidy will not cause very great changes in the rate of return at the margin. If the graphs for the

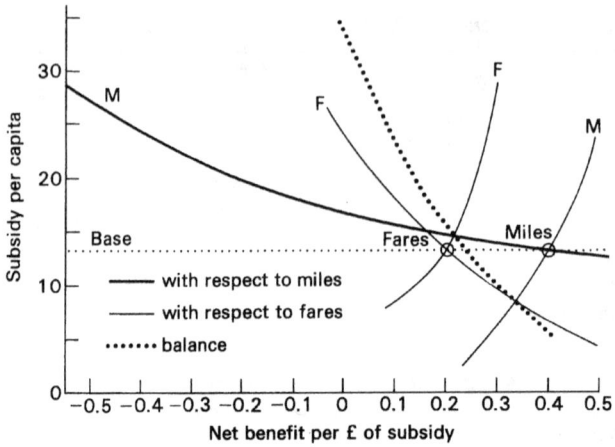

Figure 12.1 *W. Midlands*

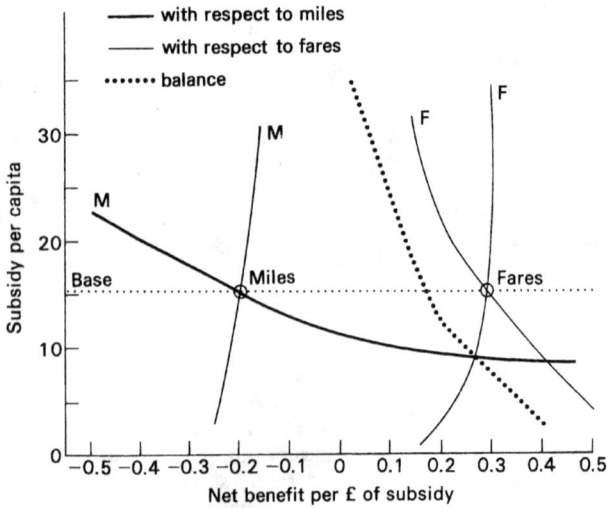

Figure 12.2 *W. Yorkshire*

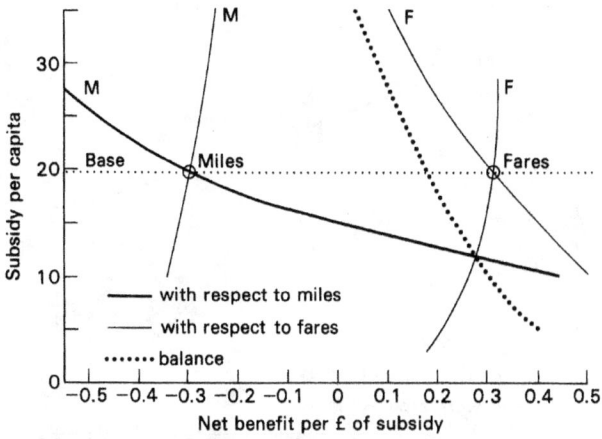

Figure 12.3 *Greater Manchester*

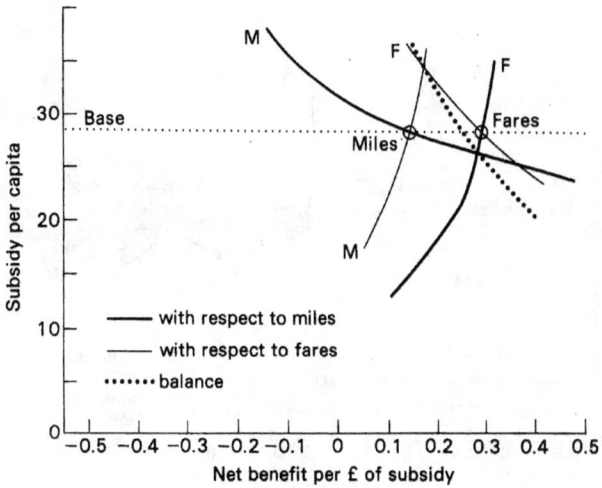

Figure 12.4 *Merseyside*

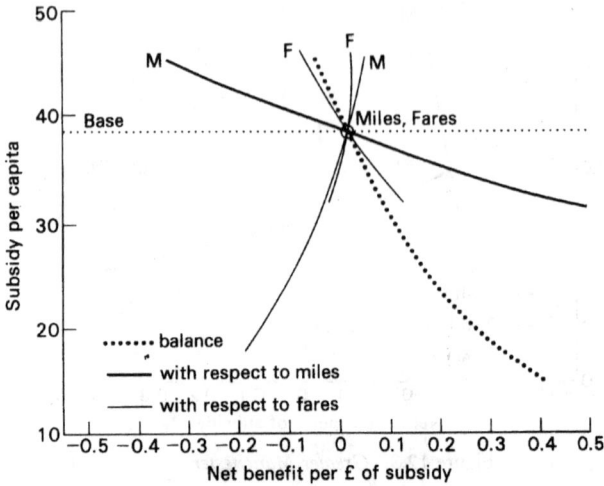

Figure 12.5 *S. Yorkshire*

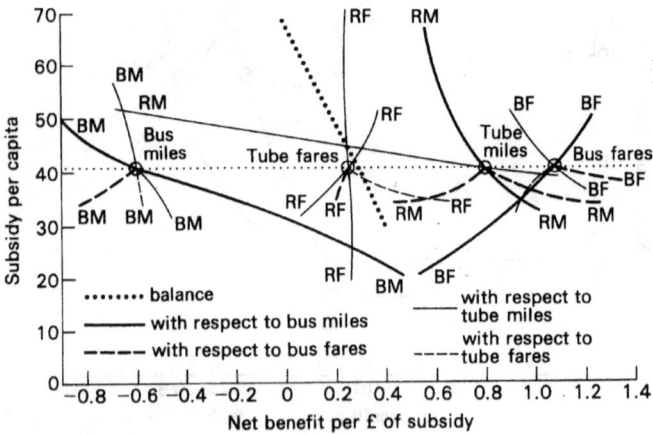

Figure 12.6 *London*

metropolitan authorities are superimposed one can see that the balance curves are quite close to one another, except that the one for Merseyside is somewhat to the north east of the others. Secondly, there is a considerable degree of imbalance in some authorities, especially the GLC. On the other hand, in S. Yorkshire the degree of balance is remarkable and, furthermore, the intersection of the curves occurs almost exactly at the point of zero net marginal benefit. Thirdly, each shadow price slopes negatively with respect to its 'own' variable and positively with respect to the 'other' variable: for example, the marginal returns to further fares reductions fall as fares are reduced, but they rise as service levels are increased. This is what one would expect. One line is consistently flatter than the others; the marginal return to improvements in service levels falls rather rapidly as service levels are improved. This is probably a reflection of the non-linear nature of the load factor effect. It has the implication that any benefits to improving service quality are relatively quickly exhausted, and any overprovision relatively easily corrected.

Table 12.5 shows how the distribution of expenditures per capita (shown in column 1) might be changed within the same total, if a variety of criteria for distribution were to be applied. It should be emphasised again that these figures must be treated as illustrations only: apart from anything else, they refer to different years for the metropolitan authorities from the GLC; capital expenditure is treated differently in the figures for the GLC; and the guidelines treat grant in lieu of concessionary fares differently. In column 2, marginal net benefits are assumed to be equalised both within and between authorities. In column 4, revenue/cost ratios are equated. In column 5, subsidies per resident capita are equated. In column 6, the guidelines issued in the White Paper (HMSO, 1982) are reproduced for comparison. Since they total to somewhat less than the total represented in each of the other columns, figures in parentheses are appended, which are the guideline figures grossed up in proportion so as to make them sum to the same total as the others.

In order to obtain an indication of how robust the results are, and to help to identify the important points of weakness, we carried out an extensive set of sensitivity tests. Not surprisingly, the valuation of service improvements was shown to be an area of doubt. The information on service elasticities is poor. Outside London, service elasticities at the lower end of the range suggested by research results (0.24–0.43) were used. The effects of modifying them towards the upper end (0.36–0.65) are that: the marginal benefits per pound of subsidy are increased by broadly £0.10 at each level of subsidy; the service cutbacks recommended in some of the areas would be about 10 per cent less (for example, 7 per cent instead of 17 per cent in

Table 12.5 *Subsidy allocations by various criteria*

Area	(1) 1980/1 per capita (£ p.a.)	(2) 1980/1 total (£m. p.a.)	(3) Equal marginal net benefit = £0.224 (£ p.a. per capita)	(4) Equal revenue/cost (64%) (£ p.a. per capita)	(5) Equal subsidy/capita (£ p.a.)	(6) Guidelines[b] 1983/4 (Cmnd 8735) (£ p.a. per capita)	
W. Midlands	13.27	35.11	14.4	15.5	28.8	10.6	(12.3)
W. Yorkshire	14.98	30.52	12.0	18.3	28.8	21.6	(25.0)
Greater Manchester	19.75	51.24	16.6	20.0	28.8	17.7	(20.5)
Merseyside	28.17	46.62	30.7	22.3	28.8	26.4	(30.5)
S. Yorkshire	38.63	50.30	22.4	19.3	28.8	30.7	(35.5)
London	40.87[a]	273.68	45.2	44.1	28.8	32.9	(38.1)
	483.47 Total	483.47	483.47 Total	483.47 Total	483.47 Total	418 Totals	(483)

[a] 1982/3.
[b] Payment for concessions for elderly and disabled excluded (included elsewhere).

Manchester); but the comparisons between the counties are not greatly affected. The load factor effect is especially important in London.

Traffic congestion was also shown to be an important element in the evaluation in London but far less significant in the other counties. Outside London, the information on speed/flow relationships and traffic flows on different road types was rather poor, but the assumptions we made would have to be in extreme error to make a difference to these findings. The two most important assumptions underlying congestion in London concern the relation between car use and LT fares and service levels, and the speed/flow relationships. Doubling the cross elasticities and increasing the slopes of the speed/flow relationships by 10 per cent did not greatly change the results.

A significant implication of these observations is that, outside London, most of the benefits from additional subsidies fall to public transport users; the effectiveness of public transport subsidies in reducing traffic congestion is limited. In London, largely because of the number of buses on the roads, balancing of fares and service levels would bring substantial benefits to commercial vehicles and cars. This applies particularly to the central area roads where a substantial improvement in traffic speeds results. Once a balanced position has been reached, then if subsidy were increased by 50 per cent, for example, about a quarter of the extra benefits would accrue to other road users.

THE ECONOMIC PHENOMENA INVOLVED

In the course of constructing the model and attempting to interpret the results, we substantially improved our understanding of the various economic phenomena involved. Although we knew some of these were important when we started, we did not appreciate the importance of others.

As Dupuit (1844) first pointed out, if there are no resource costs involved in the greater use of a facility then there will always be a net advantage in reducing the charges for its use. This must be so since the traffic generated obtains the benefit of use and there are no extra costs by assumption. If a bus or rail service is provided at a generous service level which is taken as fixed, so that the average load factor is low, then Dupuit's situation is created: one will get benefits by reducing fares so as to fill the empty vehicles. We have already observed this phenomenon in the case of fares reductions in the areas with low load factors. Note, however, that such a policy is not neutral in its impact on users as against funders of the requisite extra subsidy. In

fact, with demand elasticities substantially less than unity, as is typically the case, the benefits to generated traffic will be small relative to
the cash benefits to those who would have used the service both
before and after the reduction. They effectively receive a straightforward cash transfer. The example in Table 12.1 illustrates this: existing LT users pay £136m. per annum less, while the generated
revenues are £37m. per annum.

This raises the question of whether service levels have been set
appropriately. If fares could always be reduced at no resource cost,
then there would be an efficiency case for no charges at all. In practice, as fares fall, load factors rise. Each vehicle has to accommodate
more boardings and so its speed falls, operating costs rise and existing
passengers suffer increased times in the vehicle. More importantly,
the probability that the first vehicle to arrive at a stop will be full will
increase, and so effective passenger waiting times will increase. The
latter relationship has the property that increasing load factors have
little effect when load factors are low, but they inflict severe penalties
if the average bus load factor rises much above one-half. An additional effect on users is the dis-benefit of crowding as load factors
increase.

The 'load factor effect' thus provides the fundamental link between
fares policy and service level policy without which it is impossible to
discuss the balance sensibly. The results are sensitive to the details of
the particular functional form used and this is an area where more
research would be particularly helpful. This is an example of an effect
whose importance we had not appreciated when starting the work.

The 'second best' congestion pricing argument is well known.
Because of congestion, the user of a private vehicle imposes costs on
other users that he does not take into account when deciding whether
to travel on the basis of the cost he himself faces: the marginal social
cost of his trip exceeds the private cost. In these circumstances, some
net benefits can be created by reducing fares somewhat, providing
that this will encourage some car users to transfer to public transport.

The above argument is greatly complicated by the fact that, in
London at least, buses themselves constitute an important source of
road congestion. Thus, if bus services are expanded in order to
accommodate more diverted car users there is a danger that traffic
congestion will actually be made worse. This phenomenon is illustrated by the comparison of the examples in Tables 12.1 and 12.4. The
removal of the 37 per cent of bus miles in the second case allows an
increase in road speeds that is the reason for the fall in operating costs
of commercial vehicles and cars. This generates enough benefits to
road users to offset the considerable dis-benefits to bus users, which is

reflected in the 23 per cent increase in bus load factors and the 63 per cent decline in bus 'service quality'.

Another effect that has turned out to be more important than we had anticipated is the system economy of scale effect first pointed out by Mohring (1972). If demand were to double and services were to be doubled in response then waiting times would approximately halve. This would be a benefit to the passengers using the services before the expansion: the new users create a benefit external to themselves but internal to the system. This effect suggests a further argument in favour of subsidy in order to achieve economic efficiency.

BR rail travel is treated as one of the interdependent modes. In London, a change in LT policies will have implications for BR revenues and on user benefits accruing on BR rail. These effects enter the economic evaluation but, of course, they do not figure in the account of the implications for LT finances. In the metropolitan authorities, the institutional arrangement is different: the Passenger Transport Authority (PTA) negotiates directly with BR for the provision of rail services and finances them. Hence the financial implications for rail service of policy changes are reflected in the overall financial position of the Passenger Transport Executive (PTE). As a simplification, it was assumed in the exploratory work reported here that outside London any change in bus fares or services would also occur on rail. With a little development, one could employ the model to analyse BR fares and services in the London area. One could also integrate the treatment of BR with that of LT if one wished to take the all-embracing view that might be taken by a metropolitan transport authority.

There are a number of other effects that many will consider to be important but that are not included explicitly. These include: any energy considerations that are not captured adequately in the various vehicle operating cost calculations; accident benefits, as already mentioned; the effects of increased subsidies on labour productivity and wage costs; the long-term effects of transport policies on urban form; and the wider, social aspects of the problem. It should also be emphasised that we have accounted the resource cost of £1 of extra subsidy as being £1. This begs a whole set of important questions concerning the existence of distortions elsewhere in the economy; the alternative uses that the funds would have had; and, in particular, the efficiency cost of raising the finance through taxation.

SUMMARY AND DISCUSSION

The study described in this Chapter was developed to investigate the feasibility of estimating the economic effects of public transport subsidy and of comparing them in several urban areas. We certainly felt that we had learned a great deal about the problem in the course of what was, admittedly, a crude exercise. The results seemed to us to be generally reasonable and one can find intuitive explanations for the effects that we observed.

To summarise, in all of the metropolitan areas a positive net return to increased subsidy is shown, although this is variable and it is not established that the return is higher than that which could be earned in alternative uses for the funds. In many areas the return to extra subsidy is not as great as the return that could be attained by readjusting fares and service levels so as to obtain a better balance within the same support level. A leading cause of imbalance within areas appears to be overprovision of services, which is reflected in low average load factors. Congestion benefits are persuasive arguments for subsidy only in London. In all areas the predominant effect of fares support is to achieve a cash transfer in favour of those who would have used the services anyway.

In the event, the 1983 Transport Act explicitly embraces the notion of measurement of benefits to an extent that is unusual in legislation of this kind. Each year the PTA must agree a three-year rolling plan with its PTE that it must submit to the secretary of state. If the plan is formulated on the assumption that revenue grants will be made by the PTA to the PTE, it must be accompanied by particulars of costs, demand and, in particular, benefits expected to accrue from the grants. Further, in preparing the plan the PTE must take into account any advice given by the secretary of state on the methods of determining these. He will give guidance on the maximum revenue grant he thinks appropriate for the coming year and the PTA must take that guidance into account before determining to make any grants. In giving the guidance, the secretary of state will make reference to, amongst other things, '(a) what appears to him to be the appropriate national level of expenditure by Authorities on revenue grants; (b) the benefits which would result from the making of such grants; and (c) the levels of present and past expenditure by the Authority on such grants' (HMSO, 1983b, clause 4(6)). Although the Act itself is vague on the definition of benefits, the associated White Paper (Cmnd 8735) is a little more specific: 'considerable weight will be given to the more direct economic and social benefits which can be measured in different areas on a comparable basis. Officials in the Department of Transport will discuss with those concerned the information and procedures needed for this purpose' (HMSO, 1982, para 21).

Since the work reported here was completed, several developments have been started with the intention of improving on some of the over-simplifications. These include the separate consideration of the peak and the off peak; the division of travellers into different groups (for instance, school children and, perhaps, adults with a variety of trip purposes); the division of each metropolitan area into more than one sub-area so as to allow a more adequate representation of the more rural kind of service; a separate treatment of bus and rail services in the metropolitan areas. There is no reason in principle that the method could not be applied equally well to some of the large non-metropolitan counties.

The difficulty with all these developments is that they very rapidly multiply the number of items of data that are required and the complexity and cost of the computational effort involved. The dialogue that has now started between the Department and the metropolitan counties will undoubtedly allow considerable improvements to be made to the procedures. But it has to be said that the present lack of information on some of the matters that have been central to discussions on public transport investments and subsidies for many years is lamentable. Leading examples are area speed/flow relationships; private to public cross elasticities; service demand elasticities; what we have called load factor effects; and accident implications. It is to be hoped that the recent upheavals will have generated a great deal of new information with which we can improve our understanding of these matters.

It remains to be seen how much more insight can be attained from more complex models. Several of the phenomena involved cannot really be modelled satisfactorily at the aggregate level. It is possible that a more productive way forward would be to concentrate more on the economic and wider social evaluation of specific services, something that has been advocated and shown to be possible by a number of recent publications (Bus and Coach Council, 1982; Beesley et al., 1983). This would throw light on the important and thorny problem of cross subsidy (and hence on the implications of increased competition). It would encourage those with political responsibilities to take a more explicit view on which kinds of services should be supported – something that Gilbert Ponsonby and John Hibbs have advocated persuasively in many writings (see, for example, Hibbs, 1975, 1982; Ponsonby, 1969). The approach of this chapter assumes away the problems of production inefficiencies (failures to produce at lowest cost) and does not address the question of whether subsidy weakens the incentive to eliminate them and to innovate. The study has produced some suggestive evidence of allocative inefficiencies in the imbalance of service levels, probably caused by a reluctance to cut back services in the face of a declining market, but it is likely that the aggregate approach conceals a multitude of sins at the level of the individual bus route. On the other hand, Whitehall will inevitably retain a strategic interest in the allocation of expenditures between areas. If the kind of approach used in this chapter is to play any part in this, then it is essential that the amount of special modelling to suit the peculiarities of the individual areas be kept within bounds in order to preserve an understanding of the sources of the economic differences between them at this level.

Critics, and especially some of those with political responsibilities, will be quick and quite correct to point to the very limited nature of our analysis. No doubt some will argue that urban public transport subsidy is principally about issues that we do not take into account. This is a matter for debate, but it will certainly be of great interest to see how successfully our kind of analysis could be integrated into an account of the wider issues along the lines pioneered by Professor Lichfield's Planning Balance Sheet and taken up by the Department of Transport in the context of trunk road appraisal (see the report of the Advisory Committee on Trunk Road Assessment, 1977). The evidence submitted to the House of Commons Select Committee on Transport in connection with its uncompleted inquiry into bus subsidy policy (House of Commons, 1983) contains a great deal of constructive discussion of these issues, which demonstrates the increasing recognition that a serious problem has developed and that careful analysis can contribute to its resolution.

13 Subsidies to Urban Public Transport and Privatisation

GRAHAM CRAMPTON

INTRODUCTION

The question of the appropriate level of subsidy to urban public transport is one of the more controversial current issues in the field of public finance. In this chapter, an attempt is made to discuss the economics of the issue with reference both to conventional cost–benefit analysis treatment of efficient subsidy and to wider questions of the possible role for privatisation in urban transport.

In Chapter 12, Stephen Glaister provides an excellent example of what economists can do in analysing what the 1983 Transport Act called 'the benefits which would result from the making of such [local authority] grants' (HMSO, 1983, Pt I, *4*, 6(a)). This approach has its limitations, however. The first section of this chapter discusses some of the problems that arise in the traditional economic approach to efficient subsidy. The next section considers the relationship between recent trends in urban structure and possible areas of interest for privatisation. It shows that the extent to which private capital can be attracted into urban (or rural) local passenger transport is somewhat problematic, given the generally declining patronage of public transport in recent years in Britain. However, lack of investment (either private or public) in urban transport systems, based on pessimistic forecasts, tends to make those forecasts self-fulfilling. Most of the exciting new urban mass transit systems introduced with public capital in the US and West Germany in recent years have been orientated to providing a high-quality, time- and stress-saving congestion-free mode, using impressive modern technology and quite aggressive marketing techniques. It is possible that private capital could similarly help to 'break the mould' of British urban transport, given a sympathetic central government attitude to urban public transport.

Thus the final section of the chapter discusses government attitudes towards the financing of urban public transport systems. It seems that this attitude is the major stumbling block currently, since the central government at present seems more interested in the generalities of the 'proper balance' between rate-financed subsidies to urban public transport and fare revenues (HSMO, 1982). The possible abolition of the Greater London Council (GLC) and the English metropolitan counties would shift power in these matters even more strongly to Whitehall and further reduce the likelihood of local experimentation. One can only hope that eventually plans for both inter- and intra-city transport will be made that acknowledge that North Sea oil output will soon have peaked, and British long-run transport strategy should be orientated towards re-adopting our position as an oil importer.

PROBLEMS IN THE ECONOMIC ANALYSIS OF THE EFFICIENT LEVEL OF PUBLIC TRANSPORT SUBSIDY

One expects the economic approach to efficient subsidy of urban public transport to consist in the main of careful econometric estimation of demand functions for public transport modes using fairly standard functional forms. Once that difficult but well-researched task has been achieved, and reasonable figures are available of own-price and service elasticities, then simulations can be carried out to illustrate aggregate net benefits of various price/service strategies. An attempt may be made to specify an efficient, that is, net-benefit-maximising, fares/service mix, and estimates may be made of the subsidy required to achieve that type of service. The fare and service elasticities are at the heart of such a standard economic treatment.

The main problem with this approach is that such modelling of the urban transport system occurs largely in isolation from the economic structure of the urban area itself. Ultimately this comes down to the fact that there are likely to be *long-run* responses to subsidy changes, whether to fares or service quality, that are much more difficult to quantify precisely, both in their total amount and in the time span over which they occur. It is, of course, an example of a textbook generality that long-run elasticities are greater than short-run elasticities, but how much greater, and the form and magnitude of the long-run responses, are normally little discussed.

Possibly the most obvious longer-run relationship, and probably the most easily quantified, is the relationship between private car ownership and the level of fares and service in the urban public transport system. The typical econometric analysis of urban public transport use in effect studies short-run substitution between public transport and the *use* of the private car, which will of course be a relevant potential substitution for every car commuter (if it is the journey to work with which we are principally concerned). However, if a particular change in the public transport fare or service is expected to hold for a period of years, then long-run durable consumption decisions on car ownership, for marginal car owners, will be affected. Such a relationship may be simultaneous, in that high fares or poor service will, in the long run, increase car ownership, which will reduce demand for public transport services. Reduced demand for public transport may in turn lead to a further round of reduced services, and possibly to increased fares, although the latter depends on the economies of scale prevalent in the urban public transport system, an issue to which I return later. All this has to be taken in addition to the simple political fact of life that increased car ownership will weaken the political support for a cheap and/or good-quality urban public transport service. Just as a descriptive background statistic, it is interesting to note the 1981 Census car ownership figure for the GLC and the English metropolitan counties, with the most recent available per capita rate contribution to passenger transport (including both general subsidy and concessionary fares schemes) (see Table 13.1).

Without attempting to explain the differences (and with so few observations that is probably impossible), under the uniform Labour control of the metropolitan counties since May 1981 a pattern of subsidy has emerged in which the GLC has developed a relatively

Table 13.1 *Car ownership, 1981, and per capita estimated rate contributions to passenger transport (including concessionary fares schemes), for the GLC and English metropolitan counties, 1983/4*

County	% households with at least one car, 1981	1983/4 estimated rate subsidy of public transport (£ per capita)		
		Total	Rate fund contribution (general)	Concessionary fares schemes
W. Midlands	55.7	17.90	10.80	7.10
GLC	55.3	40.95	33.13	7.82
G. Manchester	52.8	23.00	17.69	5.31
W. Yorkshire	52.6	24.75	20.76	3.99
S. Yorkshire	50.4	54.40	44.57	9.83
Merseyside	49.9	43.57	33.96	9.61
Tyne/Wear	43.5	32.33	16.06	16.27

Sources: Car ownership: 1981 Census.
Estimated rate contributions: Chartered Institute of Public Finance and Accountacy, 1983.

generous approach. The West Midlands, in contrast, which had the highest car ownership in 1981, has retained its very parsimonious public transport subsidy strategy. Apart from the GLC, the main exception to high car-ownership counties having lower subsidy patterns is Tyne and Wear, which made substantial contributions to the debt-servicing of the newly built Metro transit system. It is interesting to note the divergence of strategy within counties of nominally similar political allegiance. Apart from the Metro transit system, Tyne and Wear has developed much the most generous concessionary fares scheme. Where such schemes include the unemployed or welfare claimants, they function as explicit attempts to raise the net welfare benefit per pound of subsidy by more precise distributive targeting. (In the case of concessionary fares for the unemployed, they may also raise the efficiency of job search. The mode of transport much favoured by a recent Secretary of State for Employment, namely the bicycle, may be less practical for job search in the largest urban areas where employment growth, such as it is, may largely occur in the suburban fringes.)

A second area of longer-run change usually neglected by conventional econometric treatments of urban public transport concerns the possible induced local real income effects of fare changes. When fare changes are distinctly non-marginal, as was the case with the GLC's 'Fares Fair' scheme and with its later abandonment, it is possible that significant localised gains or losses of purchasing power will take place where the major concentrations of public transport users reside. Local multipliers will enhance such localised real income changes. The neglect of such effects in conventional analysis of net benefit of urban public transport subsidy is an example of how rare it is for cost–benefit analysis (CBA) in Britain to take account of the employment effects of investments or price changes; in a sense British CBA (and CBA applied to other developed countries) is confined to the full employment context, in which output and employment changes indirectly occasioned by the price change under study can be called 'pecuniary externalities' and generally ignored. Whether this is still appropriate with double figure unemployment emerging as the long-run context is very much subject to doubt.

The third area in which the longer-run effects of urban public transport policy are likely to appear is probably the least well understood, and hence the least likely to be systematically included in the analysis of appropriate government guidance levels for subsidy. This is the effect of urban public transport policy on the commercial profitability of firms, and consequently on the spatial structure of employment in the urban area, both in the central business district (CBD) and in the possibly more industrial concentrations outside the commercial centre. The agglomerations of complementary activities functioning as a central business district in the major British cities are attracted together by strong locational forces, some of which will survive the trend in recent decades towards higher car ownership, higher real public transport fares and lower service quality (as represented by, for example, total vehicle miles per thousand resident population). However, a public transport system (shared by commerce, retailing and entertainment) has functioned as one of the most powerful centralising elements in the urban system, and some weakening of these centralising forces must accompany a weakening of the public transport system, in either fares or service dimension. Specifically, those employers that have enjoyed the benefits of having a wide area from which to draw a labour force, large numbers of whom commute by public transport, will have to face a local labour supply curve that will shift inwards if public transport becomes more expensive or irksome to use. In principle, the worker at work is a kind of 'delivered good', and higher generalised commuting costs will raise its supply curve.

Several important points emerge from studying the impact of the public transport system on the urban employment structure. Firstly, certain technological trends within the employment structure, most notably office automation, may be strengthened by a higher cost in 'delivering labour'. The tendency towards labour-saving technical change in the commercial sector may well be enhanced, and other sectors of CBD activity may make adjustments to relatively more expensive labour. I shall look first at the commercial sector and the CBD in particular, although there is little empirical evidence on the modal split of commuting patterns of the urban labour force in different sectors of economic activity. However, one would expect commercial and retailing activity to dominate the CBD in most cities, and the centre/radial urban public transport network is primarily oriented towards 'delivering' the commercial and retailing labour force to areas where commuter car-parking is difficult and expensive. Manufacturing areas, in contrast, whether they are on the more traditional fringe of CBD zones, or in more recent suburbanised industrial concentrations, will generally consist of lower-density employment, will be somewhat less amenable to public transport service, and will be more likely to provide free car-parking for employees. If such generalisations can be trusted, one would expect that the major commercial/retailing employers in the CBD would be the major net beneficiaries of rate-financed public transport subsidies (apart from the users themselves, of course). Although such employers might protest vehemently about their extra rate bill, they would at least be getting some of the benefit in terms of a more accessible labour force.

The principal net losers, who contribute to the rates but receive less of the benefit, apart from car-commuters themselves, would be the major employers of car-commuters. One would expect many industrial employers to be included among the net losers.

If government guidance figures were to impose a rather parsimonious overall level of subsidy on urban areas, urban public transport might well face a continued long-run increase in the real generalised cost of delivering labour to those major high-density job concentrations where car-commuting plays a minor role. In such circumstances, it is to be expected that some marginal firms in such concentrations would close, and there would be additional financial incentive to decentralise to a lower-density environment, or at least introduce labour-saving techniques if firms were tied to the high-density concentration. Ultimately, one could envisage a long-run adaptation process in the urban structure, where CBD-type functions break away from the kind of massive spatial concentration that provided urban public transport with its captive market of commuters into sub-centres specialising in the different elements of the CBD function, with the overall system of sub-centres more oriented towards private car use. This kind of 'centre-less' city is familiar in those parts of the US that developed in this century against a background of very cheap petrol and high car ownership. What one is currently required to understand in the British context is the more complicated process of how the car-oriented urban structure may emerge, through redevelopment and relocation, from an originally strongly centralised public transport-oriented structure. The long-run relationship of the whole process to the international oil market and future trends in the real price per mile of car transportation makes matters even more complex.

PRIVATISATION IN URBAN TRANSPORT

Privatisation in the form of transfer of ownership has been relatively little discussed in connection with urban public transport in recent years. This contrasts strongly with the deregulation and privatisation of inter-city bus services introduced mid-way through the Thatcher government's first term. If there had been attractive profits to be made out of private provision of particular intra-urban services or of specific routes within a larger system, then presumably proposals would have been put together, and some experimental private schemes would have been set up. Perhaps even a nation-wide lobbying of local authorities to adopt a particular package would have occurred, rather along the lines of the National Car Parks schemes in city centre parking. The main reason why this has not happened in urban public transport must be the very limited profits available. Indeed it is not fanciful to suggest that, in many areas, the average cost curve for urban public transport services may be above the demand curve, so that losses could not be avoided whatever the price level. (It is impossible to be precise about this, with observations on demand and costs being made in practice along a very limited segment of the relevant curves. Guesses about the likely functional form of the curves at extreme prices and outputs would remain guesses.) In contrast with other areas of the public service economy in which private competition has recently prospered, such as refuse disposal, health care or even education, urban public transport (at least of the type offered in major cities) has a rather low income elasticity of demand, and trends in demand over recent decades have generally been adverse. This still leaves open the possibility that a higher-quality urban public transport product could be discovered that is not so close to being an inferior good. The mass transit systems introduced over recent decades in the US and West Germany have generally emphasised speed and comfort as well as cost advantages over the car, with a relatively affluent time- and stress-conscious clientele as the principal target market. In a sense, the major British cities have been fighting a constant battle against their shoddy, aging capital stock, and have found it difficult even to test the demand for a high-quality product.

It is unthinkable that privatisation in urban public transport would involve large-scale, high-quality infrastructure projects on the scale of the Washington DC, San Francisco or Munich systems. If privatisation is to be experimented with, it will at first surely take the form of piecemeal provision of limited-scale services within a larger public system. Even with such smaller-scale experiments, it is possible that a profit may be technically unachievable, so that the economic problem shifts to one of designing contracts of a specific service to be offered at a given price over a specific time period, with a fixed capital subsidy included as part of the contract. The problems of detailed service description and quality control are no different from those that arise in the privatisation of, for example, refuse disposal, but the calculation of a capitalised subsidy to be offered with the contract, attractive enough to invite competing private tenders, does not arise in most other privatisation contexts. In theory, the most efficient way to conduct such a tendering process would be to invite the private firms that are offering to provide a detailed specific service to specify a required subsidy, and then the relevant authority could select the lowest of the subsidy bids. The major disadvantage of such an approach is that it tends to discard from the outset the energy and imagination involved in designing a *new* product, and leaves private capital with the task of providing and marketing a service that has already been described in detail.

If the advantages of privatisation are to be fully exploited, it is likely to be in those relatively unexplored sectors of the urban transport system in which small-scale operation is feasible with a profit, so that private risk capital can be addressed to introducing a new quality of service into a sector of the market previously neglected by the large public service monopolies. It is also likely that such modest moves towards privatisation would use labour unattached to the existing public transport unions and the job-maximising techniques associated with them. Of course, the privatised operation of comprehensive urban public transport systems might be experimented with for those small towns where the authorities were politically sympathetic, but the recent declines in public transport patronage in small towns would be quite discouraging.

The richest ground for inviting private capital would probably be in those directions where existing public provision works particularly badly. I have already suggested that the rather shoddy quality of infrastructure in most major British urban public transport systems makes it inevitable that the high-quality product has in general simply not been on offer. I also suggested that privatisation of whole urban systems so as to provide such a product for major cities is probably impractical. However, there are other sectors of the urban public transport system that may be more amenable to a more flexible approach, especially a more flexible price/service quality approach.

In particular, there may be unexploited economies of scale at the bottom of the service intensity scale, as well as at the top, as William Vickrey (1980, p. 393) suggested:

> Economies of scale are at their greatest at the two extremes of service intensity: with rapid transit rail service on the one hand, and with low density bus service on the other, whether in a small community with low overall demand, or at times of low demand, as with night or Sunday service in larger cities. Scale economies are at their lowest, perhaps, in cases of extremely dense bus service . . . Even here, however, economies of scale are likely to be substantial, especially in situations where the possibilities exist of increasing the variety of service offered, as is often the case during rush hours.

If it were accepted that economies of scale were strongest at the bottom and top of the service intensity scale, this would of course be a strong theoretical justification for subsidising more heavily precisely in those situations, rather than in what Vickrey calls 'extremely dense bus service'. As a general principle, this could have a far-reaching

impact on the setting of guidance figures for subsidy, both in a metropolitan county and in a more rural shire county context, although
shire counties were not covered by the 1983 Transport Act. I stress
the point because the availability of unexploited economies of scale,
with appropriately set subsidies, may be the key to attracting private
risk capital into the various forms of 'non-private car' transport, both
urban and rural. Indeed, if a small-scale experimental context is what
is sought initially, the rural/small town situation may potentially be
the most fertile ground. In addition, the recent population Census
indicates that they furnished the main population growth areas over
1971–81.

One might also suggest that there are opportunities for introducing
more imaginative service-call and routing technology in the low-
intensity market mentioned by Vickrey, which might make progress
towards capturing the available economies of scale. This is an element of the crucial area of information, public relations, ticketing and
marketing of the transportation service, which is ripe for much
improvement and modernisation in Britian. We could learn much
from the urban transport systems of West Germany (in, for example,
Munich, Nuremberg or Frankfurt), which, following substantial
investment in impressive new systems, are marketed most effectively
with highly efficient and rational ticketing arrangements and aggressive poster campaigns detailing to motorists the time/stress-saving
advantages of using the system. The Verkehrsverbund plays the same
role in West German urban areas as the Passenger Transport Authority in Britain. They have enjoyed the advantage, however, of generally having modern infrastructure. No less than twelve West German
urban areas have introduced new rail rapid transit systems since 1962
(Guhl, 1975). In several British urban transport systems in which a
British Rail line is nominally linked into a PTA network it is not even
possible to buy an integrated ticket between the two sub-sectors of
the system, much less an integrated bus–rail ticket. If the injection of
private capital will facilitate more effective marketing of urban or
rural public transport services, then it should be welcomed.

THE FINANCING OF URBAN PUBLIC TRANSPORT SYSTEMS

The problem of financing public transport systems ultimately comes
down to the central government's general policy with respect to
public transport versus the private car. In those cities where new rail
mass transit systems have been introduced in the US or West Germany, or where an older system has been raised to an impressive level
of high-quality service (e.g. Paris), there has normally been a signific-

ant central government injection of resources into the capital costs, and sometimes in operating subsidy too. In Britain, this kind of central government attitude – that the externalities and resource costs of highly congested private car operation are too important not to be central government's business – has yet to become established. Several political explanations could be offered, involving the role of the 'road lobby', but this issue is well beyond the scope of this chapter. The fact remains that privatisation will not act as a panacea, bringing private capital by magic into a sector in which deficits have seemingly become endemic. Even if private operation of deficit-making systems were to be pushed through, private capital could be attracted only if subsidies were offered with the contracts; and, if the financing of these subsidies remains strictly local, then the prospects will remain poor. It is highly unlikely that a government that ideologically favours privatisation of ownership will also favour the level of subsidy necessary to make it successful. It would also be surprising, under the present government, for a new source of revenue to be introduced that would break through the dilemma. The taxation of the development land value gains generated by the construction of new transport systems would be such a new revenue source, strongly favoured by theory. Again, Vickrey (1980, p. 401) suggests:

> . . . It does appear, however, that in the cities that are the first to follow such a policy [land rent taxation to finance subsidies], in the medium long run land rents will tend to rise by more than the required subsidies. If landlords were fully aware of their long-run interests they would be eager to tax themselves to achieve this result.

Sadly, though, such a form of taxation and subsidy will probably suffer the same fate as direct road pricing, exercising the minds more of undergraduate and academic economists than pragmatic transport policy-makers. Likewise, we have an impressive description by Berechman (1980) of the privatised Israeli bus industry. This runs on the government-specified routes and frequencies with contractual central government subsidies, and the ownership of the capital is on a co-operative, one employee per share basis. It is difficult to see subsidised bus transport co-operatives being welcomed by the Department of Transport as a solution to current British local transport problems.

It is perhaps ironic that, although the 1983 Transport Act is the major current piece of legislation addressing urban public transport problems, the most fruitful area for privatisation in transport may be in serving the low-intensity rural/small town market, where at least populations are generally growing. Government's role in this market originally emerged when Transport Supplementary Grants (TSG) introduced the concept to Britain of a direct specific central government contribution to local transport undertakings. Perhaps subsidies linked to private contracts and disbursed through the TSG may be an appropriate approach. Also, a more adventurous approach to serving evening and weekend or high-quality demand in the major urban areas, other than the conventional regulated taxi service, might prove to be attractive to private capital, particularly if the trend towards gentrification of the residential population in certain of the inner urban areas continues. These possibilities of privatisation in urban transport, including the possibility that 'privatisation' in this context may simply mean the freest possible use of the private car, seem to be rather limited. Privatisation may yet prove to play a similar role to the one it has played thus far in, for example, refuse collection – namely, a bargaining threat to use against the established public service unions, much discussed but rarely implemented.

References

Abel-Smith, B. (1967), *Labour's Social Plans* (London: Fabian Society).

Abel-Smith, B. (1976), *Value for Money in Health Services* (London: Heinemann).

Abel-Smith, B. (1983), 'Assessing the balance sheet', in H. Glennerster (ed.), *The Future of the Welfare State* (London: Heinemann) pp. 10–23.

Abel-Smith, B. and Maynard, A. (1979), *The Cost, Financing and Organisation of Health Care in the European Community*, Social Policy Series, Number 36, (Brussels and Luxembourg: Commission of the European Communities).

Advisory Committee on Trunk Road Assessment (1977), Chairman: Sir George Leitch, *Report* (London: HMSO).

Arneson, R. J. (1982), 'The principle of fairness and free-rider problems', *Ethics*, vol. 92, no. 4, pp. 616–33.

Arrow, K. J. (1963), 'Uncertainty and the welfare economics of medical care', *American Economic Review*, vol. 53, no. 5, pp. 941–73.

Arrow, K. J. (1981), 'Optimal and voluntary income distribution', in S. Rosefielde (ed.), *Economic Welfare and the Economics of Soviet Socialism: Essays in Honour of Abram Beryson* (Cambridge: Cambridge University Press).

Awan, K. and Whitehead, C. M. E. (1980), 'Policy changes and the housing market', *CES Review*, no. 9, April, pp. 25–29.

Balchin, P. N. (1981), *Housing Policy and Housing Needs* (London: Macmillan).

Barry, B. (1965), *Political Argument* (London: Routledge & Kegan Paul).

Bassett, K. and Short, J. R. (1980), *Housing and Residential Structure: Alternative Approaches* (London: Routledge & Kegan Paul).

Baumol, W. (1967), 'Macroeconomics of unbalanced growth: the anatomy of urban crisis', *American Economic Review*, vol. 57, no. 3, pp. 415–26.

Beales, A. C. F., Blaug, M., West, E. G. and Veale, D. (1970), *Education – A Framework for Choice* (London: Institute of Economic Affairs).

Becker, G. S. (1974), 'A theory of social interactions', *Journal of Political Economy*, vol. 82, no. 5, pp. 1063–93.

Beesley, M. E., Gist, P. and Glaister, S. (1983), 'Cost–benefit analysis and London's transport policies', *Progress in Planning*, vol. 19, pt 3 (Oxford: Pergamon).

Berechman, J. (1980), 'Transit subsidy and regulation, lessons from the Israeli experience', *Transportation*, vol. 9, no. 4, pp. 369–88.

Berlin, I. (1969), *Four Essays on Liberty* (Oxford: Clarendon Press).

Beveridge, W. (1942) (Chairman), *Report on Social Insurance and Allied Services*, Cmd 6404 (London: HMSO).

Blaug, M. (1970), *Introduction to the Economics of Education* (London: Penguin Books).

Blaug, M. (1981), 'Can independent education be suppressed?', *Journal of Economic Affairs*, vol. 2, no. 1, pp. 30–37.

Bone, M. and Mason, V. (1980), *Empty Housing in England* (London: HMSO).

Borcherding, T., Pommerehne, W. and Schneider, F. (1982), 'Comparing the efficiency of private and public production: the evidence from five countries', *Zeitschrift für Nationalökonomie*, vol. 91, pp. 127–36.

Bosanquet, N. (1982), 'What is the impact of trade unionism on the NHS?', *Health Service Manpower Review*, vol. 8, no. 2, pp. 11–13.

Bosanquet, N. (1983), *After the New Right* (London: Heinemann).

Bradbury, K. L. and Downs, A. (1981), *Do Housing Allowances Work?* (Washington, DC: Brookings).

Buchanan, J. M. (1968), *The Inconsistencies of the National Health Service* (London: Institute of Economic Affairs).

Buchanan, J. M. (1977), 'Why does government grow?' in T. Borcherding (ed.), *Budgets and Bureaucrats: the Sources of Government Growth* (Durham, NC: Duke University Press).

Building Societies Association (1980), *The Guideline System* (London: Building Societies Association).

Bull, D. and Wilding, P. (1983), *Thatcherism and the Poor* (London: Child Poverty Action Group).

Burghes, L. (1980), *Living from Hand to Mouth* (London: Child Poverty Action Group).

Burghes, L. and Lister, R. (1981) (eds), *Unemployment: Who Pays the Price?* (London: Child Poverty Action Group).

Bus and Coach Council (1982), *The Future of the Bus* (London: Bus and Coach Council).

Caves, D. and Christensen, L. (1980), 'The relative efficiency of public and private firms in a competitive environment: the case of Canadian railroads', *Journal of Political Economy*, vol. 88, no. 5, pp. 958–76.

Central Statistical Office (1982), 'The effects of taxes and benefits on household income, 1981', *Economic Trends*, no. 350, pp. 94–109.

Charities Aid Foundation (1981), *Charity Statistics 1980/81* (Tonbridge, Kent: CAF Publications).

Charles, S. (1977), *Housing Economics* (London: Macmillan).

Charles, S. (1982a), 'The opportunity cost of the sale of local authority rented accommodation: a comment', *Urban Studies*, vol. 19, no. 1, pp. 83–4.

Charles, S. (1982b), 'Council house sales', *Social Policy and Administration*, vol. 16, no. 2, pp. 104–14.

Chartered Institute of Public Finance and Accountancy (1983), *Finance and General Statistics, 1983–4* (London: CIPFA).

Clune, W., Coons, J. and Sugarman, S. (1971), *Private Wealth and Public Education* (Cambridge, Mass.: Harvard Educational Press).

Cohen, D. K. and Farrar, E. (1977), 'Power to parents – the story of education vouchers', *The Public Interest*, no. 48, pp. 63–79.

Collard, D. (1978), *Altruism and Economy* (Oxford: Martin Robertson).

Crew, M. A. and Young, A. (1977), *Paying by Degrees* (London: Institute of Economic Affairs).

Crosland, A. (1974), *Socialism Now and Other Essays* (London: Cape).

Cross, R. (1982), *Economic Theory and Policy in the U.K.* (Oxford: Martin Robertson).

Cullingworth, J. B. (1979), *Essays on Housing Policy* (London: Allen & Unwin).

Culyer, A. J. (1976), *Need and the National Health Service* (London: Martin Robertson).

Culyer, A. J. (1980), *The Political Economy of Social Policy* (Oxford: Martin Robertson).

Danziger, S., Haveman, R. and Plotnick, R. (1981), 'How income transfers offset work, savings and the income distribution: a critical review', *Journal of Economic Literature*, vol. 19, no. 3, pp. 975–1028.

Davies, B. (1980), *The Cost-effectiveness Imperative* (Berkhamsted, Herts: The Volunteer Centre).

Davis, O. A. and Whinston, A. B. (1961), 'The economics of urban renewal', *Law and Contemporary Problems*, vol. 26, Winter, pp. 105–12.

Deacon, A. and Bradshaw, J. (1983), *Reserved for the Poor* (Oxford: Martin Robertson).

De Alassi, L. (1980), 'The economics of property rights: a review of the evidence', *Research in Law and Economics*, vol. 2, pp. 1–47.

Department of Health and Social Security (1969), *The Functions of the District General Hospital* (London: HMSO).

Department of Health and Social Security (1983), *Report of the DHSS/NHS Audit Working Group* (London: HMSO).

Department of the Environment (1982), Consultant: Anne Power, *Priority Estates Project* (London: Department of the Envrionment).

Department of Transport (1982), *Urban Public Transport Subsidies: An Economic Assessment of Value for Money*, Summary Report and Technical Report (London: Deparment of Transport).

Donabedian, A. (1971), 'Social responsibility for personal health services: an examination of basic values', *Inquiry*, vol. 8, no. 2, pp. 3–19.

Donnison, D. (1975), *An Approach to Social Policy* (Dublin: Stationery Office).

Douglas-Mann, B. (1973), *The End of the Private Landlord*, Fabian Research Series No. 312 (London: Fabian Society).

Dupuit, J. (1844), 'On the measurement of the utility of public works', *Annales des Ponts et Chaussées*, 2nd series, vol. 8.

Edwards, C. and Posnett, J. (1980), 'The opportunity cost of the sale of local authority rented accommodation', *Urban Studies*, vol. 17, no. 1, pp. 45–52.

Esposito, A. and Thomson, W. (1976), *Parents' Choice: A Report on Educational Vouchers in East Hartford, Connecticut* (East Hartford School District).

Ferge, Z. (1979), *A Society in the Making* (Harmondsworth, Middx: Penguin).

Field, F. (1981), *Inequality in Britain* (London: Fontana).

Foreman-Peck, J. (1982), 'The appraisal of sales of local authority rented accommodation: a comment', *Urban Studies*, vol. 19, no. 1, pp. 79–82.

Friedman, M. (1962), *Capitalism and Freedom* (Chicago: University of Chicago Press).

Friedman, M. (1980), *Free to Choose* (London: Secker & Warburg).

Gallie, W. B. (1956), 'Liberal morality and socialist morality'; in P. Laslett (ed.), *Philosophy, Politics and Society*, 1st series (Oxford: Blackwell, 1970).

Gamble, A. (1979), 'The free economy and the strong state', *Socialist Register* (London: Merlin Press), pp. 1–25.

George, V. and Wilding, P. (1976), *Ideology and Social Welfare* (London: Routledge & Kegan Paul).

Gershuny, J. (1978), *After Industrial Society?: The Emerging Self-Service Economy* (London: Macmillan).

Gladstone, F. J. (1979), *Voluntary Action in a Changing World* (London: Bedford Square Press).

Glennerster, H. (1983), 'A new start for Labour', in J. Griffiths (ed.), *Socialism in a Cold Climate* (London: Allen & Unwin), pp. 6–21.

Goldberg, E. M. and Connelly, N. (1982), *The Effectiveness of Social Care for the Elderly* (London: Heinemann).

Golding, P. (1983), 'Rethinking common sense about social policy' in D. Bull and P. Wilding (eds), *Thatcherism and the Poor* (London: Child Poverty Action Group).

Goodin, R. (1982), 'Freedom and the welfare state: theoretical foundations', *Journal of Social Policy*, vol. 11, no. 2, pp. 149–76.

Gordon, A. (1982), *Economics and Social Policy* (Oxford: Martin Robertson).

Goss, S. and Lansley, S. (1981), *What Price Housing?*, Research Report 4 (London: SHAC).

Gough, I. (1979), *The Political Economy of the Welfare State* (London: Macmillan).

Greenaway, D. (1979), 'Voucher systems in education. The arguments for and against', in P. Maunder (ed.), *Case Studies in the Economics of Social Issues* (London: Heinemann Educational Books).

Grey, A., Hepworth, N. and Odling-Smee, J. (1981), *Housing rents, costs and subsidies*, 2nd edn (London: Chartered Institute of Public Finance and Accountancy).

Griffiths, J. (1983) (ed.), *Socialism in a Cold Climate* (London: Allen & Unwin).

Guhl, D. (1975), *Schnell-Verkehr in Ballungsräumen* (Düsseldorf: Alba).

Harloe, M. (1980), 'Decline and fall of private renting', *CES Review*, April, pp. 30–3.

Harsanyi, J. C. (1980), 'Rule utilitarianism, rights, obligations and the theory of rational behaviour', *Theory and Decision*, vol. 12, no. 2, pp. 115–33.

Hart, H. L. A. (1955), 'Are there any natural rights?', *Philosophical Review*, vol. 64, pp. 175–91.

Hastings, S. and Levie, H. (1983) (eds), *Privatisation?* (Nottingham: Spokesman).

Haveman, R. and Margolis, J. (1977) (eds), *Public Expenditure and Policy Analysis*, 2nd edn (Chicago: Rand McNally).

Heald, D. A. (1983), *Public Expenditure* (Oxford: Martin Robertson).

Heclo, H. (1977), 'A question of priorities', *The Humanist*, vol. 37, no. 2, pp. 21–4.

Heidenheimer, A. J., Heclo, H. and Adams, C. T. (1976), *Comparative Public Policy* (London: Macmillan).

Heidenheimer, A. J., Heclo, H. and Adams, C. T. (1983), *Comparative Public Policy*, 2nd edn (London: Macmillan).

Hibbs, J. (1975), *The Bus and Coach Industry – Its Economics and Organisation* (London: J. M. Dent).

Hibbs, J. (1982), *Transport without politics...?* Hobart Paper 95 (London: Institute of Economic Affairs).

Hicks, J. R. (1956), *A Revision of Demand Theory* (Oxford: Clarendon Press).

Higgins, J. (1981), *States of Welfare* (Oxford: Blackwell and Martin Robertson).

Hillebrandt, P. M. (1974), *Economic Theory and the Construction Industry* (London: Macmillan).

Hirsch, F. (1977), *The Social Limits to Growth* (London: Routledge & Kegan Paul).

Hirschman, A. O. (1982), *Shifting Involvements: Private Interest and Public Action* (Princeton, NJ: Princeton University Press).

HSMO (1982), *Public Transport Subsidy in Cities*, Cmnd 8735 (London).

HMSO (1983a), *The Government's Expenditure Plans 1983/84 – 1985/86*, Cmnd 8789–1 (London).

HMSO (1983b), *Transport Act* (London).

Hochman, H. M. and Rodgers, J. D. (1969), 'Pareto-optimal redistribution', *American Economic Review*, vol. 59, no. 4, pp. 542–7.

Hood, R. D., Martin, S. A. and Osberg, L. S. (1977), 'Economic determinants of individual charitable donations in Canada', *Canadian Journal of Economics*, vol. 10, no. 4, pp. 653–69.

Horobin, G. W. and Smyth, R. L. (1960), 'The economics of education: a comment', *Scottish Journal of Political Economy*, vol. 7, no. 1, pp. 69–74. Reprinted in M. Blaug (ed.) *Economics of Education 2* (Harmondsworth, Middx: Penguin Books, 1969).

Hotelling, H. (1938), 'The general welfare in relation to problems of taxation and to railway utility rates', *Econometrica*, vol. 6, no. 3, pp. 242–69.

House of Commons (1981), *Hansard* (London: HMSO), vol. 998, col. 136.

House of Commons (1983), *Bus Subsidy Policy*, Third Special Report from the Transport Committee, Session 1982–3, HC 285 (London: HMSO).

House of Commons Environment Committee (1980), *First Report from the Environment Committee 1979–80*, HC 714 (London: HMSO).

House of Commons Environment Committee (1981a), *Second Report from the Environment Committee Session 1980–81*, HC 366 (London: HMSO).

House of Commons Environment Committee (1981b), *Third Report from the Environment Committee Session 1980–81*, HC 383 (London: HMSO).

House of Commons Environment Committee (1982a), *First Report from the Environment Committee Session 1981–82*, HC 40 (London: HMSO).

House of Commons Environment Committee (1982b), *First Special Report from the Environmental Committee Session 1982–83*, HC 54 (London: HMSO).

House of Commons Environment Committee (1983), *Second Report from the Environment Committee Session 1982–83*, HC 170 (London: HMSO).

Hughes, G. (1979), 'Housing income and subsidies', *Fiscal Studies*, vol. 1, November, pp. 210–38.

Hughes, G. (1980), 'Housing and the tax system', in G. Hughes and G. Heal (eds), *Public Policy and the Tax System* (London: Allen & Unwin).

Jencks, C., *et al.* (1970), *Education Vouchers: A Report on Financing Elementary Education by Grants to Parents* (Cambridge, Mass.: Center for the Study of Public Policy).

Johnson, D. B. (1970), 'Some fundamental economics of the charity market', in T. R. Ireland and D. B. Johnson (eds), *The Economics of Charity* (Blacksburg, Va.: Center for the Study of Public Choice).

Johnson, N. (1981), *Voluntary Social Services* (Oxford: Basil Blackwell and Martin Robertson).

Jones, P. (1983), 'Political equality and majority rule', in D. Miller and L. Siedentop (eds), *The Nature of Political Theory* (Oxford: Clarendon Press).

Joskow, P. L. and Noll, R. C. (1981), 'Regulation in theory and practice: an overview', in G. Fromm (ed.), *Studies in Public Regulation* (Cambridge, Mass.: MIT Press).

Judge, K. (1981), 'Is there a "crisis" in the welfare state?', *International Journal of Sociology and Social Policy*, vol. 1, no. 2, pp. 1–21.

Judge, K. (1982a), 'The growth and decline of social expenditure', in A. Walker (ed.), *Public Expenditure and Social Policy* (London: Heinemann), pp. 27–48.

Judge, K. (1982b), 'The public purchase of social care: British confirmation of the American experience', *Policy and Politics*, vol. 10, no. 4, pp. 397–416.

Judge, K. and Matthews, J. (1980), *Charging for Social Care* (London: Allen & Unwin).

Kaim-Caudle, P. (1973), *Comparative Social Policy and Social Security: A Ten-Country Study* (Oxford: Martin Robertson).

Kapp, K. W. (1978), *The Social Costs of Business Enterprise* (Nottingham: Spokesman).

Kay, J. A. (1972), 'Social discount rates', *Journal of Public Economics*, vol. 2, no. 3/4, pp. 359–378.

Kemeny, J. (1981), *The Myth of Home Ownership* (London: Routledge & Kegan Paul).

Kent County Council Education Department (1978), *Education Vouchers in Kent: A Feasibility Study for the Education Department of the Kent County Council* (Maidstone, Kent: Kent County Council).

Kincaid, J. (1973), *Poverty and Equality in Britain* (Harmondsworth, Middx: Penguin).

King, M. A. (1980), 'An econometric model of tenure choice and demand for housing as a joint decision', *Journal of Public Economics*, vol. 14, no. 2, pp. 137–59.

King, M. A. and Atkinson, A. B. (1980), 'Housing policy, taxation and reform', *Midland Bank Review*, Spring, pp. 7–15. Reprinted with post-script in R. C. O. Mathews and J. R. Sargent (eds) *Contemporary Problems of Economic Policy* (London: Methuen, 1983), pp. 111–20.

Kirwan, R. M. and Martin, D. B. (1972), 'The economics of urban residential renewal and improvement', *CES Working Paper*, no. 77 (London: Centre for Environmental Studies).

Klein, R. (1980), 'The welfare state: a self-inflicted crisis?', *The Political Quarterly*, vol. 51, no. 1, pp. 24–34.

Knapp, M. and Missiakoulis, S. (1982), 'Inter-sectoral cost comparisons: day care for the elderly', *Journal of Social Policy*, vol. 11, no. 3, pp. 335–54.

Kramer, R. M. (1981), *Voluntary Agencies in the Welfare State* (Berkeley, Calif.: University of California Press).

Labour Research Department (1982), *Public or Private: The Case Against Privatisation* (London: Labour Research Department).

Laffont, J.-J. (1975), 'Macroeconomic constraints, economic efficiency and ethics: an introduction to Kantian economics', *Economica*, vol. 42, no. 168, pp. 430–7.

Langford, D. A. (1982), *Direct Labour Organisation in the Construction Industry* (Farnborough, Hants: Gower).

Lansley, S. (1979), *Housing and Public Policy* (London: Croom Helm).

Layard, R. and Walters, A. (1978), *Micro-Economic Theory* (New York: McGraw-Hill).

Lees, D. S. (1961), *Health Through Choice* (London: Institute of Economic Affairs).

Lees, D. S. (1965), 'Health through choice', in *Freedom or Free For All?* (London: Institute of Economic Affairs).

Le Grand, J. (1982), *The Strategy of Equality* (London: Allen & Unwin).

Le Grand, J. (1983), 'Privatisation and the social services', in J. Griffiths (ed.), *Socialism in a Cold Climate* (London: Allen & Unwin), pp. 65–80.

Le Grand, J. and Robinson, R. (1984), *The Economics of Social Problems: The Market Versus the State*, 2nd edn (London: Macmillan).

Levie, H. (1983), 'Britain goes to the sales', *Marxism Today*, vol. 27, no. 4, pp. 28–33.

Levinson, E. (1976), *The First Three Years at Alum Rock* (Santa Monica, Calif.: Rand Corporation).

LEWRG (1980), *In and Against the State* (London: Pluto Press).

Lindsay, C. M. (1969), 'Medical care and the economics of sharing', *Economica*, vol. 36, no. 144, pp. 531–7.

Lister, R. (1977), *Patching-up the Safety Net* (London: Child Poverty Action Group).

London Transport Executive (1982), *Public Transport Subsidies and Value for Money*, Economic Research Report R. 252 (London: LTE).

Lowry, I. S. (1982), *Experimenting with Housing Allowances*, R-2880-Hud (Santa Monica, Calif.: Rand Corporation).

McLachlan, G. and Maynard, A. (eds) (1982), *The Public–Private Mix for Health* (London: Nuffield Provincial Hospital Trust).

Maclennan, D. (1982), *Housing Economics* (London: Longman).

Malpass, P. and Murie, A. (1982), *Housing Policy and Practice* (London: Macmillan).

Manpower Services Commission (1982), *Youth Task Group Report* (London: Manpower Services Commission).

Margolis, H. (1982), *Selfishness, Altruism and Rationality* (Cambridge: Cambridge University Press).

Marris, P. (1982), *Community Planning and Conceptions of Change* (London: Routledge & Kegan Paul).

Marshall, A. (1961), *Principles of Economics*, 8th edn (London: Macmillan); first published 1890.

Marshall, T. H. (1963), *Sociology at the Crossroads* (London: Heinemann).

Maurice, R. (ed.) (1968), *National Accounts Statistics: Sources and Methods* (London: Central Statistical Office).

Maxwell, R. J. (1981), *Health and Wealth* (London: Heath).

Maynard, A. K. (1975), *Experiment with Choice in Education* (London: Institute of Economic Affairs).

Maynard, A. K. (1983), 'Privatising the National Health Service', *Lloyds Bank Review*, no. 148, pp. 28–41.

Mecklenburger, A. and Hostop, R. (eds) (1972), *Education Vouchers – From Theory to Alum Rock* (Homewood, Ill.: ETC Publications).

Merrett, S. (1979), *State Housing in Britain* (London: Routledge & Kegan Paul).

Merrett, S. with Gray, F. (1982), *Owner-Occupation in Britain* (London: Routledge & Kegan Paul).

Miller, S. M. (1978), 'The recapitalisation of Capitalism', *Social Policy*, November/December, pp. 5–12.

Miller, S. M. and Rein, M. (1975), 'Can income redistribution work?', *Social Policy*, May/June, pp. 3–18.

Millward, R. (1982), 'The comparative performance of public and private ownership' in E. Roll (ed.), *The Mixed Economy* (London: Macmillan).

Milne, W. H. (1975), *New Hampshire Educational Voucher Project: Final Report – Feasibility Study* (New Hampshire: New Hampshire State Board).

Ministry of Health (1944), *A National Health Service*, Cmd 6502 (London: HMSO).

Ministry of Health (1946), *The National Health Service: a summary of the proposed service*, Cmd 6761 (London: HMSO).

Minns, R. (1980), *Pension Funds and British Capitalism* (London: Heinemann).

Mishan, E. J. (1967), *The Costs of Economic Growth* (Harmondsworth, Middx: Penguin).

Mishan, E. J. (1977), 'Welfare economics and public expenditure', in M. V. Posner (ed.), *Public Expenditure* (Cambridge: Cambridge University Press).

Mishra, R. (1981), *Social Policy and Society* (London: Macmillan).

Mohring, H. (1972), 'Optimisation and scale economies in urban bus transportation', *American Economic Review*, vol. 62, no. 4, pp. 591–604.

Morris, M. (1969), *Voluntary Work in the Welfare State* (London: Routledge & Kegan Paul).

Murie, A. (1975), *The Sale of Council Houses* (Birmingham: Centre for Urban and Regional Studies, University of Birmingham).

Murie, A. (1982), 'Selling council houses', *Built Environment*, vol. 8, no. 1, pp. 12–19.

NALGO (1983a), *Profit Out of Health* (Birmingham: Birmingham and Solihull Health Branch of NALGO).

NALGO (1983b), *Qualitative Research Report* (London: NALGO).

Nickell, S. J. (1980), 'A picture of male unemployment', *Economic Journal*, December, pp. 776–94.

Niskanen, W. (1975), 'Politicians and bureaucrats', *Journal of Law and Economics*, vol. 18, no. 3, pp. 617–43.

Obler, J. (1981), 'Private giving in the welfare state', *British Journal of Political Science*, vol. 11, no. 1, pp. 17–48.

O'Connor, J. (1973), *The Fiscal Crisis of the State* (New York: St. Martin's Press).

Olson, M. (1971), *The Logic of Collective Action* (Cambridge: Mass.: Harvard University Press).

O'Malley, J. (1977), *The Politics of Community Action* (Nottingham: Bertrand Russell Peace Foundation for Spokesman Books).

Opit, L. J. (1977), 'Domiciliary care for the elderly sick – economy or neglect', *British Medical Journal*, 1 January, pp. 30–3.

Peacock, A. T. and Wiseman, J. (1964), *Education for Democrats* (London: Institute of Economic Affairs).

Peacock, A. T. (1983), 'Education voucher schemes – strong or weak?' *Journal of Economic Affairs*, vol. 2, no. 3, pp. 113–16.

Peston, M. (1966), 'The theory of spilloners in connection with education', *Public Finance*, vol. 21, nos 1–2, pp. 184–99.

Peston, M. (1972), *Public Goods and the Welfare Sector* (London: Macmillan).

Piachaud, D. (1979), *The Cost of a Child* (London: Child Poverty Action Group).

Pinker, R. A. (1974), 'Social policy and social justice', *Journal of Social Policy*, vol. 3, no. 1, pp. 1–19.

Politics of Health Group (1982), *Going Private* (London: Politics of Health Group).

Ponsonby, G. J. (1969), *Transport Policy: Co-ordination through Competition*, Hobart Paper 49 (London: Institute of Economic Affairs).

Posnett, J. and Edwards, C. (1982), 'The opportunity cost of the sale of local authority rented accommodation: reply', *Urban Studies*, vol. 19, no. 1, pp. 85–7.

Powell, E. (1966), *Medicine and Politics* (London: Pitman).

Price Waterhouse (1982), *Review of Birmingham Social Services Department* (Birmingham: Price Waterhouse).

Rawls, J. (1972), *A Theory of Justice* (Oxford: Oxford University Press).

Reddin, M. (1983), 'Pensions, wealth and the extension of inequality', in F. Field (ed.), *The Second Wealth Report* (London: Routledge & Kegan Paul).

Richter, P. C. (1976), *Education Vouchers – Bibliography* (Cambridge, Mass.: Center for the Study of Public Policy).

Ritchie, J., Keegan, J. and Bosanquet, N. (1983), *Housing for Mentally Ill and Mentally Handicapped People* (London: HMSO).

Robinson, R. (1979), *Housing Economics and Public Policy* (London: Macmillan).

Robinson, R. (1981), 'Housing tax-expenditures, subsidies and the distribution of income', *Manchester School*, vol. 49, no. 2, pp. 91–110.

Royal Commission on the Distribution of Income and Wealth (1979) (The Diamond Commission), *Report No. 7: Fourth Report on the Standing Reference*, Cmnd 7595 (London: HMSO).

Rydell, C. P. (1982), *Price Elasticities of Housing Supply*, R-2846-Hud (Santa Monica, Calif.: Rand Corporation).

Samuelson, P. A. (1954), 'The pure theory of public expenditure', *Review of Economics and Statistics*, vol. 36, no. 4, pp. 387–9.

Schwartz, R. A. (1970), 'Personal philanthropic contributions', *Journal of Political Economy*, vol. 78, no. 6, pp. 1264–91.

Seldon, A. (ed.) (1980), *The Litmuss Papers* (London: Centre for Policy Studies).

Sennett, R. and Cobb, J. (1974), *The Hidden Injuries of Class* (London: Cambridge University Press).

Short, J. R. (1983), *Housing in Britain* (London: Methuen).

Sinfield, A. (1978), 'Analysis in the social division of welfare', *Journal of Social Policy*, vol. 7, no. 2, pp. 129–56.

Sinfield, A. (1979), *What Unemployment Means* (Oxford: Martin Robertson).

Sleeman, J. F. (1979), *Resources for the Welfare State* (London: Longman).

Social Democratic Party (1983), *A Strategy for Housing* (London: SDP).

Social Services Committee (1980), *The Government's White Papers on Public Expenditure: the Social Services*, Vol. II, HC 702 (London: HMSO).

Spann, R. M. (1977), 'Public vs. private provision of government services', in T. Borcherding (ed.), *Budgets and Bureaucrats: the Sources of Government Growth* (Durham, NC: Duke University Press), pp. 71–89.

Stafford, D. C. (1978), *The Economics of Housing Policy* (London: Croom Helm).

Stretton, H. (1974), *Housing and Government*, 1974 Boyer Lectures (Sydney: Australian Broadcasting Commission).

Struyk, R. J. and Bendick, M. J. (eds) (1981), *Housing Vouchers for the Poor* (Washington, DC: Urban Institute Press).

Sugden, R. (1982), 'On the economics of philanthropy', *Economic Journal*, vol. 92, no. 366, pp. 341–50.

Sugden, R. (1984), 'Reciprocity: the supply of public goods through voluntary contributions', *Economic Journal* (forthcoming).

Sutton, J. and Whitehead, C. M. E. (1982), 'The sale of council houses: a cautionary note', *Applied Economics*, vol. 14, no. 3, pp. 295–303.

Tawney, R. H. (1964), *Equality*, 4th edn (London: Unwin Books).

Taylor, M. (1976), *Anarchy and Cooperation* (London: Wiley).

Taylor-Gooby, P. (1983), 'Public belt and private braces', *New Society*, 14 April, pp. 51–2.

Taylor-Gooby, P. and Dale, J. (1982), *Social Theory and Social Welfare* (London: Arnold).

Thorns, D. (1981), 'Owner-occupation: its significance for wealth transfer and class formation', *Socialist Review*, vol. 29, no. 4, pp. 705–28.

Titmuss, R. M. (1963), *Essays on the Welfare State*, 2nd edn (London: Allen & Unwin).

Titmuss, R. M. (1968), *Commitment to Welfare* (London: Allen & Unwin).

Titmuss, R. M. (1970), *The Gift Relationship* (London: Allen & Unwin).

Titmuss, R. M. (1974), *Social Policy* (London: Allen & Unwin).

Tobin, J. (1970), 'On limiting the domain of inequality', *Journal of and Economics*, vol. 13, no. 2, pp. 263–77.

Townsend, P. (1967), *Poverty, Socialism and Labour in Power* (London: Fabian Society).

Townsend, P. (1975), *Sociology and Social Policy* (Harmondsworth, Middx: Penguin).

Townsend, P. (1979), *Poverty in the United Kingdom* (London: Allen Lane).

Townsend, P. (1981), 'Elderly people with disabilities', in A. Walker and P. Townsend (eds), *Disability in Health* (Oxford: Martin Robertson), pp. 91–118.

Townsend, P. and Davidson, N. (1982), *Inequality in Health* (Harmondsworth, Middx: Penguin).

Treasury (1979), *The Government Expenditure Plans 1979/80 to 1982/3*, Cmnd 7439 (London: HMSO).

Treasury (1982), *Economic Progress Report, No. 145* (London: HM Treasury).

US Office of Economic Opportunity (1971), *Feasibility Study for the Design and Implementation of an Education Voucher System in Rochester, New York* (Washington, DC: OEO).

US Office of Economic Opportunity (1973), *The Feasibility of Implementing a Voucher Plan in Seattle* (Washington, DC: OEO).

Vaizey, J. (1962), *The Economics of Education* (London: Faber).

Van Fliet, W. and Smyth, J. A. (1982), 'A nineteenth century French proposal to use school vouchers', *Comparative Education Review*, vol. 12, no. 3, pp. 95–103.

Vickrey, W. (1980), 'Optimal transit subsidy policy', *Transportation*, vol. 9, no. 4, pp. 389–409.

Walden, L. J. (ed.) (1982), *Housing Policy: Papers and Discussion From Two British–Scandinavian Seminars* (Gävle: National Swedish Institute for Building Research).

Walker, A. (1979), 'Private care: whose freedom to choose?' *Nursing Mirror*, 18 January, pp. 14–16.

Walker, A. (1980), 'The social creation of poverty and dependency in old age', *Journal of Social Policy*, vol. 9, no. 1, pp. 49–75.

Walker, A. (1981a), 'Social policy, social administration and the social construction of welfare', *Sociology*, vol. 15, no. 2, pp. 225–50.

Walker, A. (1981b), 'The social origins of impairment, disability and handicap', *Medicine in Society*, vol. 6, no. 2, pp. 18–26.

Walker, A. (ed.) (1982a), *Public Expenditure and Social Policy* (London: Heinemann).

Walker, A. (ed.) (1982b), *Community Care* (Oxford: Blackwell and Martin Robertson).

Walker, A. (1983), 'Labour's social plans: the limits of welfare statism', *Critical Social Policy*, vol. 3, no. 2, pp. 45–65.

Walker, A. (1984) *Social Planning* (Oxford: Blackwell and Martin Robertson).

Walker, A. and Townsend, P. (1979), 'Compensation for disability: the wrong course', in M. Brown and S. Baldwin (eds), *The Year Book of Social Policy in Britain 1978* (London: Routledge & Kegan Paul), pp. 57–80.

Walker, A. and Townsend, P. (eds) (1981), *Disability in Britain* (Oxford: Martin Robertson).

Walker, A., Wintford, S. and Pond, C. (1983), 'Conservative economic policy: the social consequences', in D. Bull and P. Wilding (eds), *Thatcherism and the Poor* (London: Child Poverty Action Group), pp. 13–26.

Webb, A., Day, L. and Weller, D. (1976), *Voluntary Social Service Manpower Resources* (London: Personal Social Services Council).

Webster, D. (1980), 'The financial consequences of council house sales', *CES Review*, no. 9, April, pp. 39–46.

Weiler, D. *et al.* (1974), *A Public School Voucher Demonstration: The First Year at Alum Rock* (Santa Monica, Calif.: Rand Corporation).

West, E. G. (1965), *Education and the State* (London: Institute of Economic Affairs).

West, E. G. (1967), 'Tom Paine's voucher scheme for public education', *Southern Economic Journal*, vol. 33, no. 3, pp. 378–82.

West, E. G. (1968), *Economics, Education and the Politician* (London: Institute of Economic Affairs).

Whitehead, C. M. E. (1977), 'Neutrality between tenures', *CES Review*, no. 2, December, pp. 33–36.

Whitehead, C. M. E. (1979), 'Why owner-occupation', *CES Review*, no. 6, May, pp. 33–41.

Whitehead, C. M. E. (1983), 'Housing under the Conservatives: a policy assessment', *Public Money*, vol. 3, no. 1, pp. 15–21.

Wilensky, H. (1975), *The Welfare State and Equality* (Berkeley, Calif.: University of California Press).

Williamson, O. E. (1975), *Markets and Hierarchies: Analysis and Anti-Trust Implications* (New York: Free Press).

Wilson, E. (1977), *Women and the Welfare State* (London: Tavistock).

Wiseman, J. (1959), 'The economics of education', *Scottish Journal of Political Economy*, vol. 6, no. 1, pp. 48–58. Reprinted in M. Blaug (ed.), *Economics of Education 2* (Harmondsworth, Middx: Penguin Books, 1969), pp. 360–72.

Wiseman, J. (1960), 'The economics of education: rejoinder', *Scottish Journal of Political Economy*, vol. 7, no. 1, pp. 75–6. Reprinted in M. Blaug (ed.), *Economics of Education 2* (Harmondsworth, Middx: Penguin Books, 1969), pp. 373–81.

Woodhall, M. (1977), 'Alternatives in the finance of education: vouchers', *The Finance of Education: Open University Course Economics and Education Policy IV* (Walton Hall, Milton Keynes: Open University Press), pp. 65–115.

Index

Index

accident rates, and public
   transport subsidy 184
accountability
   effects of privatisation 40
   public sector problems 8, 49, 61
'act utility' 80–1
altruism 9
   and voluntary activities 71–2, 75,
   86
Australia, health care expenditure
   26

Beveridge, W. 2, 22, 33, 47
Birmingham, cost effectiveness study
   of social services department
   38–9
blood donation study 26, 38, 86
Buchanan, J. 7
Buckingham University 156
BUPA 106, 107, 108
business development, and urban
   public transport policy 204–5

Calderdale, hospital laundry services
   109
Canada
   health care expenditure 26
   railroads study 8
cancer research 72
Cancer Research Campaign 79
capitalism, recapitalisation of 28, 30
car ownership, and public transport
   systems 202–4, 206
Castle, B. 108
charitable behaviour
   conventional theory of 75–80
   'principle of fairness' 83–4
   'private benefits' theory 80–3
   'rational commitment' theory 83
   see also altruism
charitable trusts 74

Chester, study of attitudes to public
   services 31–2
choice
   and charitable behaviour 75–80
   and education vouchers 162, 167,
   173
   freedom of 32
   'Public Choice School' 7
community
   concept of 55
   and the welfare state 13–14
community development 50–1
   aims 54, 55
   and constitutional structure 52–3
   and resource allocation 53
Community Development Projects
   85
consensus politics, and welfare state
   reforms 56–7
Conservative Party 70
   and concept of self-help 86
   policies on health care 97, 100
   see also Thatcher Government
consumers
   exploitation of 38
   stigmatisation of 40, 41, 42
contracting out, and the NHS 95–6,
   109
co-operatives 50
   in housing 53
cost-effectiveness
   of public and private education
   156, 157, 167
   and public services 19, 85
   and urban transport systems
   179–97
council housing 5, 23, 92, 144–5
   comparable efficiency of 120–6
   concept of 'non-profit' 138
   finance of 139–41
   ideological basis for 134–6,
   138–9

For Product Safety Concerns and Information please contact our EU
representative GPSR@taylorandfrancis.com
Taylor & Francis Verlag GmbH, Kaufingerstraße 24, 80331 München, Germany